The Billy Gazonas Story

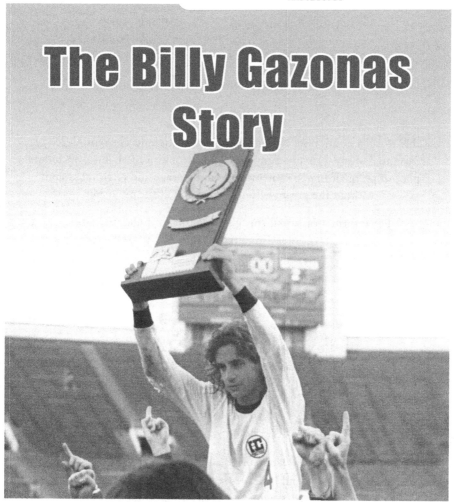

A Soccer Journey from Tears and Humiliation
to National Champions and Hermann Trophy Winner

BILLY GAZONAS
"The Greek"

The Billy Gazonas Story
A Soccer Journey from Tears and Humiliation
to National Champions and Hermann Trophy Winner
by Billy Gazonas ("The Greek")

© 2021 Billy Gazonas

All rights reserved.

This work is nonfiction. No part of this publication may be reproduced or transmitted in any form or by any means, electronic or mechanical, including photocopy, recording, or any information storage and retrieval system, without the prior written permission of the publisher.

For information about special discounts for bulk purchases, please contact Polemistis Press at info@billygazonas.com.

Published by

POLEMISTIS PRESS

P.O. Box 1365
Princeton, N.J. 08542
Website: www.billygazonas.com
Email: info@billygazonas.com

Book design by Nick Zelinger, NZ Graphics
Editing by Bruce Goldberg
Cover photo by Ed Clough

The original document for all photographs taken by
Ed Clough and James Parsons, Jr. are located in the
Paul F. Cooper, Jr. Archives, Hartwick College, Oneonta, NY.

ISBN 978-1-7342228-2-1 (paperback)
ISBN 978-1-7342228-3-8 (ebook)
Library of Congress Control Number: 2021911148

First Edition
Printed in the United States of America

In loving memory of my parents
James and Connie Gazonas

None of this would have been possible without your love,
nurturing, guidance and encouragement to pursue my dreams.

CONTENTS

FOREWORD

December 4, 1976: The metallic click of soccer studs reverberating off the walls was the only sound as the Hartwick College soccer team despondently walked into the locker room. We had just lost 2-1 to Indiana University in the NCAA national semifinal. The silence was palpable as players slumped on benches and stared straight ahead. I looked over at Bill Gazonas; there were only tears.

The ensuing weeks built a burning resolve and trajectory for Bill's path to the 1977 season. When asked by a professor why Bill wasn't his usual smiling self, he replied, "I'll smile when we win the national championship."

Bill's quest to win that national championship is a story of passion, tenacity and a ruthless desire to compete. Always fighting the perception that a 5-foot-3 soccer player was too small to compete at the highest level, he immersed himself in the rich and intense soccer environment surrounding Trenton, N.J. A hotbed of soccer, Trenton was the place for an aspiring player to develop his skills while competing against some of the best players in the country.

Year by year, Bill became a better and more complete player. During those development years, Bill came under the influence of some exceptional soccer personalities and coaches. Most notably, the reader will meet the legendary Glenn "Moochie" Myernick and Bill's mentor, "Ping Pong." Both had a lasting impact on Bill's development and future.

As his very successful playing career at St. Anthony's High School came to a close, choosing a college loomed on the horizon and Bill faced the agonizing search for the right one. He admitted that his priorities for selecting a college were first to further his soccer career, and second for the education.

Seeking advice from loving parents, Bill ultimately made the decision himself and chose Hartwick. The Hartwick soccer program was one of the most successful in the country. Not only was it close to home,

Hartwick also had a number of prominent New Jersey players attending, including his friend Mooch Myernick. The coach was the well-known and respected Timo Liekoski, probably the best soccer mind in the nation's colleges and universities.

Bill wasn't heavily recruited by Hartwick. In the preseason training of his freshman year, Bill had to fight to even train with the varsity. He eventually made the team and worked his way up the roster.

Frustrated with being a substitute, Bill demanded a meeting with Timo and said, "I should be starting!" Timo gave Bill his chance, and he never sat on the bench again. Eventually he was moved to the middle of midfield, where his skill and tactical acumen emerged to make him the team engine. Bill became the tactical center around which the Hartwick team revolved. His midfield dominance created the rhythm and pace of team function.

In spring 1976, Timo left Hartwick to coach in the NASL and I became the new coach of the Hartwick soccer team.

We went undefeated in the 1976 season until the heartbreaking loss to Indiana. With Mooch leaving for the NASL and the 1977 season on the horizon, I had to choose our next captain. Without a second thought, Bill Gazonas was now the captain of the Hartwick soccer team.

Bill and I had parallel views on style of play, tactics and the type of training that would further develop the Hartwick way of playing. Bill became my sounding board for tactical and personnel decisions. He and I made a good team!

Through the end of 1976 and into 1977, Bill committed a part of every day to train. Often by himself, Bill and the ball become one. Spring 1977 meant going home every weekend to play for his club, Trenton Extension, the "EX."

Soon, the 1977 season approached. We went through the 1977 regular season undefeated and stormed through the early rounds of the national tournament to reach the Final Four. A decisive 4-1 defeat of Brown University in the semifinal brought us to the final versus two-time defending champion San Francisco University.

The final was an intense, combative game. Bill dominated the midfield, with the first half ending 0-0. Three minutes into the second half, a goal by Trenton native Art Napolitano put us up 1-0. Midway through the second half, a goal by Stephen Long put us ahead 2-0. San Francisco scored to make it 2-1, which became the final score—and Hartwick was the national champion.

Bill's compelling journey from the fields of Trenton to the pinnacle of college soccer is a story of relentless courage and perseverance to achieve a dream. Through supreme self-confidence and force of personality, Bill refused to be a prisoner in that perceptive box, "He's too small." He pushed back that barrier to become a national champion, Hermann Award winner and professional player.

Through the prism of Bill's experience, the reader will discover that this entertaining and inspirational story is a portal for anyone pursuing a dream. Enter, follow the Bill Gazonas lead and you will achieve your dream.

Jim Lennox

January 2020

1

Cold Feet

Sitting on the curb at the corner of Commonwealth and Roebling Avenue with knots in my stomach, I was oblivious to the numerous cars zipping past me in this middle-class, blue-collar neighborhood in Trenton, New Jersey.

I was scheduled to leave the next week for the beginning of pre-season soccer camp at Hartwick College. A recurring question kept invading my thoughts. *Am I good enough to play for Hartwick College? Am I good enough to play for Hartwick College?*

Hartwick College is a small, private, liberal arts school in upstate Oneonta, New York, that just happens to be a soccer powerhouse. The student population is approximately 1,500. Hartwick's men's soccer team was the school's only team to play at the Division I level; all other Hartwick teams competed in Division III.

Soccer is a whole other story. The soccer program was like a finely tuned factory that produced great players and coaches.

New Jersey was one of the top areas in the country for youth soccer. It was fertile ground for Hartwick's recruiting efforts. Kearny, Harrison and the greater Trenton area typically produced not only the top players in the state but also in the country, as did St. Louis, Missouri.

Timo Liekoski, head coach for the Hartwick College soccer team, made it very clear to me that he did not feel I was good enough to play at Hartwick. I knew he was wrong and that I would have to prove it to him.

The only reason I was invited to preseason camp is because I was friends with Glenn "Mooch" Myernick and Art Napolitano. Mooch and Art were Timo's most prized recruits that year. Mooch may have been the most talented player in the country. He did not attend Hartwick College the previous year because he tore up his knee in a junior league game for Tom Hamnetts (a soccer association in Lawrence Township, NJ) and decided to spend the year at Mercer County Community College to rehabilitate it.

Mooch has been a soccer legend since age 14. I will never forget the first time I had the privilege to see Mooch play in a soccer game after hearing almost unbelievable stories about how great he was. It was 1970 and I was playing on a select team from Mercer County in the 14-year-old bracket at a tournament in Howell, New Jersey. Teams came from as far away as Canada.

Although Mooch was only one year older than me, he played as a guest for the Trenton Extension Juniors in the 18-year-old bracket. From his first few touches of the ball I could see how special he was. His technical skill was impeccable and he had the physical maturity of a player in his prime. Mooch was a man amongst boys.

This was the first time I had played in a tournament that was outside of Mercer County, New Jersey. We ended up tied with the local Howell team and the championship was to be decided by penalty kicks.

The fans circled the field, literally standing on the field from 25 yards out and all the way around the goal. I had never experienced anything like this and was quite nervous when our coach, Mr. Kemo, had me take the first penalty kick for our team. I sent the keeper the wrong way and slotted the ball to his left for the first goal. We eventually lost, with Napolitano missing the fifth kick.

I could not have imagined at that time that four years later I would possibly get the opportunity to play with the legendary Mooch Myernick. Napolitano would be attending Hartwick College, along with Zeren Ombadykow, Angrik Stepanow and Kenny Ivanchukov from the Howell team.

What if? What if I hadn't had a painful injury that season? Would Timo have recruited me with open arms? Are most of the players on the team like Mooch? Sitting on the curb and thinking all these thoughts—none more daunting than *'Are most of the players as talented as Mooch?'*—gave me an idea that temporarily took the knots out of my stomach. I would tell my dad that I wanted to start college next year. That would give me a year to train and become that much better before I went to Hartwick. *What will my dad say? Could he lose the tuition money? Should I take a walk to the Hamilton Sweet Shoppe to see my dad?*

My grandfather, John J. Gazonas, bought the Hamilton Sweet Shoppe in 1940 for $8,000. The Sweet Shoppe sat on the corner of Hamilton Avenue and Chambers Street. Trenton Central High School was across the street and St. Francis Hospital occupied another corner to the right of the shop. Six months after my grandfather purchased the store, he had a heart attack in his sleep and passed away. My father, James J. Gazonas, had to put off going to college to become an attorney and instead took over the business, along with my uncle George J. Gazonas. The shop always has been an important part of our family. My brothers John and Andy, and me, all had our first jobs there.

As I walked back up Commonwealth Avenue towards the shop, I stopped by our home at 312 Commonwealth Ave. I found my mother Connie Gazonas getting ready to prepare dinner.

"Mom, do you mind if I go to the store and eat dinner with Dad?"

"No Billy that is fine. I am still cooking so if you are hungry later, there will be food for you."

Growing up in a Greek-American household, you never have to worry about not having enough food to eat. As I walked the two blocks to the shop from my house, my great idea suddenly didn't seem so wonderful. I stopped dead in my tracks. Staring at St. Francis Hospital, I wondered what Dad would say.

He knew that from a young age I loved sports. Baseball was my favorite sport from ages 7 to 12, then I fell in love with basketball. For as long as I could remember I always wanted to be a professional athlete.

Though I was quite short for my age and also not very good at basketball, at 14 I figured that if I grew three inches each year for the next five years, I would be 6-foot-2 and tall enough to play in the NBA.

Dad suggested I become a physical education teacher. His thoughts were that I could stay involved in sports, coach if I liked to, and perhaps even more importantly, have weekends and summers off. My dad made great sacrifices for our family. He worked seven days a week for many years after taking over the store. I know he did not want me to have to work the tremendous hours that Uncle George and he worked.

My passion for soccer and desire to become a great player was so intense, though I was going to Hartwick first and foremost because of soccer and not academics, my father remained silent about my decision. Hartwick did not offer a teaching degree.

When I saw my dad's smile, I knew everything would work out.

"Hi, Dad. Can I have a cheesesteak with fried onions and French fries?" "Yes. What would you like to drink?"

"I'll have water. I'll get it."

As I finished my sandwich, I decided there was nothing to discuss with my father.

I was going to Hartwick the next week.

The summer going into my high school junior year, I went to the Rider College soccer camp. That is where I met the two head coaching instructors, Charles "Ping Pong" Farrauto and Manfred Schellscheidt. It was a life-changing experience for me.

After one week with Ping Pong and Manfred, I had fallen in love with the game of soccer. My perspective of the game changed so dramatically, it was as if someone turned on the light bulb and I finally understood what this beautiful game of soccer was all about. I improved dramatically since then and continued to train every free minute.

A week after visiting Dad at the store, I was putting my last piece of luggage into my parents' car for the trip up to Oneonta. I turned and looked one last time at the house I had lived in my whole life. I hoped not to see my home again until Christmas.

If I was home for Thanksgiving, it would mean either I did not make Hartwick's varsity soccer team and/or we were eliminated early in the NCAA Tournament. It was a given that Hartwick College qualified for the NCAA Division 1 soccer tournament every year.

As I got comfortable in the back seat for the drive up to Hartwick, I wondered how Liekoski, one of the premier soccer coaches in the country, could be so wrong about me. He saw me play one time, and that was my first game back after I spent five months rehabilitating my left knee. I suffered ligament damage in the state championship game for St. Anthony's High School. How could he possibly have evaluated me correctly?

It was a cold, windy day on Nov. 17, 1973, when St. Anthony's High School was playing Union Catholic in the Parochial A state championship game. It was to be a very special day for me because the Saturday morning game meant my parents could attend my last high school game. In fact, due to my father's long working hours and the store being closed on Saturdays, it would be the only one of my high school games that he would see.

The game was scheduled for 10 a.m. Coach Potenza had the team report to our locker room at Saint Anthony's High School at 7 a.m. As we stepped off the team bus at Mercer County Park in West Windsor, New Jersey, it appeared that the wind had picked up dramatically since earlier in the morning.

During the warmup, I glanced across the field to look at the opposing team. I was shocked to see how big many of their players were. The wind was so strong that during the coin flip, the game ball the referee put down on the ground for the kickoff started blowing away with such speed that he had to run after it. We lost the coin toss and Union Catholic took the wind. I knew we would have to keep the ball on the ground and keep possession of it as best we could. If we could keep them from scoring when they had the wind in the first quarter, we would be in good shape to win this game.

We did a really good job of keeping possession of the ball during the first quarter and limited the opportunities for them near our goal. When we changed ends for the second quarter, the game changed dramatically. We started knocking the ball around better than we had all season, with many of our possessions ending up with good chances on goal. The strong wind made us all feel much more confident that we could shoot from much greater distances than in normal weather conditions.

Midway through the second quarter, after we squandered several good goal-scoring chances, I received a pass at the top of the D and beat the first defender. As I beat the second defender, I pushed the ball a little too far in front of me. As the third Union Catholic defender went down to slide tackle me, I toe-poked the ball, jumping over the tackle and watched as the ball slowly trickled into the corner of the goal for the first score of the game. We were all over them for the rest of the second quarter, but couldn't get the second goal.

Coach Potenza gave us a fiery halftime speech and had us believing we could walk through fire, if necessary, to win the game. It didn't matter that Union Catholic had the wind at its backs for the third quarter. We were getting ball possession and made them chase the ball, and they expended a lot of energy. Five minutes into the third quarter, Denny Kinnevy gave Juan Hauser a great pass and our Argentinean-born winger dribbled around Union Catholic defender Tom Ryan, beating the keeper to give us an important second goal.

Several minutes later, there was a loose ball between me and Union Catholic's biggest player. I went into the tackle with every ounce of energy I had, sliding right through the ball. My follow-through caught him and sent him airborne; he landed awkwardly on top of my left knee. I momentarily felt an excruciating sharp pain and at the same time felt a sensation as if my left knee had turned 360 degrees.

The game was stopped. Coach Potenza and our trainer, Charles Clerke, rushed out to attend to me. Coach Potenza immediately asked what happened. I replied, "Coach, he fell on my knee and I had this sharp pain for a few seconds, but it doesn't hurt too much now."

Clerke grabbed my knee almost with a fatherly touch, gently feeling and squeezing different parts of it instead of doing a draw test or another technique to test the stability. Although Clerke was our trainer, I did not believe he had any specialized medical training. The benefits from Clerke tended to be more spiritual than physical.

Clerke asked me, "Billy, do you feel any pain or discomfort when I am moving your knee around?"

I lied and told him no.

I had played most of the regular season with unbelievable pain in my left calf, before the pain finally went away near the end of the regular season. Although I did have a throbbing pain in my left knee, it was not nearly as painful as my calf injury was and I did not want to come out of the game.

Coach Potenza got close to me and stared into my eyes, asking, "Billy do you think you can keep playing?"

I said, "It's the state championship game and my parents are here. Of course I am going to keep playing. It will take more than this to keep me from finishing this game."

I got up and as Coach Potenza and Clerke ran off the field, all I could think about was how close we were to winning the state championship. The third quarter ended with us up 2-0 and the wind at our back for the fourth quarter. Between quarters, I hoped Clerke did not ask me how I was feeling, because I did not want to lie again. Sure enough, just as I was about to run back out onto the field, he asked me if I felt OK. I just smiled and nodded, and ran out onto the field.

Midway through the fourth quarter, JoJo Tuccillo, our left midfielder, who was playing his first year of organized soccer and having a brilliant game, buried a left-footed shot from 25 yards out for the third goal of the game. Shortly after that, our rock-solid goalkeeper Mike Magee kicked a long, wind-aided punt. It fell to Jerry Hustak, who played a through ball to Denny, who buried the shot into the back of the net for his team-leading 33rd goal.

It was only appropriate that Denny score in the state championship game. Denny and his family introduced me to soccer and his parents drove me every Sunday to our club team games. Denny was one of the best center forwards in the state.

With the score 4-0 and the wind at our backs, this game was decided. As the game neared its end, I experienced a constant throbbing pain, and something did not seem right with my knee. As the final whistle blew, I located my parents in the stands and we made eye contact. Having my parents attending the game and experiencing our state championship win made the day much more memorable. Little did I know when walking off the field that day how much it would affect my future.

In the afternoon Denny, several other teammates and I went and watched Steinert High School play its semifinal game of the state tournament. Many of the players on Steinert High School were teammates of ours on Hamilton Post 313, our junior league team. Steinert was the top team in the state and undefeated. The only blemish on its record was a tie with us. As we left the Steinert game, the pain in my knee started to intensify dramatically.

As we got into the early evening celebrating our state championship, the pain in my knee became unbearable and I asked Denny to take me home.

When I got home, I told my parents that something was wrong with my knee. I didn't tell them how bad the pain was because I didn't want them to worry. My father had to get up early for work the next day, so we decided that my mother would take me to the hospital. St. Francis Medical Center was only two blocks away, so Dad said, "OK, walk to the hospital with your mother." I truly wanted to drive to the hospital, but I knew parking at the hospital could be a real problem, so I did not say anything to my father.

We waited in the emergency room for what seemed like an eternity. Then a technician took me for an X-ray, after which I met the emergency room physician. After looking at the X-rays, the doctor told me that I had broken my patella. I was in shock. He said I would have to stay in the hospital overnight and in the morning, a specialist would re-examine my X-ray.

I was put into a room with a very old man who was in extreme pain and hollered, cried and whined the whole night. Between his discomfort and my concern how this injury would affect my soccer career, I did not sleep one minute. I thought how I had spent almost the whole high school soccer season dealing with pain in my left calf and when I finally felt good, I broke my kneecap. I couldn't believe this was happening to me. I trained every day of the year and now I had no idea what my future looked like. The morning sunlight could not come soon enough.

Dr. Fasulo, an orthopedic specialist, told me I had been there not too long ago with a broken fibula. I told him that he was wrong, that the only time I had been in the hospital other than being born in St. Francis Hospital was when I had my tonsils out. He looked at me and said that my X-ray clearly showed I had recently fractured my fibula and showed me the calcification, an indication that it had healed. My mind immediately raced back to our trainer, Clerke.

In our second game of the season, against Hopewell High School, I was shielding the ball when defender Harold Driver kicked me squarely on the side of my left calf muscle. That injury worsened day by day. By the middle of the season, I could barely walk out for the coin toss because the pain had become so severe.

Clerke was a religion teacher who volunteered to be a trainer for the soccer team. When Driver injured me, his recommendation was for me to take hot water baths and soak my leg. In the second half of the season, the pain slowly diminished. As we entered the state tournament, I was finally pain-free. Now I realized why I had been in such pain. I played almost an entire high school season with a fractured bone in my leg.

I looked the doctor and told him, "Doctor, you're right and wrong. I never came to the hospital but I had an injury to my left calf muscle, which would explain all of the pain I experienced."

The doctor did several tests on my right knee first and then my left. "Bill, you did not break your kneecap. You have irregular-shaped kneecaps and that prompted the physician last night to incorrectly read the X-ray. You have suffered ligament damage."

I was numb. I had no idea which injury was worse. Was I supposed to be happy that I did not break my kneecap, or sad that I damaged a knee ligament?

"Bill, we are going to put your leg in a cast for a month and then after that, you will have to rehabilitate your knee by strengthening the muscle groups around your knee."

All I heard from the doctor was, "We are going to put a cast on your leg for a month."

As we drove past Scranton, Pennsylvania, on our drive up to Hartwick, my dad startled me out of my deep thoughts about my high school injuries.

"Billy, are you hungry and would you like to stop for lunch?"

I knew that after my parents dropped me off, they would have to immediately turn around and drive back to Trenton.

"No, that's fine, Dad. I will eat with the team when we get there."

The truth was I was so nervous, I was not hungry. Going away to college was a nerve-wracking experience. Compounding it with walking into the preseason camp of one of the top teams in the country, with a coach who tells you that you are not good enough, did not inspire tremendous confidence in me.

Oneonta is a beautiful, historical college town nestled in the Susquehanna River Valley. As we approached the campus, my emotions rose like a flood of water from my feet, through my body to my throat. We found Dewar Hall and my dad pulled up to the entrance of the dormitory that would be home through preseason. We emptied the trunk of my bags and my father hugged me.

"Billy, I love you. Good luck. I know you will be fine."

My mother was crying and I used all my willpower to fight back the tears as I hugged her and kissed her goodbye. My dad told my mother to get back into the car because he wanted to return before dark. As the car pulled away, I observed the surrounding area and was thankful that Timo was not in the vicinity. All I needed was for him to see me with tears in my eyes. He would send me packing right to the junior varsity.

As I entered Dewar Hall, someone greeted me. "Hi, I am Charlie Lang. I am the soccer team's manager, and you are?"

"Hi Charlie. Nice to meet you. I am Billy Gazonas."

"Billy, let me check the list and see what room you are in and who your roommate is. You are rooming with Duncan MacDonald. Here, let me help you with your bags. Duncan is from Liverpool, England. Hopefully he's in the room."

Charlie knocked on the door. As we entered the room, I saw a guy with the reddest hair I had ever seen in my life. Duncan jumped off the bed and extended his hand to me. Charlie made the introductions and quickly left. Duncan immediately began to tell me where he was from and numerous facts about his upbringing.

Duncan was extremely friendly and exuded a lot of energy. His personality made me feel a bit at ease as I unpacked my soccer gear. All of my other attire would remain in the suitcases until preseason was over and I went to my dormitory room in Van Hess Hall. Dinner was not for several hours and Duncan decided to go see his fellow Englishman Jeff Tipping.

As I sat alone in this cinderblock wall college dormitory room, my nervousness reappeared. I wonder if Mooch had arrived yet. I had the opportunity to train with him most of the summer and initiate a friendship with perhaps the most charismatic individual I had ever met. I could not bear to sit in this room alone for another minute. I found Charlie Lang and he told me Moochie had not yet arrived. I decided to take a walk up to the soccer field.

Elmore Field was hallowed ground located at the top of the hillside of Hartwick's campus. The view is breathtaking. The field had bleachers built into the mountainside, with team benches situated on the opposite side next to a huge drop off and an almost endless sight of the Susquehanna River Valley. It's never more spectacular than with the fall foliage and changing of the leaves.

I was told that all home games were sold out. Excluding the bench side of the field where there was nowhere to stand behind the benches, there would be a wall of human bodies two to three deep.

I stepped onto Elmore Field and felt the grass. I slowly walked towards the center circle, getting excited about what the atmosphere must be like to play in. As I reached the center circle, I slowly turned in all directions. My emotions fluctuated between excitement and nervousness. I had trained every day that summer to strengthen my knee and improve my technical ability. The next day, I would get the opportunity to show Timo how wrong he was.

I sat in the middle of the bleachers for the fans' view of the game. I liked it. I then walked around the field and headed down to Dewar Hall. I quickly realized that on this campus, walking downhill is much easier than walking uphill.

There were numerous players standing at the entrance to Dewar Hall. I spotted Michael Angelotti, who's from Lawrence, New Jersey. He and I had driven up to visit the campus the previous winter. Angelotti was one of a small group of players who had trained at Nottingham Junior High with Charles "Ping Pong" Farrauto. I was so glad to see Michael, who introduced me to numerous players as we walked over to the commons for dinner. Finally Mooch arrived and I suddenly felt much better.

After dinner Timo and Alden Shattuck, the assistant coach, addressed the team. They reviewed our daily training schedule and our preseason exhibition games. Our training routine for the first week would be to get up at 7 a.m. and go for a cross-country run up into the woods behind the far goal on Elmore Field.

After breakfast, we would train from 10 a.m. to noon, followed by lunch, rest and training from 2 to 4 p.m. Tomorrow would be the exception to the rule. After breakfast, we would go through a physical fitness test up at the track that surrounds Elmore Field. I was very disappointed to find out that we would not train on Elmore Field.

At this point, I was feeling pretty good about things, until Timo said, "Not everybody in this room will be on the varsity roster at the end of preseason camp."

Although I knew this, hearing it directly from him put a knot in my stomach. I knew there were 24 players in camp, and Timo did not mention a specific number of players that would remain on the varsity. As I looked around the room, I recognized many of the players from New Jersey. Most of the freshmen from New Jersey were first team all-state selections and/or an All-American.

Timo, when he had visited New Jersey in the spring on his recruiting trip, raved about the three Mongolian players from Howell—Zeren Ombadykow, Khyn Ivanchukov and Angrik Stepanow. Duncan and Jeff Tipping were recruited from England and I had to assume they were very good players. Mooch was by far the greatest American-born player I had ever seen.

I wondered how good the returning players were. If they played anything like Moochie, then my chances of making the team were slim. I was told that if you play for the junior varsity, it was very difficult to get called up to the varsity and that the JV team was comprised mostly of players from prep schools in New Jersey and throughout New England. I saw a sleepless night coming.

As we stood up from the table, Mooch grabbed my arm and leaned over to ask quietly, "How are you feeling, Billy?"

"I feel good Mooch."

He sensed my uneasiness. He put his arm around me and with that big smile of his told me, "Just play as if you are at Nottingham; you will be fine!"

"Thanks Mooch. I'll see you in the morning."

Back at the room, Duncan was talking a mile a minute, while I was trying to relax and hopefully get some sleep. As Duncan turned off the lights, I said my prayers, asking God to allow me to make the varsity, among other things, including looking after my family. The next thing I knew, the alarm clock went off. I must have been so tired from the worrying the last few nights that I slept through the night.

2

Time to Prove Timo Wrong

Today would be the exception to our daily training schedule. We went directly to breakfast and were to skip the cross country run. I decided to have a crumb cake and some orange juice. At breakfast, we were told we did not need our soccer cleats for the morning fitness test. Our flats would do.

Up at the track, everybody looked so fit. I got through the first four fitness tests feeling quite good. A shuttle run was our final test. Five yards and back, 10 yards and back, 15 yards and back, 20 yards and back, and 25 yards and back.

I felt good after the first four tests, but as I finished the shuttle run, I realized I should not have eaten a crumb cake for breakfast. I ran to the side of the track, got on my knees and vomited for what seemed like a very long time. As I finish wiping my mouth and stood up, Timo was standing right behind me.

"Billy, are you OK?"

"Yes, Timo. I am fine."

He abruptly turned and walked away. At our dinner the night before, I noticed Timo went around the room and talked to what appeared to be everyone except me. Well, by getting sick, I realized at least he remembered my name!

My teammates ribbed me as we walked back to the dorm. That didn't bother me at all. What *did* bother me was that I had a feeling Timo actually resented the fact that he invited me to preseason. It was as if he couldn't even hide it from me. He probably wished he could cut me before I even touched a soccer ball.

At lunch I decided that for the rest of preseason, I would eat a very light breakfast and lunch. At dinner, I would eat whatever I wanted.

Most of our preseason training would be held at Neahwa Park, home to historic Damaschke Field, where the Oneonta Yankees Double A minor league team plays. The soccer team rarely trained on Elmore Field.

For every training session, we would walk up to Binder Gymnasium, where we would take vans to Neahwa Park. We were told the vans would leave promptly at 9:45 a.m. and 1:45 p.m—and we better not be late. As I walked up to Binder with Duncan, my thoughts wandered away from our conversation. I realized I would have to be at the top of my game for every training session. In Timo's speech at dinner the night before, he implied that he probably would not make any decisions on who made the team until the end of the two weeks, at the earliest. I knew I may or may not have had two weeks to impress him.

We reached the top of the hill, where three school vans were waiting to take us to practice. As I squeezed into the back of the van, I sat next to Ralph Hartzog. I immediately noticed the huge disparity in the size of our thighs. Ralph's thighs appeared to be twice the size of mine and chiseled out of stone. I could feel the nervous tension starting to flow through my body.

We pulled up to the training fields and as I stepped down out of the van, Timo yelled to me, "Billy, get the balls out of the back of the van."

As I did so, I noticed Lange, our team manager, and Shattuck both getting balls out of their vans. My nervousness quickly changed to anger, as I was the only player to be told to retrieve balls.

Timo told us to stretch for 10 minutes before we started the team warmup. Angelotti leaned over next to me so no one else could hear him as he whispered, "Don't let Timo bother you. He can be hard and as cold as ice to players. Just focus on all of the training you've done."

"Thanks Michael," I said. "Once I start touching a soccer ball, I think I will feel better."

After our stretching, Angelotti led the team through a long warmup. Timo then broke up the players into three groups to play some possession soccer. As I should have expected, I was the last player called to go with the third group. It was obvious that the first two groups were the players that Timo felt would be the nucleus of the team. My group was the players trying to survive the cuts and remain on the varsity.

The minute I touched the ball I was relieved. Over the last two years, my love of soccer had grown greater every day. Excluding when I had been injured, I had not missed one day of training and working on my technical skills. Even the day before, when my parents and I traveled up here, I went to Wetzel Field at 7 a.m. and trained for an hour before the trip.

In the keep-possession exercise, every touch of mine felt perfect and my concentration was very good. I knew what I was going to do before I received the ball. Playing two-touch possession soccer does not give you much time on the ball and your first touch needs to go exactly where you want it.

My first touch over the past year had improved dramatically. I owed that to Ping Pong. There were days when he and I were the only two at Nottingham to train, and training with him was always about mastering the soccer ball. I will never forget the first time Ping Pong told me to go stand in front of the six-foot chain link fence. I was not sure what he was going to do. He dribbled a ball over and, standing approximately seven to eight yards away, struck a ball that bounced off my knee before I could react. Ping looked at me and laughed. "Billy, trap the ball!"

"OK, Ping."

I remember getting on my toes and Ping started striking balls at me. Ping started slowly and kept the balls on the ground. The goal was to trap the ball perfectly still with one touch and play it back with a second touch. As the days and months passed, we built upon that initial training. Ping eventually would strike the ball with such velocity that I could barely react and balls were no longer just played on the ground. At times balls were played as high as my chest, with Ping constantly changing the location of his kicks. We would do this exercise for 10 to 15 minutes.

Ping had a saying: "You have to control the ball like it was Alabama cotton," meaning just as cotton would fall to the ground and stop dead still, so must the ball.

This training exercise evolved from trapping balls dead still in front of me to moving traps to get away from pressure. Ping Pong had a brilliant soccer mind. He constantly talked about being two to three plays ahead of the game. Know what you are going to do with the ball well before you receive it. When it came to playing two-touch possession soccer, I felt that I had an advantage over the other players.

During the 1974 World Cup, Ping Pong drove us to Philadelphia to watch the games on closed-circuit TV. Ping and I were so caught up in my mastering the first touch that we studied Franz Beckenbauer's body mechanics when receiving a ball.

Beckenbauer, who revolutionized the sweeper position, epitomized controlling the first touch like Alabama cotton. His first touch—in fact all of his technical skills (perhaps excluding heading the ball)—were impeccable.

We noticed a subtle movement that Beckenbauer did before receiving a forceful pass or shot from an opposing player. A fraction of a second before he was to trap a ball with the side of his right foot, he would slightly hop off the ground with his left. At the moment of impact, his total body weight was off the ground when the ball made contact with his right foot. It was so subtle, I have to believe most of the world never realized that Beckenbauer had both of his feet off of the ground when he was trapping a ball out of the air. I will never forget the next time Ping Pong and I trained together. We were so excited, we could not wait to try to emulate the technique, which we named the Beckenbauer Trap.

As our Hartwick two-touch possession training session progressed, my confidence was growing. After what seemed like 20 minutes, I still had not given the ball away to the opposition. That was the positive. The negative was that Timo and Alden had not come over to our group for even one minute to observe our session.

We broke for a water break, with a shooting drill to follow with the whole team. I thought Timo did not watch one minute of our two-touch session, which was the strong point of my game, but now he would watch my shooting. Shooting from distance and long passing of the ball were my weak points, which I knew I had to improve dramatically.

Ping Pong and I had a long discussion prior to my leaving for Hartwick. "Billy, you have to improve your long-range passing of the ball," he said. "If you don't, you will be limiting your effectiveness on the field. Look how dynamic Mooch is. Part of his greatness is his ability to make pinpoint, accurate 60-yard diagonal passes cross field." It is ironic because I had a similar conversation with Mooch and he told me he would help me with my long-distance passing.

The shooting exercise involved two players out wide playing a one-two, with one of them getting to the end line and cutting the ball back into the 18-yard box, and a third player running onto the ball and striking it first time. The first five players struck nice shots on goal and then Mooch ran to the ball and hit a laser into the back of the net. Steve Jameson, our English goalkeeper from Liverpool, never even moved. The training session momentarily stopped with everyone in awe of Mooch's rocket of a shot. I followed Mooch and, leaning back, struck the ball 10 yards over the goal. Running back to the other line, I told myself to stay over the ball and strike it with proper technique. I played great for 20 minutes in the two-touch session, but this is what Timo saw of me.

As the shooting session continued, Timo complimented pretty much everyone who struck their shot on goal. My crosses were perfect and my remaining shots on goal were struck well. But Timo remained silent, although Alden complimented me on my crossed balls.

As the session ended, Timo was walking towards me, my thought being that I had done a good job and he was going to tell me that I played well. Was I wrong. "Billy, help Charlie pick up the balls," and he turned and abruptly walked away. It was like after I vomited and he asked if I was all right.

I am my harshest critic and I know I had played quite well, other than the first shot on goal. After dinner, I went back to my room knowing that not only did I have to play really good soccer, but I had to figure out a way to get Timo to notice my good play.

The very positive comments he made to his highly recruited players should not have been a surprise to me. That past spring during Timo's recruiting trip to New Jersey, he watched me playing for Hamilton Post 313 in my first game back since I damaged my ligaments in my high school state championship game in November.

My discussion with him after that game was more about how great his recruits were, not about my ability and my chances of playing at Hartwick. He actually told me if any school offered me any money, I should take it and go to that college. I felt like I showed up at a party whose host didn't want me there and made sure I knew it.

I hoped I would sleep. I said my prayers and went to bed before Duncan got back to the room.

The alarm sounded and Duncan and I were out of bed in a heartbeat. That morning, we would be going on our first cross country run. Duncan and I quickly dressed and went to Binder Gymnasium. We went out on the track and stretched while we waited for the last few players to arrive. Alden would be leading us on our cross country run. He attended Springfield College, located in scenic Western Massachusetts. Springfield is famous for being the birthplace of basketball.

We started our run into the woods behind the far goal on Elmore Field. Jim Harrison, a senior from Kearny, New Jersey, jogged alongside me. From what I had heard. Jim, known as Harry, was by far the funniest guy on the team. Ten minutes into the run, I turned to Harry and told him that "all I have heard is how difficult this run is, but it does not feel that hard to me." Jim said, "Wait. It will gradually get more difficult as we make our way to the top of the mountain."

Two minutes later I looked up and the running trail appeared to be at least a quarter-mile straight up the mountain. The group slowed dramatically, although watching Alden separate from us you would think he was running downhill. Halfway up the mountain, my thighs started burning. I had never run on terrain like this, never uphill. My long-distance preparation this summer was walking over to Trenton High School and running around the track. Players' conversations abruptly ended.

What started out as a beautiful cool summer morning in Oneonta heated up dramatically. The only noises were our feet striking the ground and collective heavy breathing of the players. If misery loves company, then this was the epitome of that phrase.

No one stopped running. But near the top of this incredible ascent, the pace had slowed significantly. I did not think I could take another stride uphill when I made it to the top. The rest of the run was straight downhill. Slowly the burning in my thighs dissipated and I eventually caught my breath. Needless to say, my conversation with Harry did not continue until we finished the run. My first thought upon completing the run was: Do I have any energy left to train today?

After breakfast we headed back over to Neahwa Park for our morning training session, which consisted of a lot of technical work, with fitness incorporated into each exercise. At the end of the morning session, Timo told us what to expect for the afternoon session, including that we would scrimmage the last 30 minutes. He also said that early the next week, we would travel to play State University of Albany in our first scrimmage of preseason.

On the ride back to campus, all I could think about was the afternoon scrimmage. If I could get Timo's attention during our team scrimmages, it could lead to some playing time in the Albany scrimmage the following week. Hopefully I would slowly change his mind about my playing ability.

Timo addressed the team before the scrimmage. He talked about how in transition, specifically when we lose the ball, everybody should immediately get behind it. I instantly thought of Ping Pong, who told us that one of the biggest changes in the game tactically from the 1970 World Cup to the 1974 World Cup is that in the latter, when teams lost the ball, they would instantly get behind it and all 11 players were expected to defend. Timo said when the opportunity presented itself, we needed to counterattack with speed before the opposing team got all 11 players behind the ball. If not, than we needed to slow the game and keep possession.

When Timo said, "This is how we are going to line up this afternoon," it sent a jolt of nerves through my body. I thought, just put me in the first

22. The choices for the midfield for the first 11 were pretty obvious from his numerous comments the previous few days.

Timo continued with, "and in the midfield I want Mooch at central midfield, Brian as the right-sided midfielder and Zeren on the left side." Brian Doyle was being touted as a possible All-American candidate and after Mooch, Zeren may have been Timo's most highly recruited player. From the first time I saw Zeren play in the Howell tournament through all the games with the Pinelanders, Zeren's junior club team played indoors at the Trenton Civic Center, I always felt he was such a gifted player. Zeren had fabulous technical skills and an immense Afro that would have caught your attention even if he was not a great player.

Timo's selection of the above three in midfield for the first 11 was not a surprise to me. I was very aware of Mooch and Zeren. From what I was told, Doyle, who was going into his senior year and had not been a starter for several years, had worked very hard on improving his game. Brian was very technical with good vision and appeared to have loads of confidence.

I did not expect to be in the first 11 and be a starter in my freshman year at Hartwick. My goal was to make the varsity. Timo announced the second 11 and I was not included. Mark Rowley, son of our team doctor Dr. Douglas Rowley, and I were the two players not selected in the first 22 to start the scrimmage.

As the scrimmage was about to start, Timo turned to me and said, "Billy, help Charlie get the balls that go out of bounds." It was not exactly what I was hoping for when Timo called my name.

As I alternated between chasing balls and watching the scrimmage, I noticed how physical the scrimmage had become. Excluding the previous day's session of two-touch possession, this was the first training session where players were physically competing head to head. After 25 minutes of chasing balls, I heard Timo shout, "Billy, go in on the right side of midfield for the second team." I got one touch over the next five minutes and Alden blew the whistle to end the scrimmage.

After helping Lang collect the soccer balls, I was walking to the van when Doyle approached me with some words of encouragement.

"Billy, don't let any of this get you down. Just train hard and try to improve yourself as a player every day. I know what it's like to come into this program when you are not one of the highly recruited players. It's taken me years to get into the position that I am finally going to start. It is obvious to me your technical skills are good enough to play for Hartwick. You just have to have patience and make the cut. You will improve more training with the varsity versus being the best player on the junior varsity."

I replied, "I know, Brian. That is my goal. Thanks, I appreciate it."

That evening, I was having dinner with Mooch when Timo came over and sat down next to me, across from Mooch. Timo and Mooch begin analyzing the attacking role of Beckenbauer as the sweeper for West Germany. Beckenbauer had revolutionized the position. Although I was not part of the conversation, it was an enlightening experience learning their thoughts on the expanding attacking role of the sweeper position.

Although Ping and I had spent all summer dissecting the World Cup and many of the subtleties of Beckenbauer's game, I chose just to listen and learn from Mooch and Timo. Although I strongly disagreed with Timo's analysis of me as a player, I still recognized that he had a brilliant soccer mind and I wanted to learn as much as I could about the game I had come to love so much.

When under defensive pressure, Beckenbauer often would do this classic pirouette move to make space for himself, doing a circular motion with the ball almost attached to the outside of his right foot. The movement was so simple yet so effective.

Ping Pong felt that in order for me to become a very good midfield general, I had to master that pirouette move. We had spent countless hours the previous summer attempting to master the move, first with the outside of my right foot and then with the inside of my right foot. Thanks to Ping Pong, I incorporated into my game the Beckenbauer trap and pirouette move. I was in my glory listening to Mooch and Timo analyze everything about The Kaiser's game and it may be the only time getting ignored by Timo did not bother me at all.

The remainder of the week was physically grueling. High school preseason was like being on vacation compared to this. Timo precisely followed his preseason training schedule itinerary for the team. We entered a stretch of extremely hot weather and with the pressure of players competing for starting positions, playing time and in my case just to make the varsity, there were no friends on the soccer field. Tempers were short and tackles were getting harder by the minute.

Timo continued to ignore me. Despite this, I started to receive some encouragement from Alden. I felt every day that I was playing a little better than the day before. Mooch and Angelotti made it a point to let me know after every training session that I was playing good soccer and to stay focused. Doyle took a liking to me and suggested ways for me to improve my game.

I could feel my confidence starting to grow. Although Mark Rowley and I were by far the smallest players in preseason camp, I made it a point to go into each tackle with every ounce of energy I possessed. I would not allow myself to be intimidated by anyone, including Mooch, who was becoming a very good friend, mentor and confidant.

There was another important point that started to raise my confidence. Three of Timo's most highly regarded recruits were Art Napolitano, Zeren Ombadykow and Randy Escobar, all very talented players, with Art having received the New Jersey High School Soccer Player of the Year award our senior year.

I sensed that as our training sessions became more physical, the three were getting a bit intimidated. Timo loved Art, so he would be starting no matter what. Randy was a forward with dazzling dribbling skills, born in Peru but raised in New Jersey. With Randy being a forward, I really was not directly competing with him for playing time, but I was competing for a spot on the roster.

The real encouragement for me came from Zeren not performing up to his superb soccer skills. I was sure that in Timo's mind, Mooch and Zeren would form the nucleus of the midfield for the next three years. Zeren was not comfortable with the physical nature of college soccer and I could see it in his game.

I would know if my assessment of my teammates was correct after the next day's scrimmage. Timo announced the player lineup for the afternoon scrimmage, and there were no changes from the first scrimmage of preseason. It was as if Timo had his mind made up before preseason even started who would play and in what positions. Timo also made it clear to me that I was to help Charlie chase balls that went out of bounds. Once again, I received only a few minutes of playing time during the afternoon scrimmage after expending most of my energy chasing balls.

Still, I had a good night's sleep and was very excited getting in the van for the 80-mile trip to Albany for the scrimmage. The first thing I noticed stepping out of our team van was the breathtaking blue sky canvassing the bright orange sun. It had rained very hard overnight, but there was not a cloud in the sky now.

We had a nice long warmup, led by our captain Angelotti. The field was very soft and soggy in certain areas. Timo huddled us together and announced the starting lineup. No surprises here; it was the same lineup from the first day of our scrimmages.

Although this was an exhibition game for us, it was much more than that for Albany. We were Hartwick, a superpower in college soccer playing a minnow. The game started out very sloppily, with the ball stopping dead numerous times in puddles of water.

Ten minutes into the game, a lanky defender for Albany sprinted towards Bob Isaacson as Ike received a ball played through the midfield. As Ike turned with the ball, the defender went over the top of the ball with two feet and crushed Ike in the tackle. Ike crumpled to the ground and Timo exploded off the bench, hollering at the defender and referee that the infraction deserved a red card.

Fifteen minutes into the game after numerous fouls, I realized our very physical training sessions at Hartwick practices were child's play compared to some of the tackling going on in what was supposed to be a friendly exhibition game. The field conditions didn't allow us to keep possession of the ball for long periods of time and our goal-scoring chances were more from bad weather conditions than good individual and combination play.

The first 11 played the whole first half. At halftime, Timo made some tactical adjustments, and told us he would be freely substituting in the second half and everybody would get some minutes. As the second half began, I stood behind the bench stretching and trying to keep loose. The second half felt like an eternity, with Timo freely substituting everybody on the team but me. I finally heard that strong Finnish accent directed towards me. "Billy, warm up. You are going in for Zeren on the left side of midfield."

My body instantly filled with nervous excitement. There were five minutes left in the game. Two minutes later, I stepped on the field for my first actual intercollegiate action. I was located on the left side of the field, where there were many puddles. My first sprint after the ball made me feel like I was running in quicksand. My thighs became so tight I felt like I was in slow motion. I played very simply with the few touches of the ball that came my way and was glad when the referee blew his whistle to end the game. I never felt so tight in a game and I was not sure if it was the muddy conditions or just nerves. In those three minutes of playing time I did not do anything to endear myself to Timo.

On the ride back to Oneonta, I did not talk to anyone. I just tried to analyze the game. I knew that I was right about Artie, Randy and Zeren. The Albany game confirmed my belief that the extreme physical nature of college soccer would affect their special talents until they could adjust to it. For me, being strong in every tackle could be a way to get Timo's attention. Although I did very little, I knew it was due to lack of playing time and my extreme tightness, hopefully just due to the field conditions.

The training leading up to our next scheduled scrimmage, against Mitchell Junior College, was very intense. The competition was fierce and my window of opportunity to impress Timo and get his attention was getting smaller day by day.

For me, it was a repeat of the Albany game. I went in with about five minutes left to play; everyone else on the team got significant playing time. I had little involvement, getting few touches. The only positive was that I felt really loose compared to the Albany game. But I was on an emotional roller coaster. I knew in training I was playing well and at times very well, which gave me the confidence that I could make the team. But on the other hand, there was zero acknowledgment from Timo, and his opinion was the one that would decide my soccer future at Hartwick.

As Timo addressed the team with his postgame analysis of our performance against Mitchell, all I could think about was that he was not going to give me an opportunity to prove myself to make the team. I was not sure if I heard anything he said. I was the last player left in the locker room after showering when Alden walked in and sat next to me.

"Billy you did not get many minutes today but you will get more playing time against Cortland." I responded with, "That's good. I need some playing time to show what I am capable of. Alden, what is their playing style?"

He said, "Billy, they are a physical education school, meaning they will be very physical, very fit, and play 100 miles an hour with lots of long balls. They will high-pressure everything and will commit a lot of fouls against us to disrupt our playing style."

As he walked away, Alden said, "By the way, some of the older players on the team are impressed with your play. Keep it up."

"Thanks, Alden."

After two weeks of constant nerves and worry, with my confidence vacillating like a seesaw, I think I had indirect confirmation from Alden that I belonged on the varsity. Was that Alden's way of telling me I was a player of Hartwick caliber? It would come down to Timo's opinion regardless of what Alden or anyone else thought. The fact that Cortland State was very aggressive was good for me. Its style of play would make Artie, Zeren and Randy uncomfortable and give me the opportunity to show Timo that the physical nature of college soccer did not intimidate me in the least.

Several hours later, Mooch came up and put his arm around me. "Billy, sit with me for dinner tonight," he said.

"OK, Mooch."

We took a table away from all of the players. "Billy, you have a real fight on your hands to make the varsity. I spoke to Timo about you. I explained to him that you are a much better player than when he saw you in the spring but he feels you aren't Hartwick College material. You have to play really good in the next exhibition game. Timo mentioned dropping you down to the junior varsity right after the Cortland State game."

As soon as Mooch finished, I felt an intense knot in my stomach. I was feeling much better after my conversation with Alden, and now this.

"Mooch, I think I have been playing good in training, but in the preseason games I am always the last player to go in and only for a few minutes at the end of the game. It's hard to make an impression under those circumstances."

Mooch said, "I know it is, but you have to go out there and prove to Timo that he is wrong."

"That's what I am going to do. I spoke to Alden before I left the locker room and he told me that I would get more playing time against Cortland. Thanks, Mooch."

The next day would be our first break after two very intense weeks of preseason camp. Preseason was officially over and that Sunday, we all would move into our dorms or apartments and get ready for classes, which began the next day. Walking back to the dorm after dinner with Mooch, all I could think about was that I had one more day of training and then one exhibition game against Cortland to convince Timo that I deserved to stay on the varsity.

That night, as I packed up my things to get ready to move out in the morning, Duncan came in the room and told me that he heard Timo would make all of his roster decisions on Wednesday. "Duncan, is that before training or after training?" I asked. He replied, "I don't know whether it is before or after training ends." Timo probably would send me down to the junior varsity before training even starts on Wednesday.

As I twisted and turned in bed that night trying to get some sleep, I not only felt the constant pressure of trying to make the varsity, but also the anxiousness of meeting my roommate. I was a little apprehensive. What if we do not get along? Throw in the excitement that in two days classes would begin, and I didn't foresee a great night of sleep.

The next morning after I moved all of my belongings into my room, the door opened and in walked a tall, blond-haired individual. He introduced himself as Joe from Scarsdale, New York. We spoke for several minutes. Joe seemed on the shy, quiet side. Later in the morning after long periods of silence in our room, I asked Joe if he would like to go to lunch with me. As we went to the cafeteria, I noticed numerous parents gasping for air as they walked the physically challenging campus.

I had a nice lunch with Joe and we got to know a little bit about each other. The break also took my mind off of soccer and allowed me to relax a little bit. I was physically exhausted from preseason but decided to go to the lower field and do some secret training on my own. Once I started training, I felt much better. There is something about having the soccer ball at my feet.

Classes started the next day, and I felt the nervousness that I think any freshman would feel their first day of college. The excitement of starting classes was a great distraction for me. I finally had a reprieve from the constant worry of possibly not making the varsity.

After two classes and a light lunch, I went to Binder to change for practice. On the ride over to Neahwa Park, the reality that it might be my last training session with the varsity really sunk in. As we exited the vans, I did not hear Timo holler for me to get the balls. I realized that the last few training sessions, Timo had not asked me to carry the balls or any other tasks to help Charlie Lang, tasks more in line with an equipment manager than a Division 1 varsity soccer player. I took that as a good sign.

Perhaps Timo was starting to realize that I actually could play this game and hopefully, down the road, I could contribute something to the team. That thought was quickly erased when Timo announced lineups to scrimmage that afternoon. I was not on either of the first two announced teams. I played very little in the scrimmage and questioned whether Alden was right with his comment that I would get to play a lot against Cortland.

After class the following day, we boarded Hartwick's bus Bluebird to go to Cortland State. I intentionally picked a seat where I could sit alone.

I just wanted to go over in my mind what I would do when I got into the game and all of the positive things I would contribute.

We got to the game two hours prior to kickoff and Timo ran us through a light training session, with lots of focus on our restarts. As we got close to kickoff, it started to get dark. I was amazed at how many fans were there for the exhibition game. Timo huddled us together, reviewed the starting lineup and discussed tactics.

Timo started with, "We know that they want to play the game at 100 miles per hour and it is our responsibility to not allow that. When we have the opportunity to counterattack with speed and we have numbers, we need to play fast. Most of the time we need to slow the game up, keep possession of the ball and make them do a lot of running. Alden, do you have anything to add?"

Alden said, "Yes, Timo. We know that they are going to commit a lot of fouls and it is very important that we keep our composure and not let them disrupt our flow of the game. We worked really hard this preseason. Let's go out and enjoy the game. Good luck."

As our starters were ready to walk on the field, Mooch came by and said, "Billy, just be ready when your name gets called. Know what you want to do with the ball before you receive it because this team is going to play very fast and aggressive."

"Thanks, Mooch," I said.

Although everyone emphasized how fast Cortland State would play, I was stunned by the high pressure it put on us the minute the whistle blew. Ten minutes into the game, I don't think we had put five passes together. They were the ultimate kick-and-run team and very athletic.

About 20 minutes into the game, we started to settle down a bit and string more passes together, but it was obvious Timo was not happy at all. I had thought with the team playing so poorly that I might get a chance to play in the first half. But that was wishful thinking.

What became 100 percent clear to me was that Artie and Zeren, who started, and Randy Escobar, who went into the game at around the 25-minute mark, were very uncomfortable with the physical nature of the game. Cortland State made repeated fouls.

While Albany State had many clever foreign players who were able to make their fouling look unintentional to the referees, Cortland State players were not disguising anything and literally just running through players. There could have been several red cards in the first half, yet the referees just verbally reprimanded the aggressive play by Cortland State and allowed play to resume. It was 0-0 at halftime and Timo was livid with our play.

He substituted freely at halftime, and the second team played much better than the first team. At 20 minutes into the second half, I finally got into the game. Despite never having experienced high pressure like Cortland State displayed and the huge importance for me to play well, I felt very relaxed once I got into the game. The game ended 1-0 in our favor and Timo actually complimented several players who were not in the starting lineup. I felt I played pretty good. The last words out of Timo's mouth before we boarded the bus for the ride back to Hartwick was, "After training tomorrow, I will meet with every player and make decisions on who is on the varsity and who will go down to the junior varsity."

The minute I got back to my room and put my head down on my pillow, I realized I would not be getting much sleep. I last looked at the clock at 4:12 a.m. The next morning, I arose early for my 8 a.m. American Government class with Professor Sugwon Kang.

My thoughts in class were all over the place. One minute on Kang's lecture the next on my future with the soccer team. On my second day of class, and I couldn't concentrate on his lecture at all. At lunch, I had a few bites of a tuna fish sandwich. I just wanted to know my future.

Three o'clock couldn't arrive soon enough. Training started with some two-touch possession, something I'm normally very good at, but I felt the pressure getting to me.

My concentration was very poor and I had a hard time thinking ahead before I received the ball. I gave away more balls in 20 minutes than I did all of preseason. We then reviewed set pieces and I was not even in the second 11 defending against our starting 11. This definitely was not a good sign.

As training ended, players mingled in small groups, waiting for Timo to start calling over individuals. Timo predictably started with all of the players who appeared to be in the starting lineup. Most conversations lasted not more than a couple minutes or so, with lots of smiling.

Then Timo started with the remaining players. Some would be substitutes and several would be going down to the junior varsity. One by one, I studied each player's facial reaction when Timo talked to them, and I intensely watched their reaction as their conversation ended and they walked away from Timo.

It was as if time was still. Every second seemed like minutes. I had not even thought about what I would do if I didn't make the varsity. I went to Hartwick only for the soccer program and if I wasn't good enough, I really should have been at another college. I knew my priorities were a bit backwards, but soccer was my life. Player after player was called while I waited to hear Timo call my name.

I was the last player left when Timo finally called my name. "Billy, come."

I slowly walked over to Timo.

"Billy, I know you had a knee injury last year and were just coming back from that injury when I saw you play in New Jersey. You have had over two weeks here for me to watch you and you seem like you have physically fully recovered from that injury. I don't see you playing at all on the varsity."

With that sentence I felt like my life was over, I felt numb, speechless. I just continued to look right at Timo, and after what seemed like an eternity of silence Timo said, "But I will give you a choice. You can go down to the junior varsity and you will probably be one of the better players on the team and you will play a lot, or you can stay on the varsity, but you're most likely not going to play at all."

Without any hesitation I looked right into Timo's eyes and told him, "I'll stay on the varsity." I then turned and as I started to walk away, emotions started swirling inside me when I heard, "Billy, if you change your mind let me know."

I immediately turned back to Timo and replied, "Timo, thank you, but that will never happen."

Walking away, I had numerous thoughts flowing through my mind. As I approached the door going into Binder Hall, Mooch was waiting for me.

"Billy, let's take a walk on the track. What did Timo tell you?"

"Mooch, he gave me a choice. The choice was stay on the varsity and I most likely would never play or go down to the junior varsity and be one of the better players on the team." Mooch asked, "Billy, what did you tell him?"

I replied, "Mooch, you know I love soccer. Where am I going to become a better soccer player, playing on the junior varsity playing kick and run, or getting to train with and against you every day in training?

"You know, Mooch, before I came to preseason, I thought the majority of the players on the team were as good as you and I got cold feet and almost was going to sit out the year. But having gone through preseason, no one else on the team is remotely as good as you are and I know I not only deserve to be on the varsity, but feel I should get some playing time."

"I agree," Mooch said.

As Mooch and I walked back into the locker room, I noticed Charlie Lang was going around the room asking the freshmen players for their height and weight so he could put the information into the home game brochures. My mind started racing 100 miles per hour. I knew that many colleges were not interested in me as a soccer player because they felt I was too small. If someday I was good enough to play at the professional level, my size or lack thereof may be even a bigger negative against me. I was 5-foot-3 3/4 and weighed 125 pounds. But I decided to tell Charlie I was 5-foot-5 and 132 pounds.

"Billy, what is your height and weight and your hometown," he asked. "Charlie, I am from Trenton, New Jersey, 5-foot-5 and I weigh 132 pounds."

As soon as I finished eating dinner, I headed straight for a pay phone to give my parents the great news that I had made the varsity. My parents could sense my excitement and were really happy for me. Now that I had made the varsity, my parents would get to see me when we played Montclair State University in our first regular-season game.

Although I knew in my heart that Timo did not want me on the varsity, I was very excited to be on the team nonetheless. I reached my first goal and it was time to train harder than ever to reach my second, which was to get some playing time and eventually start. My ultimate goal was to win a national championship with Hartwick.

That Saturday, we went to Philadelphia and played in the Leaness Tournament held at Temple Stadium. We played three 45-minute exhibition games. We lost to Temple 1-0, Philadelphia Textile 1-0 and 2-0 to the University of Pennsylvania. We were really struggling in the attack and had a very difficult time creating quality chances. I received a few minutes of playing time at the end of each game—once again the last player to get into each game.

The following Monday at training, Timo made a few changes and took Zeren out of the first team midfield and inserted Jeff Marshall into Zeren's position. Without the pressure of worrying about making the varsity, I was so much more relaxed in training. Every day, I felt like I was playing a little better than the day before.

Midweek, we had our final exhibition game before the regular season started on that Saturday at Montclair State University. Our Friday training was light, and we went over set pieces. Saturday couldn't come soon enough for me.

We boarded Bluebird at 8 a.m. for the three-hour bus ride to Montclair. Despite Timo telling me that I probably never would play on the varsity, I tried to rationalize why I would get some playing time against Montclair State. We should win the game easily, I thought.

This may have been one of the few easy games on the schedule, where Timo may be comfortable substituting a lot of players. If we got a big lead, why wouldn't Timo give me some playing time?

It also was the only game to be played in New Jersey that year and my parents would be there. I hoped we'd get a two- or three-goal lead so I could play more than the last five minutes in the second half. And this game was extra special for all of the freshmen on the team from New Jersey.

We arrived at Montclair at 11:30 a.m. We relaxed a little bit and then went through our warmup. I watched for my parents and spotted them 15 minutes before game time. I waved to them and finished the warmup. I was really excited. I was on the varsity soccer team of Hartwick, one of the perennial powerhouses of college soccer, ranked seventh in the country, getting ready to play my first official college game, and my parents would get to watch this game. On top of that, Manfred Schellscheidt was the coach of Montclair State. Manfred, along with Charles 'Ping Pong" Farrauto, were the two head instructors at the Rider College soccer camp that had opened my eyes to what soccer was all about. That was the moment when I fell in love with the sport. Manfred was also the New Jersey state coach and considered one of the best coaches in the country. I hoped one day to get picked to play on the New Jersey State team. I knew it was going to be a great day.

There were no surprises with our starting lineup. Ten minutes into the game, it was apparent that we were a much better team, although Montclair State had some very good individual players, none more so than Dickie Moore. We created good chances but couldn't seem to finish good buildups with a goal. Timo must have sensed that a goal or two would be coming shortly, as he started to substitute freely at around the 20-minute mark. Several more substitutions were made before halftime. I had to believe I would get some playing time in the second half. We outshot Montclair by a huge margin but at halftime, the score was 0-0.

The second half started like the first, with us dominating possession of the ball. Timo continued to make numerous substitutions and I still eagerly waited to make my official debut in a Hartwick uniform. Midway through the second half, every player on Hartwick but me had played a fair amount of time.

I started to get a little anxious when at the 72-minute mark, Zeren served a perfect cross to Jim Harrison standing on the 18-yard line. Harry controlled the ball off of his chest, turned and volleyed the ball into the side netting. Harry dropped to his knees and raised his arms to the sky exactly like Gerd Muller did in the 1974 World Cup final for West Germany against Holland.

Teammates mobbed Harry on the field. I thought it was only a matter of time before I would enter the game. I stood behind the bench and started to stretch, one, to make sure that my muscles were nice and loose and two, to make sure Timo saw me.

With 15 minutes left in the game, Timo made more changes. Ten minutes left, I got concerned that I might not get in, although in several preseason games, I did not go in until there were five minutes left. I was fixated on the amount of time left in the game. Eight minutes, five minutes, two minutes, one minute and then the referee blew the whistle to end the game.

I could not believe it. I did not play for one minute. I was in shock. I was the only player on the team not to get into the game.

This was supposed to be such a special day for me. I collected my thoughts, controlled my emotions and made my way over to Jimmy Harrison to congratulate him on the game-winning goal. I was genuinely happy for Harry because he had worked really hard and was in his senior year and hoping to get into the starting lineup.

I congratulated Mooch and Mike Angelotti on a game well-played, then headed to my parents. I could feel disappointment and humiliation taking over my emotions as I approached them. I fought those feelings and gave my mom and dad big hugs. My dad sensed that I was very upset and asked me, "Billy how are your classes? Are you happy with the professors you have?" "They are good, Dad. I like my classes and professors."

That's my dad. He knew I was upset, so the last thing he was going to do was bring up that I was the only one on the team not to play.

Then my mom chimed in.

"I have a care package for you, koulourakia and the September edition of *World Soccer Magazine*."

"Thanks, Mom."

I love my mother's koulourakia. They are Greek butter cookies. *World Soccer Magazine* was my favorite publication. I had read every word of every edition since my junior year in high school.

In the background I heard Alden shout out, "Everybody needs to be on the bus in five minutes." My dad, sensing that it was only a matter of time before my mother started crying, told her to hug me because I had to get on the bus. I was the first one on the bus. I headed to the back and watched my parents make it to their car out the back window.

What I thought was going to be a very special day for me turned out to be a humiliating experience. I was the only player on the team not to play. If I knew I was not good enough, perhaps it would not have been as painful as it felt at this moment. But I knew I deserved to be on this team and to get playing time.

My eyes filled with tears as my teammates stepped on to the bus one after another, hollering, laughing and planning their night at the Rail Bar when we got back to Oneonta.

Then Harry stepped into the bus and everyone chanted "Harry, Harry." He sat next to me. The irony was that Harry scored the game-winning goal and may have been the happiest member of our team at this moment, and I was the only one who did not play and most likely was the unhappiest team member.

Harry looked at me and saw that my eyes were filled with tears. He leaned over to me and whispered, "Billy, there have been many great players at Hartwick College who have gotten screwed. You should transfer to another school."

With my voice cracking, I replied, "Harry, I do not know what I am going to do." The bus ride back to Oneonta was extremely loud with lots of talking and laughing.

The majority of the players would meet this night at the Rail.

The Rail was one of 58 bars in downtown Oneonta. At the time, the legal drinking age was 18, and the majority of Hartwick and Oneonta State University students ended up downtown at one of the bars most weekends and many weeknights also. The bars typically catered to one of three groups: Hartwick students, Oneonta State students or residents of Oneonta, and the surrounding small towns that comprise Central New York State. The Rail was a Hartwick bar and Nate, the owner, was a huge fan of Hartwick soccer. Nate was very generous, according to the older players.

I was deeply absorbed with my thoughts and didn't utter one word the entire trip back to campus. I realized that transferring would be the same as quitting, and quitting is the last thing I was going to do, especially when I knew I was good enough to play at Hartwick. I had to get to a playing level that would convince Timo that I not only belonged on the varsity but should be playing.

As I stepped off the bus, Mooch was waiting for me.

"Billy, we are going to meet at the Rail around 9, so we will see you there?" "Mooch thanks, but I am going to pass."

"Billy, don't let today get to you. Just keep training hard and you will get your opportunity to prove Timo wrong."

"I know Mooch. I am going to show him how wrong he is about me and thanks, but I have some things I want to do."

Such as do some secret training that night at Neahwa Park, which I decided to do on the bus ride back. The park had a well-lit grassy area near the entrance, so when it got dark, I still could train.

When I got back to my dorm room, I changed into training gear, put on training flats, grabbed my soccer ball and made the 25-minute walk downhill to Neahwa Park. I got to the park right around 8:30 and planned to train for a good hour. While stretching, I couldn't get the thought out of my mind that I was the only player on the team not to play and how humiliating it was.

I spent about 10 minutes dribbling before starting a juggling exercise. I began with one touch with my right instep, flicked it up to my right thigh for one touch, to my forehead for one touch, down to my left thigh for one touch and down to my left instep for one touch. I repeated the process in reverse, from left instep one touch to left thigh to my forehead back down to my right thigh to my right instep.

I repeated the process, taking two touches with my right instep, right thigh, forehead going over to the left side and back. I followed with three touches, etc. The goal was to get to 10 touches with each part of my body without dropping the ball. Maybe someday I would reach that goal, but I knew it would not happen this night.

Next training exercise, I took four or five juggles before kicking the ball 10 to 15 feet in the air—and simultaneously, I made sure to take quick glances over my right shoulder and left shoulder, then gave a body swerve as if I was going to take the trap in one direction when I actually was going to do a moving trap in the opposite one.

After controlling the ball off of the moving trap, I accelerated 10 to 15 yards and ended the move with one of the Beckenbauer pirouettes to get away from my imaginary defender. I did 50 repetitions with the ball using the inside of my right foot, followed by 50 repetitions with the ball using the outside of my right foot.

This was one of my favorite training exercises, especially when I trained alone and didn't have access to a wall. It incorporated so many aspects of the game. I practiced my touch with the juggling, worked on my vision with my quick glances, made body swerves to send the defender in the wrong direction, worked on my traps controlling the ball out of the air, my acceleration and ended the move with a Beckenbauer pirouette to make space for myself. If I accelerated and exploded off of the trap at top speed for 10 to 15 yards, it added a fitness component to the exercise, especially if I did it uninterrupted for one repetition, immediately followed by the next repetition.

Although I had planned to train for one hour and then walk back up hill to campus, I could not stop. The embarrassment I felt in the afternoon gave me this energy and I just kept training and training until I looked at my watch and it was 11:20 p.m. I decided to finish with fitness work. I ended the night doing 10 repetitions of the shuttle run we did in preseason, when I ended up vomiting with Timo standing over me. I got back to my dorm after midnight and I was exhausted.

The team had Sunday off. I spent most of the day studying, then went down to the lower field to do three hours of secret training before it got dark. I was more determined than ever to prove Timo wrong. Monday couldn't arrive soon enough. I was looking forward to my second full week of classes and that Friday, we would play Penn State University at its field under the lights. They had many players from Bucks County, Pennsylvania, which is across the Delaware River from Trenton.

Players included the Bahr brothers, Chris and Matt, from Neshaminy. Chris was also the kicker for Penn State's highly ranked football team. Their father and coach Walter Bahr was a U.S. soccer legend, having played on the USA Men's National team that beat England in the 1950 World Cup.

Penn State's team also included Randy Garber, a super skillful player from Abington, Pennsylvania, who spent two years playing for Mercer County Community College, and two very dangerous wingers, Johnny Marsden and Richie Reice, who had played club soccer for the Trenton Italians. Their Mercer County representative was Ciro Baldino, of Italian American descent, who also played for the Trenton Italians.

During the previous summer, I had been a guest player for the Trenton Extension Tavern Men's team, which included Hartwick teammates Mike Angelotti and Mooch. We played against the Trenton Italians in several local tournaments and the games were very skillful, physical and nasty. The nucleus of the Trenton Italian team was comprised of many older, experienced ex-professional foreign players from Italy, Argentina and Ecuador. In the previous summer, they had added the two wingers from Penn State: Ciro Baldino in the midfield and an outstanding goalkeeper, Larry Keller, who played for Lehigh University. I had matched up against Rich Reice in two of the games, and handled his speed and dribbling skills quite well in both contests.

Training sessions during the week brought no big surprises, as Timo stuck with the same starting lineup in scrimmages as against Montclair State University. As the week went on, you could feel the tension building. Both teams were ranked among the nation's top 10 college soccer programs. It promised to be a great game, Hartwick being a traditional powerhouse and Penn State a relatively new powerhouse.

There was a lot of talk of the matchup of Randy Garber with Brian Doyle in the midfield. Brian had played great all of preseason and there was talk of him being a potential All-American candidate. He was a very skillful player and brimming with confidence. It was his time to shine. This was his senior year and he finally was in the starting lineup.

Surprisingly Brian's performance against Montclair was nothing to write home about and you could sense that he put a lot of pressure on himself with high expectations. As the week progressed, I felt like the invisible man in Timo's eyes. He said nothing all week concerning my play, but had numerous positive words and made confidence-building remarks to the rest of the players on the team.

That Thursday night during the bus ride to University Park, I couldn't help but wonder if Timo was hoping to make me feel that there was absolutely no hope for me to ever play on the varsity, and that I would ask him to put me down onto the junior varsity. Timo's personality towards me was as cold as the winters in his native Finland—and I could feel the frostbite setting in.

As we got off the team bus Friday night, I couldn't believe how beautiful the Penn State soccer field was. The grass was as immaculate as a putting green, and much longer and wider than Elmore Field. Fifty minutes before kickoff, the bleachers were packed.

To avoid another upsetting bus ride back to Oneonta, I came to the realization that we probably would win a close game and I wouldn't get any playing time. Training sessions are where I would have to impress Timo.

I had a real nice warmup and felt really good. There was something about playing on big fields with real nice grass. It gave you confidence that you could do anything you want with the ball and that the opposition couldn't get it from you.

Several minutes into the game, it was obvious Penn State was much more talented than Montclair State. In the third minute, Mooch played a perfect 50-yard diagonal pass, hitting Artie perfectly in stride and getting behind the defense. Artie took one touch to control the ball and then struck a perfect shot into the lower left-hand corner of the goal to give us a 1-0 lead.

We felt good about ourselves when minutes later, Ciro Baldino ran onto a ball at the corner of the 18-yard box and hit a laser of a shot into the far upper corner for a goal. The goal lit a fire under Penn State. After that, they were all over us. Randy Garber orchestrated everything from the midfield. Their wingers Johnny Marsden and Richie Reice started shredding our defense, continuously beat our outside defenders, reached the end line and served dangerous crosses into the box. They came at us in waves when Chris Bahr, who could strike a ball as hard as anyone in the country, hammered a shot that exploded off of the crossbar and thankfully bounced away harmlessly.

A minute later, Johnny Marsden took a corner kick and Penn State defender Bob Viehweger headed it in for a 2-1 lead. Seven minutes after Penn State's first goal, Johnny Marsden finished a flurry of shots in front of our goal to score and put Penn State up 3-1.

We settled down for a few minutes and created two very good chances, first by Timmy Kevill and then by Mooch, which produced two outstanding saves by Penn State keeper Tim Dantzig. On the subsequent counterattack, Penn State attacked our sweeper Jeff Tipping three on one, leaving Steve Jameson helpless to stop Johnny Marsden from scoring Penn State's fourth goal of the half.

Halftime couldn't come soon enough. We were fortunate to be down by only three goals.

I wasn't sure how Timo would address the team at halftime. The team appeared in shock as Penn State had totally dominated us, from time of possession, to creating goal-scoring chances, to the score. Timo had a very calm demeanor as he spoke to the team.

The first change was to put team captain Michael Angelotti in the lineup, after Timo had surprisingly omitted him from the starting 11. Michael would go back to his sweeper position, playing behind Johnny Bluem. Timo had started the game with Jeff Tipping playing behind Johnny. Jeff was a great defender, with that uncanny ability to hang in the air for head balls and was great in the tackle.

I did not remotely understand the game of soccer like Timo did, but when he announced the starting lineup I couldn't understand why he would play two traditional stopper backs in the middle of the defense. In the first half, we had had a very difficult time playing the ball out of the defense. Putting Michael into the game was meant to resolve that problem.

Michael was an extremely skillful, intelligent player who always had a solution to compensate for his lack of speed. If Michael ever was exposed and was the last line of defense, you could be sure that the man or the ball might get past Michael, but never both at the same time.

With Michael in the sweeper position, we started to do a much better job of playing the ball out of the defense and keeping possession, But we still couldn't stop Penn State's attacks. Timo began to freely substitute, including taking Jamie out of the goal and bringing in the very talented Keith Van Eron. Despite having given up four goals, Steve Jameson actually played very well in goal, with numerous brilliant saves to keep the score from getting even more embarrassing.

Matt Bahr scored a goal with 10 minutes remaining to make the score 5-1. Every Hartwick player but I had had some playing time.

Then I heard these words from Timo: "Billy, warm up! You are going in the next time we can substitute."

I jumped off the bench and started stretching. Thirty seconds later, the ball went out of bounds near the Penn State 18-yard line. I ran onto the field and stood at the top of the D above the 18-yard line. Off the throw-in, Mooch one-touched a beautiful cross right to the six-yard line. I timed my run perfectly, cut in front of a Penn State defender, and with my first official collegiate touch of a soccer ball, headed the ball down towards the corner of the goal. I watched as my first touch was inches from crossing the goal line for a score. Penn State goalie Tim Dantzig flung himself airborne to the far corner and flicked the ball out of bounds for a corner kick.

I was disappointed that I did not score but also so excited that I was in the game. I played quite well the last few minutes of the game, winning several tackles and never losing possession of the ball.

Final score: Penn State 5, Hartwick 1.

I don't think Hartwick had ever been so dominated and embarrassed. A much better team totally humiliated us. I was happy with my performance, although it was only for nine minutes, but also very upset with the team's performance. I came to Hartwick to win a national championship, and this was not the road I expected to travel to get there.

Few Hartwick players could say they played a good game. Randy Garber thoroughly dominated Brian Doyle in the midfield, and Brian appeared to have lost his confidence. Mooch had a very quiet game, considering his immense talent. It did not help that Penn State controlled the ball for long periods of time. Mooch had spent a considerable amount of time chasing the ball and defending.

Timo didn't have much to say after the game and the bus ride home was eerily quiet, which is not typical for a bunch of college kids. This game validated my opinion that Zeren, for all of his wonderful technique and vision, was not nearly ready for the physical nature of college soccer. At the same time, I could envision a future Hartwick midfield consisting of Mooch, Zeren and myself, which sounded very exciting, if I could convince Timo I could play at this level.

Duncan, who I thought was the best player on the field against Montclair and did not seem to have any weaknesses in his game, had a very difficult time defending Richie Reice, a player I had handled with relative ease that past summer. It was at that moment on the bus ride home to Oneonta, I realized that I should be playing for this team. Little did I know that the coming week would reshape my destiny at Hartwick.

Our next game was the following Wednesday at home against University of Connecticut. UConn was undefeated, ranked second in the country and boasted two of the top players in the country: second team All-American Frantz Innocent, a brilliant dribbler who also could finish in front of the goal, and Timmy Hunter, a tall, skillful midfield general.

Timo decided to give the team the whole weekend off. Saturday, I spent most of the afternoon studying at the library and then went down to the lower field to do some training before it got dark.

We were not supposed to train on Elmore Field other than when the team trains there, but on Sunday morning I got up at the crack of dawn —probably before anyone else on campus was awake—and went to Elmore Field to do some secret training. I had heard so much about the atmosphere at home games being unbelievable. While I trained, I imagined the field being surrounded by a wall of students. I was excited thinking about what the atmosphere would be like that afternoon, until reality hit me that although I expect Timo to make some significant changes, I still was the last player to get into the Penn State game and only when the result had already been decided.

3

The Opportunity Presents Itself

When I walked into the locker room that Monday, I expected a somber atmosphere due to the horrific performance by our team the previous Friday night, and it seemed even gloomier than that. As I changed, I was focused on how I had to have a great training session that day. I didn't pay attention to several quiet conversations going on around me. Walking out of Binder heading for one of the vans, Mooch grabbed me by the arm, pulled me to the side and said, "Did you hear about BD?" BD is Brian Doyle's nickname.

"No Mooch. I have not seen anyone on the team since I got off the bus Friday night until I just walked into the locker room, and it's like a morgue in there. What's going on?"

"Brian quit the team."

"What did you just say, Mooch?"

"Brian went to see Timo this morning and he quit the team, that's all I know." "That's terrible, Mooch, just because he had a bad game? The whole team played terrible. He worked so hard to get in the starting lineup and he quits after a bad performance. I don't understand that. He will regret that down the road."

"Billy, do you know what that means?" "No. What, Mooch?"

"There is an opening in the midfield!"

"I did not think of that. I felt really bad for Brian. He helped me a lot and always gave me confidence that I can play at Hartwick."

I decided I would approach Timo after training that day.

With every substitute on the team feeling they may have had an opportunity to get into the first 11, and many of the starters realizing that their starting positions were in jeopardy, training was very intense, with players going into tackles as if their lives depended on it. Tempers were very short and Timo had to stop training on several occasions. I was in total control of my emotions and despite the physical play, I just concentrated on knowing what I would do with the ball before I received it.

As soon as training ended, I went to Timo and asked him if I could have a few words with him in his office after I shower. As soon as Timo replied "yes," I felt a surge of nervousness. While I showered, I couldn't figure out what I actually wanted to say to him.

But I knew I should have been playing more than I was for this team. Actually, with Brian gone, I felt I should be starting.

I quickly dressed and headed straight for Timo's office. I decided I was going to tell one of the best soccer coaches in the country that his evaluation of me as a player was totally wrong and I should be playing. Inexplicably, the anxiety and heart pounding I felt in the shower was gone, and I felt a calmness and focus as I knocked on the door.

"Come in, Billy."

I closed the door and sat in a chair facing Timo's desk. "So Billy, what do you want to talk to me about?"

"Timo, I should be playing. I should be starting for this team."

I was not sure what Timo may have expected—perhaps that I wanted to go down to the junior varsity. But I knew that it was not that I should be starting. Timo's face had a shocked expression and there was total silence in the office for at least 10 seconds, while he collected his thoughts. Timo finally said, "Billy, why do you say that?"

"You are giving lots of playing time to players who are timid out there and playing scared."

"Richie Reice destroyed us on Friday night."

"I have played against him several times this summer for Trenton Extension and every time I have played against him, I have put him in my back pocket."

Timo hesitated momentarily, then said, "Do you think you can mark Timmy Hunter?" I immediately replied, "I have never seen him play but I am sure that I can."

Timo said, "Then Wednesday you will start. Your job will be to mark Timmy Hunter and take him out of the game."

"That is fine. I am ready, Timo." I got up and walked out of the office.

When I got to the cafeteria, I was so excited I could hardly eat. I had a million thoughts swirling through my mind. I decided not to say anything to anyone, including Mooch, about my starting Wednesday. I was hoping Timo wouldn't change his mind.

At Tuesday's training session, we had a long warmup followed by some technical work. Then Timo announced the starting lineup so we could go over free kicks. There were several changes to the lineup, but none more surprising to the team than when Timo announced my name in the midfield. He then told the team that I would be marking Timmy Hunter all over the field.

Near the end of the training session, I stood in the wall defending free kicks when I stretched to block a shot, and the ball caught the tip of my foot and bent it back severely. A sharp pain ran through my body, and the thought of getting injured and not being able to play the next day immediately ran through my mind. I limped off the field and our trainer George "Mitch" Mitchell examined my foot, then taped it up. I sprinted back on the field to finish training. I didn't want to give Timo any reason to change his mind about my starting. After training ended, I iced my foot for 20 minutes before showering and heading for the cafeteria.

A cafeteria employee gave me a big bag of ice and smaller plastic bags. Back in my room, I kept icing my foot for 20 minutes every hour until all of the ice melted. The whole time, all I could think about was that the next day would be my first start for Hartwick on the famous Elmore Field, where there have been so many historic games played. The icing on the cake was that I also would mark one of the best players in the country.

The first thing I did the next morning was inspect my right foot. The swelling had gone down significantly, which was a good sign. I stood up and jogged in place to see how it felt. I had a fair amount of pain, but nothing was going to keep me out of the game.

After breakfast, I went to my Colonial Experience class, but it was hard for me to concentrate. All I could think about was our 3 p.m. kickoff against UConn. When class ended, I headed to Binder, and after changing, I went to the trainer's room to have Mitch tape up my foot.

We had a 45-minute warmup in the gymnasium, which is a Hartwick tradition. It's a great idea, especially when we had those frigid late-November games with temperatures close to or below freezing. Then the team ran out onto Elmore Field with the song "Glad" by the English band Traffic blaring through the stadium. As I ran onto Elmore, the field was packed with fans, the stands were full and the hillside was a blanket of human bodies. It is the environment I had envisioned when I knew I wanted to come to Hartwick.

They announced the starting lineup and most of my teammates receive a thunderous applause. When I finally was introduced, there was a smattering of clapping. It is obvious that the Hartwick fans had no idea who I was. That's fine. All I cared about was playing in the game and winning. That was all that mattered to me.

With the game about to start, I went over a mental checklist of my priorities on the field. First and foremost was to limit Timmy Hunter to as few touches as possible. Two, when he did receive the ball, make him play square or back. Three, when I did win the ball, look to play the ball early and forward, keeping possession for Hartwick. We didn't do this against Penn State.

In the first few minutes of the game, Timmy Hunter intercepted a pass from Mooch and pushed the ball a little too far in front of himself. I went in as hard as possible with two feet, going right through the ball and him, sending Hunter airborne. No foul was called, to my surprise. As I got up and jogged away, Timmy Hunter sent numerous expletives my way. I just ignored him.

The rain over the previous few days made the field wet and treacherous. No one on the field took advantage of this more than Frantz Innocent.

Midway through the first half, Innocent put on a dribbling exhibition and eventually was fouled in the penalty box. He scored on the ensuing penalty kick to put UConn up 1-0.

Several minutes later, I felt the tape on my foot shifting and it became extremely uncomfortable. I hollered over to the bench that I had to briefly come off so Mitch could re-tape my ankle. Timo substituted for me and as Mitch taped my ankle, UConn was awarded a corner kick. Before I could re-enter the game, Hunter scored off the corner kick with a header. Timo wasted no time in getting me back out onto the field. UConn led 2-0 at halftime.

Walking off the field at the end of the first half, I was satisfied with my play. I had a lot of success in limiting Hunter's touches and when he did receive the ball, I was able to force him to play the ball square or back. On the attack, I hadn't given away a ball.

Although the first half felt like it was a fairly even game, we were down 2-0 and had a difficult time creating chances. Timo made several adjustments at halftime, and as I walked out of the locker room, he told me I was doing a real good job and to keep it up.

After six weeks, Timo finally had some encouraging words for me. It made me feel good and I was determined to have a strong second half and help us win this game.

We started out the second half with a lot of fight and were doing a better job of keeping possession. We were playing good between the 18-yard lines, but still couldn't create any good chances on goal. At the 33-minute mark, a poor clearance by our defense led to a third UConn goal. Although our fans remained extremely vocal, urging us on, we couldn't get back into the game. Final score: UConn 3, Hartwick 0.

Following our blowout the previous week against Penn State, we were dropped from the top 20 rankings in the nation for the first time since its inception in 1968. This embarrassing loss to UConn wouldn't get us back into the top 20 anytime soon. It was almost hard to conceive that Hartwick had lost the last two games by a combined score of 8-1.

I was not sure what to expect in the locker room after the game. After the Penn State game Timo was very calm, but we had been blown out again and on Elmore Field, which is unheard of. Timo never gave any indication how upset he was and began talking about all of the positives we could take from this game. He remained very calm and positive throughout his talk and made us feel like things were about to improve dramatically.

Walking to the cafeteria, I thought about Timo's comments and hoped he was right.

Although I knew I had a good game, the embarrassing loss overshadowed my individual performance. I hated to lose and I knew that would never change.

Our next game was a Saturday contest at home against Brockport State, a Division III powerhouse that had developed a strong rivalry with Hartwick. The majority of its players were from Long Island.

Just before we started practice that Thursday Timo came up to me. "Billy, I thought you had a good game yesterday," he said.

"Thank you, Timo."

"Billy, I am going to have you man-to-man mark Nelson Cupello on Saturday. Do you think you can mark him?"

"Timo, I have never seen him play but I am confident I can mark him out of the game.

"Thanks, Timo."

Alden took us through a long and thorough warmup. Timo then reviewed the lineup for the first 11 for our scrimmage and there were numerous changes from the team that lined up against UConn. I was happy once again to hear my name in the starting 11.

Other than Mooch, every team member had to feel they were competing for playing time, and it showed in the intensity of our scrimmage.

For the UConn game, Timo had brought up Bucky Worthen from the junior varsity team, which occurred rarely at Hartwick. In the scrimmage that day, Bucky displayed some blinding speed. At the end of the training session, Timo talked about our tactics against Brockport State and that I would be marking Nelson Cupello.

After training ended, Johnny Bluem and Mike Angelotti come over to me and said I needed to be aware that the Brockport games were very physical and that they had several dirty players who frequently go over the ball in tackles.

The year before, my reply to hearing about over-the-ball tackles would have been, "What is an over-the-ball tackle?" Having played for Trenton Extension in numerous tournaments in the summer before joining Hartwick, I received firsthand experience playing against many older, ex-professional foreign-born players. Many were just as happy to aim their cleats at my knees as they were tackling the ball. For many of the tournaments Trenton Extension played in the past summer, we were the only team with American-born players. It was a wonderful opportunity for me to learn to protect myself on the field and develop as a player.

The Hartwick men's soccer team received unbelievable fan support, including the entire student body attending home games and alumni that traveled significant distances to attend home and away games. We also had a substantial fan base from local residents in Oneonta and surrounding areas that had become fanatical about the team. None were more supportive than Neil and Cindy Buzzy, and their close friend Mary Mitchell.

A Saturday home soccer game typically was preceded by a team meal on Friday nights at the Buzzys' house, with the assistance of Mary Mitchell. That Friday was to be the first dinner I would experience at the Buzzys' house and to meet them for the first time.

The instant I met the three, I could sense the passion and love they had for the soccer program. Considering that we had just lost our last two games by a combined score of 8-1, it may have been the perfect environment for the team to relax a little bit. This also would be the first home-cooked meal many of my teammates and I had had since the beginning of preseason. I looked forward to every bite of my grilled cheeseburger and homemade potato salad.

Mooch, Art Napolitano, Johnny Bluem and Steve Jameson, our English goalkeeper, all lived in one of Neil and Cindy's rental properties on Depew Street, located on the other side of the railroad tracks and not the preferred side of Oneonta. It was the area of the less-fortunate, with railroad tracks 30 feet from the back door of the house. When the train came through Oneonta, behind the house on Depew Street, the house literally shook.

Fortunately, the freight trains didn't come through Oneonta at night and disrupt my teammates' sleep.

Mooch was holding court with Neil Buzzy and his roommates. They laughed hysterically at every story Mooch told. Mooch may have been the most charismatic person I ever met, and by far the best soccer player I ever played with and against. It was a great night, with none of the pressure that would come the next day when we stepped onto Elmore Field.

The minute I stepped into the locker room that Saturday afternoon, I could feel the tension in the air. There was talk that if we had another loss this early in the season, we may have had a very difficult time qualifying for the NCAA tournament.

Listening to the seniors, I got the impression that we were evenly matched teams and that Brockport State was a very big, physical team. The expectations were that it would be a war out there with a lot of nasty fouls.

After returning from the gymnasium warmup, Timo gave us a few last-minute tactical instructions. We headed out to Elmore Field for our annual Homecoming Day game, with Glad blasting from the intercom. The field was packed with fans.

Michael Angelotti pointed out Nelson Cupello to me, and reminded me there could be lots of over-the-ball tackles that day and for me to prepare. I thanked Michael. They announced the starting lineups and I was shocked to hear the applause for me when I was introduced. It made me feel good that the UConn game made an impression on some of the fans.

During the national anthem, I thought how important this game was for the team and myself. It is hard to believe that if we lost today, a game in early October, we might not get into the NCAA Tournament.

I was not one of Timo's highly recruited blue-chip prospects and I knew that if I was not playing well, he would yank me off the field in a heartbeat. I understood that one good game played against UConn had not changed Timo's opinion of me as a player and that *every day*, I had to prove him wrong. Whether it was in a game or a training session, *every day* I had to work to get a little bit better.

The game was extremely physical from the opening kickoff. There was little time and space to play in, and the game had numerous stoppages for fouls by both teams. Nelson Cupello was very strong physically and with his long legs, it was difficult for me to get the ball when he shielded it.

Although he could hold the ball, I did not allow him to turn and play balls forward into the attack. I did a good job when I had possession of the ball and was able to jump and avoid several hard tackles.

The second half started out the same way, with lots of play between the 18-yard lines, but no real scoring chances for either team. At the 80-minute mark, the crowd started chanting. At first, I didn't know what they were hollering, but as it got louder and louder, bordering on thunderous, I finally realized what they were chanting. "Let's go Wick." "Let's go Wick." "Let's go Wick."

I had not heard that at all during the UConn game. The crowd continued chanting and we could sense the energy it gave the team as we dug down deep to try to score a goal and win.

The intensity throughout this game from both teams culminated with Jeff Marshall and Kevin Gannon, an outstanding midfielder for Brockport, getting into a fight. Both were sent off in the waning moments of the game, which ended 0-0.

Once again after a game, Timo found all of the positives in the game and concluded his talk with, "We have to figure out a way to score some goals." We had not scored a goal since the three-minute mark of the Penn State game. That was 267 minutes without a goal.

Angelotti did a great job organizing the defense from his sweeper position and Ron Hardy, our left back, who had been battling injuries since preseason, was brilliant, but without goals, we could not win games.

Walking to the cafeteria, I felt physically beaten up from the game and wrestled with whether I should rest the next day and skip secret training. By the end of dinner, I decided I would just study all day and rest my body.

A lot of the players were going to the Rail to have a few drinks and relax a little bit. I joined them later. The Rail was packed shoulder to shoulder with Hartwick students.

Many of my teammates wanted to buy me a beer and I kept telling them I didn't drink beer. For many, their standard reply was, "Well, you will eventually acquire a taste for it." I never could understand why they thought I would drink something that tastes disgusting, just so one day, I would find the taste tolerable.

I found Mooch and Johnny at the foosball table. Johnny looked like he had drunk a fair number of beers, but he was terrific on the foosball table, beating one opponent after another.

Mooch, as usual, was holding court, telling stories that left people laughing hysterically. It was good to see many of my teammates relaxing, especially the seniors. There was so much pressure on the team and the seniors had to feel it the most. I settled for a Coke and nursed it until I decided to head back to campus.

On Sunday, after five hours of studying in the library, I realized I couldn't take the whole day off without touching a soccer ball. I quickly gathered my books, headed to my dorm room, changed and went to the lower field while there still was some light out.

While training, it hit me that Mooch was way too unselfish as a player and probably needed to be a little more selfish on the field. I decided I would say something to him at training.

The first thing I did when I got on the field for training Monday afternoon was to approach Mooch. "Mooch, I need to talk to you," I said.

"What is it, Billy?" Mooch said.

"Mooch, you are way too unselfish and it is hurting the team."

"Why do you say that?"

"Mooch, you are the best player in the country. You should have more of the ball, especially when we get into the attacking third of the field."

"Billy, there are a lot of great players across the country." Mooch said.

"Mooch, OK, I am not going to argue with you if you are the best player in the country or not. What I know is that you need to keep more of the ball, attack players and look to get forward more. As long as I am playing in the midfield whenever you go forward, I will slide over into the central midfield position and be the holding defensive midfielder. We are a lot more dangerous with you going forward than me."

Mooch hesitated, then replied, "Billy, what you are saying makes sense."

I said, "Mooch, I do not know if I am starting tomorrow. The last two games, I was marking someone. I don't know if Cornell has a midfielder that needs to be marked all over the field."

Mooch replied, "Billy, you have been one of our better players the last two games. Timo has to play you."

"Mooch, you know Timo has all of these recruits that he loves and if we didn't get off to such a horrible start, I never would have gotten off the bench for even one minute.

"Timo is not my greatest fan, but he is desperate right now to find the right combination of players to win a game."

"You are right, Billy," Mooch said.

Our game against Cornell the next day would have a huge effect on whether or not we qualified for the NCAA tournament. On defense, Cornell was led by All-Ivy first team goalkeeper Jon Ross. Cornell also had an outstanding defender in sweeper Jay Holbrook. On attack, Cornell had two highly skilled players in Joe Mui and David Sarachan.

Timo was said to be a brilliant tactician and during our scrimmage, he moved players around into numerous positions and team alignments. I didn't think most of us had any idea what the starting lineup would be.

He started announcing the starting 11 for Cornell. I waited anxiously for him to get to the midfield, wondering if my two starts were my last ones of the season and if I would return to the bench.

Timo finished with the back four and then said, "In the midfield, Mooch will be the central midfielder, Jeff will play on the right side and Billy will play on the left side."

I felt such a relief and excitement, knowing I was going to start in my third consecutive game. But I also had mixed emotions on whether Timo was changing his opinion of me for the better. I would start again. But on the other hand, Timo never complimented me during training and constantly encouraged the majority of the players, in particular the blue-chip freshmen.

We started creating scoring chances from the kickoff against Cornell, and it seemed it was only a matter of time until we would score.

But Jon Ross, Cornell's outstanding goalkeeper, was up to every challenge. On defense, our central backs Johnny Bluem and Mike Angelotti were terrific. Ron Hardy again was outstanding in his left back position. But midway through the first half he pulled a hamstring and left the game.

The more I saw Ron play, the more I realized how good a player he really was. After battling injuries since preseason and finally getting healthy, he got injured again. That would definitely hurt the team.

We shut down Cornell's attack and got scoring opportunities, but had nothing to show for it at halftime. We were frustrated as we walked into the locker room.

One of the bright spots was that Mooch was looking to attack more. That was a big part of why we did much better in the attacking third of the field.

The second half started the same way the first half ended, with us primarily attacking the Cornell defense. In the 51st minute, Cornell defender Howard Reissner was called for a handball. The goal drought was about to end, as we were awarded a penalty kick.

Timo selected Jeff Marshall to take the penalty kick. Jeff approached the ball and as he struck it, Ross dived to his right, pushing the ball wide of the post.

Our disappointment was short-lived because Ross moved too soon, before the referee's whistle. Timo had Mooch replace Jeff and take the kick. I knew we were going to score and get the weight of this goal drought off the team.

Mooch placed the ball on the penalty spot, took four steps back and then slowly approached the ball. I expected him to hit a rocket that Ross would barely see. But instead, Mooch struck the ball with the side of his foot, placing it to Ross's left side. Mooch did not strike the ball with a lot of power. Ross again flung himself airborne and made the save.

The Ross save deflated us and energized Cornell. Now Mui and Sarachan were getting more of the ball and attacking our defense. The game became more end to end. In the waning moments, Tim Kevill was called for a handball right outside of the penalty box.

David Sarachan took the free kick, bending the ball around the wall. Our goalkeeper Steve Jameson clearly was beaten as the ball sailed toward the far post.

But the ball struck the corner of the crossbar and bounced out of danger. A minute later, the referee blew his whistle to end the game.

Another tie, another goalless game. The locker room was like a morgue, until Timo and Alden came in to address the team. Timo emphasized how the goals would start coming and said we could have scored two or three goals if not for Cornell's outstanding goalkeeping.

We had gone 357 minutes without a goal. The pressure and frustration were growing. I felt I had another good game and liked the fact that without having to mark one individual all over the field, I had more freedom to get involved in the attack.

4

Tension Mounts

The next morning, the Oneonta Star newspaper said it best in the headline:

Wick ties and tension mounts

During Wednesday training, the consensus among the seniors was that if we did not win Saturday against Colgate, we would not get an NCAA bid.

The team felt unbelievable pressure. Saturday would be only our sixth regular-season game and it was do or die. We could feel the pressure on the team coming from everywhere—in the locker room, on the field, on Timo and Alden's faces.

I was not as well-known as my teammates, but students on campus stopped me repeatedly as I walked to class, sat in a classroom and ate at the cafeteria. They had the same concerns: *What is wrong with the team? Why can't we score a goal? Are we going to win Saturday?*

The soccer team was such a huge part of the identity of Hartwick. With every question I was asked, I could feel the passion and love they had for the soccer team. Every time I was stopped, it just made me want to play harder and start winning for them as much as for my teammates.

As training ended that afternoon, Timo told me to come by his office after I showered. I didn't have any idea why he wanted to talk to me and it made me a little anxious. I quickly showered and walked to his office. The door was open. I walked right in and sat down. Timo started the conversation with "Billy, you know I have to make changes to the lineup." All I could think of was that he was going to drop me from the starting lineup.

"Billy, I am thinking of taking Jamey out of the goal and pushing him up front. I also am considering changing our alignment. We created a lot more chances against Cornell but we could still not score. For the game Saturday I am taking you out of the midfield and I am putting Jeff Marshall in the left-sided midfield position."

Timo then hesitated, and my initial thought was, *Why am I getting dropped from the team?*

My mind was racing as to what I should say to Timo, if anything. He continued with "because I want you to play left back against Colgate."

I gave a huge sigh of relief.

"Billy, you said you played left back for Trenton Extension and marked Richie Reece out of the game. Are you comfortable playing there?"

"Timo, I played left back in two tournaments this summer for Trenton Extension. I am comfortable back there."

"Billy, tomorrow I am going to experiment with playing two right-wingers. If we use that alignment, you should have a lot of space to run into and support the attack from your left back position."

"That's fine Timo, wherever you want to play me."

I knew Timo was going to make changes and I was happy I still had a position in the starting 11.

Prior to our warmup that Friday afternoon, Timo gathered the team and began with, "We are going to experiment with a variation of our 4-3-3 alignment."

"Up front we are going to play with Ike as our center forward and two right wingers."

The players were bewildered because we were desperate to score goals and Timo may have created an alignment that never had been implemented in the history of the game. He explained that by playing two players out wide on the right, it would cause the opposing defenses to face tough decisions. They had to mark both players, so did that mean that the stopper back would have to come out wide and mark one of the two wingers? Or would their right back come over to mark one of our wingers? Timo felt this would leave a lot of open space on the left side of the field for us to attack.

During our scrimmage, Jamey was taken out of the goal and was put out wide on the right with Artie. I was the left back. Having two wingers on the same side of the field was very different and we were very uncomfortable with the alignment. We finished up training going over our free kicks. In the locker room after training, you could sense a lot of the players questioning Timo's tactics.

That Saturday morning, we boarded Bluebird for our one-hour drive to Hamilton, New York. The bus ride was unusually quiet. You could feel the pressure on the team. I had nervousness that I had not felt since the UConn game. I felt it was more how we would do as a team than how I would play.

After the warmup, Timo reviewed the starting 11 and our alignment. We really were not sure how Timo would line us up, but he stayed with our traditional 4-3-3 setup with a winger on each side of the field.

Right from the kickoff we were so tight, we gave away balls even when we were not under pressure. The longer the half went on without us creating any good scoring opportunities, the more pressure we felt.

At the 22-minute mark, Barry Small, Colgate's talented and extremely fast attacker, made a clever pass into the box to Dave MacKenzie. He received the ball with his back to the goal, but in one motion turned and shot on goal, beating Steve Jameson to the far post for a 1-0 Colgate lead.

We were stunned. This had to be the low point of our season and possibly in the history of the storied Hartwick soccer program.

In the next 10 minutes, we started stringing more passes together but could not create anything in the attacking third of the field.

With 12 minutes left in the half Timo changed goalkeepers. He put Keith Van Eron, our very athletic backup goalkeeper, in the goal. Steve Jameson went up front to play as a second right winger alongside Artie. Minutes later Timo inserted Jeff Tipping, who had been out with a shin injury, and put him into the midfield. That was to allow Mooch to get more forward into the attack. Over the last six or seven minutes of the half, we started to get into a rhythm. The half ended with us down 1-0.

I thought Timo was brilliant at halftime. Although our team had not won a game in three weeks and had not scored a goal in over 400 minutes, Timo had us believing it was only a matter of time before we scored and we would win this game.

Timo brought on Bucky Worthen to play at right wing. Timo also made a point that he did not want Jamey too close to Bucky. He wanted Jamey to position himself almost equally between Ike in his center forward position and Bucky on the touchline.

We started the second half as an entirely different team. Right from the whistle, we kept possession of the ball for extended periods of time. Mooch started to take control of the game.

Timo was prophetic when he told me that I would be able to exploit the open space where the Colgate right back normally would be playing. Five minutes into the second half, I made a run out wide into the attacking third. Mooch played a perfect 60-yard diagonal pass to me right in stride, as if he had handed the ball to me on a platter.

I took several touches before serving the ball into the box. Ike made a run to the near post, beating his Colgate defender to the cross, and had the Colgate keeper beaten, with his header grazing the corner of the goal post but going out of bounds for a goal kick.

This sequence seemed to energize the team even more as we pressed for that elusive goal. Mooch stood in the middle of the field like a maestro, elegantly dissecting the Colgate team with one brilliant pass after another.

At the nine-minute mark of the second half, Bucky Worthen won a ball in the attacking half, beating several defenders before serving a low, hard-driven cross into the 18-yard box. Jamey timed his run perfectly, cutting in front of the Colgate defender and redirected the ball past Colgate goalkeeper Tom Visconsi. The elation we felt as a team watching the ball hit the back of the net was indescribable. It was as if this huge weight finally had been lifted off of our shoulders.

We were relentless in the attack, coming at the Colgate defense in waves. At this point it appeared that Colgate Coach John Beyer would settle for a tie. Barry Small was the lone attacking player up front, with the rest of the Colgate players defending for their lives. As the game wore on, I felt more like a left winger than a left back as Mooch repeatedly found me overlapping down the left sideline.

The Colgate keeper was outstanding with one great save after another. Frustration started to set in, as we knew time was running out for us in this must-win game to qualify for the tournament.

We were awarded a corner kick at the five-minute mark. Mooch sprinted over, demanding to take it. His service was perfect, with Ike soaring head and shoulders above the Colgate defenders and emphatically heading the ball past a beaten Tom Visconsi in goal.

The exhilaration I felt the moment we scored was immeasurable. I think my mind went blank for a few seconds as we all sprinted over to hug Ike. We then went into lock-down mode the last few minutes of the game, just waiting for the referee to blow his whistle. We finally heard that whistle.

Timo had followed the team bus to Colgate in his car. He was planning to go on a scouting trip immediately after the game and gathered us together quickly to address the team before he departed. We could see a much more relaxed coach. As he finished up his talk, he turned towards me and said, "Billy, you were the player of the game today."

I was speechless. I just nodded my head and smiled. On the bus ride back, I was thinking how it was only three weeks before that I was the only player on the team not to play, sitting in the back of the bus with tears in my eyes as we drove back from Montclair. Three weeks later, I was starting and Timo named me player of the game. To say I was excited was an understatement.

Mooch made it a point to come sit with me and tell me how good I had played. A lot of it had to do with Mooch's tremendous passing, skill and vision in making those 50-to-60-yard diagonal passes to me. We had a week to prepare for Bridgeport University at home on Parents Day.

The transformation from desperately trying to make the team, then being the last player on the team to get any playing time, to now being a fixture in the starting lineup, had invigorated me and had a positive effect on me in the classroom. I noticed I had much better concentration in my classes and considerably more energy at night to get through my school-work. I was starting to really enjoy being at college.

The success on the soccer field had brought numerous invitations to pledge for several fraternities.

Jimmy "Harry" Harrison asked me to pledge his fraternity Delta Sigma Phi. I told him yes, but I started to get cold feet as the deadline neared for me to give a definite decision. The thought of having individuals (future fraternity brothers) I hardly knew giving me orders and having to do silly, embarrassing acts on and off campus started to bother me.

The day before commitment deadline, I had a very uneasy feeling as I lay in bed thinking about becoming a fraternity brother. After several hours of twisting and turning in bed and trying to get to sleep, I realized that joining a fraternity was not the right choice for me. I felt relief. In the morning, I went to the cafeteria to tell Harry that although I truly appreciated the offer to join Delta Sigma Phi, I had decided to decline the offer to join. I felt a huge relief and immediately realized I had made the right decision.

That Monday afternoon as I walked from class to the cafeteria, I had seen her again.

She was 50 feet away and walking right towards me. I saw this girl four or five times on campus and thought she was the most beautiful girl in the school. I wanted to talk to her, but I lacked the courage to say anything to her.

My mind raced as to what I could say to her, and I felt nervousness setting in. I told myself next time I saw her I would say something. As I got within 10 feet of her, I forced myself to stop staring and just looked down as we were about to pass each other. She stopped and said, "You're Billy, right?"

She totally took me by surprise. I was momentarily tongue-tied before I could respond, "Uh, yeah. I'm Billy. Uh, what is your name?"

"I'm Sue, Sue Foote."

"Where are you from, Sue?"

"I'm from Long Island. Do you think that you guys are going to win on Saturday?"

"I think so, Sue. We played much better the last game."

"Well, Billy, I have been wanting to meet you. I would like to talk some more but I am going to be late for class."

"It was nice to meet you, Sue. Bye."

"Bye, Billy."

Playing on the soccer team definitely had some benefits. I felt like I was walking on a cloud. I was so excited yet so nervous. I could not stop thinking about Ms. Sue Foote from Long Island and it showed in practice later in the day. I had a poor training session. Alden approached me afterwards.

"Billy, is everything OK? You had a great game Saturday but today you seem to be struggling a bit."

"I know, Alden. I am having a hard time concentrating. I will be better tomorrow."

"Are you sure everything is OK?"

"I am fine, Alden. Thank you."

The last thing I was going to do was tell Alden that I had just spoken to the most beautiful girl on campus and my concentration had turned to mush. Though I had a lackluster training session, I still walked to the cafeteria excited about meeting Sue. I knew the next day I would have to be at my best in training. I couldn't take starting for granted and had to get back to proving myself to Timo every day.

Bridgeport University was one of the special games I marked on our schedule. Kevin Welsh, one of Bridgeport's top players and an All-American candidate, was one reason I was playing at Hartwick. Besides my playing with Kevin Welsh on Trenton Extension in summer tournaments, he was also one of the players who trained with Ping Pong and I all summer at Nottingham Junior High.

Kevin's greatest skill was dribbling past players, and he could attack you one on one as good as any attacking player in the country. Kevin spent countless hours that summer taking me on one versus one, and for the most part beat me every opportunity he had.

Over and over again, day after day, week after week. Near the end of the last day we trained together at Nottingham before leaving for preseason Kevin said, "Billy let me take you on."

"All right, Kevin."

Kevin got the ball, attacked me at top speed and as he threw a body swerve, I tackled the ball and sent him flying. Kevin was relentless and got off of the ground and said, "All right Billy. Again."

I replied "OK, Kevin."

He ran at me again at top speed and I timed my tackle perfectly, winning the ball as Kevin stumbled. I slowly dribbled away, laughing, knowing that Kevin was such a competitor he would not want to stop.

"Let's do it again, Billy."

I had just stopped Kevin two times in a row, which is something I did not do once over the past two months. I looked at Kevin and said, "I'm done Kevin, I am ready to go to preseason."

We had a good laugh.

Thinking about it, I felt so unbelievably lucky and fortunate that I not only had the opportunity to train with such gifted players as Ping Pong, Mooch, Michael Angelotti and Kevin Welsh every day during the summer, but that they were also so willing to help me become a better player.

The rest of the week flew by as we prepared for our game with Bridgeport on Saturday. Ron Hardy was still injured, so I assumed I would be starting in the left back position again.

Due to the terrible playing condition of Elmore Field, our Parents Day game with Bridgeport University was moved to Damaschke Field in Neahwa Park, home to the Oneonta Yankees.

As we walked off the team bus onto Damaschke Field, we could feel the electricity in the air. There was not a single empty seat in the stands. The noise was deafening as we walked onto the field.

Like Hartwick, the Bridgeport team was comprised of many players from New Jersey, including the very talented Hughie O'Neill from

Kearny. Having Kevin Welsh and Hughie O'Neill up front for Bridgeport would put our defense under constant pressure. That combination surely was as talented as any attacking combination in college soccer. I was hoping to get to mark Kevin, but he lined up for Bridgeport out wide on the left side.

Mooch took control of the game right from the kickoff and pulled the strings from his midfield position. Eric Swallow, Bridgeport's outstanding freshman goalkeeper, was under siege from a relentless attack we'd lacked all year. In the 16th minute, Mooch served a perfect cross that Bob Isaacson powerfully headed past Swallow for the first goal of the game.

We continued to attack the Bridgeport goal. But 10 minutes later, Bridgeport was awarded a free kick. Wayne Grant served it into the box. Michael Angelotti and Johnny Bluem both started for the ball but hesitated, allowing Hughie O'Neill to rise above them and head in the equalizer. I think that was the first time that season that Michael and Johnny had any miscommunication.

We did not allow the goal to affect our confidence. We continued to control the game for the rest of the half. The 1-1 score at halftime was not an indication of our dominance in the first half. Timo was very happy with our first-half performance.

The second half began the way the first half ended and it seemed only a matter of time before we would score. Midway through the second half, a Mooch cross found the chest of Howie Charbonneau. Howie controlled the ball before going around Bridgeport defender John Wilson and finished by beating Eric Swallow to his left.

With 11 minutes left in the game, The Glenn Myernick Show continued with Mooch blasting a 40-yard free kick past Eric Swallow to put us up 3-1. It appeared that we were going to have a stress-free end to the game when with only minutes left in the game, Michael called for the defense to push up and catch Bridgeport in an offside trap.

As I sprinted forward from my left back position, I slipped to the ground, allowing Esteban Sebourne, the player I was marking, to remain onside. Sebourne received the pass played over the top of the defense and made his way into the box. His shot deflected off Johnny Bluem, beating Steve Jameson to make the score 3-2. I felt awful. My mistake just cost the team a goal.

The last few minutes seemed like forever. I was so happy when the referee finally blew his whistle to end the game. Pure relief. This was the first time this season we had won two consecutive games and we were finally starting to score goals.

As a team, we were starting to regain our confidence and it showed that Tuesday afternoon, when we went to Ithaca on a beautiful fall day and hammered a weak Ithaca College team 5-0. Although we had won three consecutive games, the intense pressure on the team has not really subsided. Timo felt an upcoming game on Saturday at East Stroudsburg, followed by a midweek game at Adelphi, were must-wins if we were going to qualify for the NCAA tournament.

After training on Wednesday, several teammates noticed money had been stolen from their lockers. Our locker room was adjacent to the general male student locker room for Binder gymnasium and our door was never closed, let alone locked. The thief could have been any male that walked into Binder.

Ron Hardy was declared fit to play and that Friday, Timo announced the starting lineup for the East Stroudsburg game. I was going back into the midfield. This would be my seventh consecutive start and I felt I was slowly gaining Timo's trust in me as a player.

East Stroudsburg State University was coached by the legendary Dr. John McKeon. He had an illustrious career coaching college soccer and also was the vice president of the United States Soccer Federation.

The first thing I noticed stepping onto the field was that the East Stroudsburg field was narrow and bumpy. There also was a very strong wind. Field conditions thus favored the less-skillful Stroudsburg team, which was led by an outstanding goalkeeper in Bobby Stetler.

Despite the poor playing conditions, we dominated, but seemed to revert back to not being able to finish our chances. Against the run of play, East Stroudsburg's leading scorer Charlie Kish scored his 11th goal of the season for a 1-0 lead at the half.

We continued to control the game and 18 minutes into the second half Artie scored the equalizer. We were all over East Stroudsburg, looking for the go-ahead goal, and it appeared certain we would get that goal. Bobby Stetler was terrific in goal for East Stroudsburg, making one save after another.

As the game wound down, Blaz Stimac, East Stroudsburg's outstanding midfielder, hit a wind-aided rocket from 25 yards out, beating Jamie in the goal with two minutes left in the game. It was a devastating blow to the team and an eighth straight NCAA Tournament invitation was in serious jeopardy.

Our record stood at 4-3-2 and our confidence was severely jolted. An upcoming game against Adelphi University would have a huge influence on whether or not we would qualify for the tournament.

Timo did his best to point out the positives in his post-game speech to the team but this loss really deflated us. We stopped at Dr. McKeon's favorite Italian restaurant for dinner before our ride back to Oneonta.

During dinner, the older players talked about Adelphi with great respect. Adelphi is led by head coach Dr. Mel Less, a citizen of Israel, and assistant coach Abe Reiss. Its roster was comprised of many former top high school players from New York City and Long Island, plus several outstanding older players imported from Israel.

They shared stories of some of the great games we had played against Adelphi the last few years. The seniors said without a doubt, Adelphi would have more talented individual players on its roster than any other team we played during the regular season.

Once we got back to Hartwick, most of the players planned to go downtown and have some drinks to drown their sorrows. I declined my teammates' serious arm-pulling to join them downtown. I was going to get up real early again on Sunday morning and sneak on to Elmore Field for some secret training while most students still were asleep.

There was something special for me being on Elmore Field with the soccer ball at my feet.

At Monday's training session, Timo's scouting report mentioned several key players for Adelphi. Up front, Ron Atanasio was described as a very powerful and fast attacking player who was very difficult to defend against in one-on-one situations.

Nimrod Dreyfuss, who was rumored to be an Olympic water polo player for the Israeli national team, played in the midfield and defense, and supposedly had an indefatigable work rate. The scouting report said Dreyfuss was a physical specimen.

In goal, Adelphi had a very talented goalkeeper in Eugene DuChateau. Adelphi would be the best team we had played since UConn and be a good barometer of how far we had come since the beginning of the season.

Tuesday morning, the weekly New York State rankings came out with Binghamton State No. 1 and Adelphi No. 2. There were four Division I schools ahead of us in the rankings; the top four would earn invitations to the NCAA tournament. It was apparent that a loss would end our tournament chances.

We had been in these do-or-die games almost all season, and you could feel the pressure permeate the locker room.

Timo's starting lineup surprised us, with Long Island native Keith Van Eron in the goal and Steve Jameson moved up front.

We were intense from the start and controlled the game for long stretches but could not produce any goal-scoring opportunities. There were numerous bone-crunching tackles by both teams. The first half ended 0-0.

The second half began the same way as the first half ended. We controlled the ball, but had a difficult time breaking down Adelphi's defense in the last third of the field. Minute by minute, we could feel the game getting more intense. Every 50-50 ball was challenged with a harder tackle than the previous one.

Fifteen minutes into the second half, Mooch soared through the air to head a ball and had a nasty clash of heads with an Adelphi defender. The game was stopped. It appeared Mooch may have broken his nose and gotten a concussion. He was taken off the field. When play resumed, the intensity went up another notch, as it was hard to know if Mooch's injury was accidental or intentional.

Minutes later, there was a loose ball in the middle of the field. I sprinted towards it, with two Adelphi players also in the chase. I beat both of them to the ball and timed my slide tackle to go right through the ball and the defender running towards me. As I slid, one Adelphi player jumped over the tackle. And Adelphi's Nimrod Dreyfuss, who looked like his body was chiseled out of granite, came from the side and slid down, his knee crashing into my thigh.

It felt like a Mack truck drove through my right thigh, which I grabbed as pain pulsated through my body. The game was stopped and Mitch came out to attend to me. It seemed like an eternity because of the amount of time it took me to limp off the field with Mitch's assistance.

Within minutes, two-thirds of our midfield has been knocked out of the game.

The game became even more physical, and the referees tried to keep it under control. At the 14-minute mark, Jamey played a long diagonal ball to Howie Charbonneau out wide on the left. Howie took several touches, controlling the ball, and then played a perfect through ball to Artie sprinting in the box. Artie was heading straight for goal when Carl MacDonald, Adelphi's huge sweeper, had no choice but to take Artie down for a penalty kick.

Timo selected Jamey to take the penalty kick, and our goalkeeper/ forward buried the ball past Eugene DuChateau, Adelphi's outstanding goalkeeper, to put us up 1-0.

Adelphi had no choice but to push everyone forward into the attack as it looked for the equalizing goal. With 10 minutes left in the game, Keith Van Eron, who had been outstanding in goal all game, misjudged a crossed ball and we all watched helplessly as the ball floated to Nimrod Dreyfuss, who stuck out his barrel chest and redirected the ball into the empty goal. It tied the game up at 1-1 and was very disheartening.

Both teams pushed for the winning goal in the waning minutes but neither could score. Although as a team we were disappointed that we did not win the game, the tie most likely would help us qualify for the NCAA tournament.

Ping Pong attended the game and Michael, Mooch, Artie and I spent a few minutes with him before we had to get on the bus. Ping grabbed my arm and said, "Billy, you made a very poor decision on your choice of going into that tackle and that is why you got hurt."

"I know, Ping, I really thought the defender in front of me would be the player going into the tackle and the other defender from the side would slow up," I said.

"Billy, other than that poor decision, I thought you played very well. You did not give one ball away all game."

"Thanks, Ping. Let's get together over the Christmas holiday. See you."

I iced my thigh on the bus ride back to Oneonta. I could not help but think about Ping Pong's comment about my poor decision. He was absolutely right and I vowed that I would never let anyone get the best of me in a tackle again.

I needed to analyze tackling as Ping would: Consider all the factors, including my size, my opponent's size, the timing of the tackle, putting every ounce of energy into the tackle and avoiding tackles, if necessary.

The next morning I could barely get out of bed and it took me forever to walk to the cafeteria for breakfast. At training that afternoon, Mitch gave me treatment. I knew there would be no chance that I would be fit enough to play that Saturday against Lehigh University. The rest of the week, I received treatment and watched training. On Friday, Timo's starting lineup included Steve Jameson staying up front in the attack with Keith Van Eron in goal. Mooch was cleared to play, and Jeff Marshall was inserted into my position on the left side in the midfield.

Saturday morning, I rushed up to Binder to get treatment before my teammates who were playing received theirs. Today would be another must-win game for us against a Lehigh team that had an outstanding goalkeeper in Larry Keller, who happened to be the Trenton Italians' keeper.

I sat on the bench in street clothes, and it was absolute torture knowing I would not be playing. Bob "Ike" Isaacson scored on a header three minutes into the game and the rout was on. We destroyed Lehigh 5-0 and the team played very well. Keith Van Eron made two outstanding saves in goal and Jamey playing up front seemed to make a big difference in our attack.

Timo finished up his post-game talk to the team with, "We have to beat Binghamton State next Saturday to get into the tournament." I thought how appropriate it was that it all came down to our last game of the regular season.

That Monday, I was allowed to do some light jogging for the first time since my injury. I felt better on Tuesday and on Wednesday I was allowed to sprint and felt little tightness. Mitch cleared me, so on Thursday, I finally got to train with the team again. I couldn't wait. I hadn't touched a soccer ball for over a week and it was driving me crazy.

I felt pretty good training on Thursday and I went into Friday's practice with the mindset that I had to prove to Timo I deserved to be in the starting lineup, that I was 100 percent healthy.

Near the end of training, Timo selected the first 11 to go over our free kicks and I was not on the first team. I was disappointed because who would not want to play in such an important game, on a packed Elmore Field? But Jeff Marshall, who was starting again at left midfield, was a very good player, and the team played outstandingly the previous Saturday. I could understand Timo's decision and I had to be prepared mentally and physically if I got the opportunity to get into the game.

Saturday morning, the campus was buzzing. It would be like playing a NCAA tournament game; we had to win or we were done. As I walked into the locker room, it hit me that this could be the last time the seniors ever put on a Hartwick uniform and played on Elmore Field.

It was really exciting, even though I was not starting and didn't know if I would get any playing time. Timo asked me once during the week how I felt. But otherwise, there was no hint if he planned for me to play or if I was being pushed to the end of the bench.

When we ran out onto Elmore Field, the fans erupted. The place was packed and the fact that I might not play really sank in.

After the national anthem, I sat down on the end of the bench and kept telling myself to be positive, that we would win this game, qualify for the NCAA Tournament and that I would get some playing time.

Binghamton was a big, aggressive team. Charlie Lineweaver, who was the second-leading scorer in New York State, led its attack. Johnny Bluem was assigned the job of marking Charlie out of the game. The key player for the Colonials in the midfield was Marty Friedman, whose passes tended to find Lineweaver in good positions in and around the penalty box. Binghamton also had a strong defense with an outstanding goalkeeper in Dan Goldstein.

The game started out fast and physical, with not a lot of ball possession for us—everything Binghamton State hoped for. You could sense the nervousness on our part as we gave the ball away much too easily and had a difficult time getting the ball to Mooch. We were at our best when the ball was at Mooch's feet. But we were not controlling midfield.

Despite the sloppy play, we created several good scoring opportunities early on that we could not finish. Binghamton followed our near-misses, squandering two quality goal-scoring chances. Fifteen minutes into the game, Timo turned toward the end of the bench and hollered, "Greek, warm up. You are going into the game. You are going in for Jeff."

I was so excited when I heard Timo call my name that I jumped off the bench to start warming up. Several minutes later, we had the opportunity to make a substitution and as I ran on to the field, I sensed that Jeff Marshall was very upset he was getting taken out of the game. Who would not be mad that they were getting taken out of such an important game?

In my first minute, I received a ball from Ron Hardy, turned and played a give-and-go with Mooch, then changed the direction of play with a pass to Jeff Tipping out wide on the right side of the midfield. Any nerves I had entering the game quickly disappeared. We started to keep better possession of the ball and found our rhythm.

Minutes later, Mooch went into a ferocious tackle in midfield, winning the ball and finding Duncan overlapping out wide on the right side. Perfectly in stride, Duncan one-touched the ball to Jamey, who timed his run impeccably, getting behind the Binghamton defense and bearing down on Colonial goalkeeper Dan Goldstein. Jameson drew Goldstein off his line before playing a square ball across the box and Art Napolitano one-touched the cross, burying the ball into the back of the net for a 1-0 lead. Elmore Field exploded in joy.

We continued to push forward in the attack and eight minutes later were awarded a free kick out wide on the right. Duncan took the free kick and the clearing header found the feet of Bob Isaacson at the 18-yard line. In one motion Ike controlled the ball, turned, and fired a hard, low shot towards the far post, just past the diving Goldstein, to put us up 2-0. Once again Elmore Field erupted.

Shortly after play resumed, Mooch won a ball in midfield and played a 40-yard through ball with the outside of his right foot, perfectly splitting the two Binghamton central defenders, and putting Jamey through on a foot race with the oncoming Goldstein. Goldstein beat Jamey to the ball by a millisecond, followed by a huge collision. Tempers flared and the referees had to intervene to calm the situation. When play finally resumed, the intensity level picked up significantly.

We were pushing forward, looking for a third goal, when Binghamton caught us on a counterattack at the 31-minute mark. Marty Friedman found the feet of Charlie Lineweaver in the box. Lineweaver was able to hold off a hard challenge by Johnny Bluem and laid off a pass to Joe Bolan, who hit a rocket right above Keith Van Eron's head into the goal.

Binghamton was back in the game. We knew they had a lot of heart and would fight to the end. The half ended 2-1.

At halftime, Timo was very focused on making sure we kept numbers in the defense and did not get caught in a counterattack again. We knew the game was going to get progressively more physical and it was important that we kept our composure. You could feel the emotion in the locker room. Such a pressure-packed season and we were 45 minutes from getting into the NCAA Tournament. I was really excited and could not wait to step back on to the field and hear the referee blow his whistle to start the second half.

The second half would be a game of opposites, each team trying to impose its will on the other. Binghamton tried to mark us as tightly as possible all over the field with constant high pressure, challenging for every ball, looking to win the ball or foul us and disrupt our rhythm.

We sought to keep possession of the ball, patiently waiting to find openings in their defense and look for that elusive third goal. The last 45 minutes were even more physical than we anticipated. The referees were giving out yellow cards like M&Ms. Thirteen minutes into the second half, Binghamton defender Charlie Dawson and Art Napolitano were given red cards for kicking and punching each other.

The game ebbed and flowed, with us stringing multiple passes together, with Binghamton chasing the ball, getting it back and sending long balls into the direction of Charlie Lineweaver. Johnny Bluem, with his terrific vertical jump, was up to the challenge and repeatedly won those aerial duels.

In the last 10 minutes of the game, the Colonials sent everyone except the keeper into the attack. They repeatedly sent long balls into the box, looking to win the header or get to the next touch following the headers. Michael Angelotti, our captain and sweeper, kept us organized and composed on defense, and we were delighted when the referee finally blew his whistle to end the game.

I was amazed at the physical effort and heart that the Binghamton team displayed. Although they lost, the team had nothing to be ashamed of. They had my utmost respect.

There was an immense sense of relief and excitement in our locker room. Not only did we know that we would qualify for the tournament, but also there was a high probability that we would get the first or second seed and have the first round played at Elmore Field.

You could see the pressure evaporate from Timo's face. Alden had a big smile and hugged everyone. I was really excited. This was the reason I came to Hartwick, to play in the NCAA Tournament and hopefully win a national championship.

Most of the team planned to go to the Rail to celebrate our victory. After dinner, I walked downtown to the Rail. It was so packed I could not open the door to get in.

Eventually I was able to force my way inside. Every three steps, a Hartwick student offered to buy me a drink. I politely declined. It was hard to tell if my teammates were more excited than the student body. We had the most amazing fans and our student body loved the soccer team.

I stayed for about an hour, then left. I was craving a meatball parmesan sandwich, so I stopped at Joe Ruffino's Pizzeria to get one for the walk back up to campus. I absolutely loved their meatball parm sandwich and if Joe Ruffino's was closer to campus, I probably would have eaten one every day.

On the walk back up to campus, while I was savoring every bite of my sandwich, I could not help but wonder if I would be put back into the starting lineup. I knew I needed to have a great week of training. I still felt that every day, I had to prove to Timo that I deserved to be in the starting lineup. I often wondered if that ever would change or remain the situation for my four years there.

I was very tired at the end of that game and knew that the one-week layoff from my thigh injury had affected my fitness. My weekly Sunday secret training on Elmore Field awaited the next morning, and I would incorporate fitness into my technical work.

Trentonian photo

I captained Junior High School number two to the city championship.
Here, Principal Dalba Brilliantine handed the trophy to me.

George O'Gorman

To protect my left calf during my senior year of high school, I wore heavy
padding-and didn't even know I had fractured my fibula.

Iron Mike Booter
Proves Iron Man

Billy Gazonas didn't get much of a chance to celebrate the biggest win of his soccer career.

Gazonas, the fine senior midfielder who scored a goal that helped St. Anthony win the NJSIAA Parochial Class A state title Saturday, is in St. Francis Hospital recovering from crushed knee ligament damage which he suffered in the third period.

Gazonas, who played the rest of the game unaware of the injury, was taken to the hospital Saturday night and had the leg placed in a cast. He will be on crutches for a month.

He also learned that he had played the final six weeks of the season with a broken leg bone that had slowly healed during the season. "The worst part is that I won't be able to start playing junior ball (with Post 313 of the Hamilton Junior League), for at least eight weeks," Gazonas said.

Copyright *The Times of Trenton.* Reprinted with permission.

James and Connie Gazonas. I feel so fortunate to
have had two wonderful parents.

The coaching staff of the Bronco Soccer Camp led by Manfred Schellscheidt and Charles "Ping Pong" Farrauto. Manfred is in the back row fourth from the left and Ping Pong is to Manfred's left. The impact the two had on me is beyond words. I am sitting in the front row, far right.

George O'Gorman

I'm dribbling in the high school state championship game, with my parents right behind me in the crowd.

Ed Clough

Standing in front of the airplane flying us to St. Louis in 1974.

James Parsons, Jr.

**The 1974 Hartwick College team won third place
in the NCAA Tournament.**

Ed Clough

Receiving a third-place plaque in the 1974 NCAA Tournament.
Little did I know it would take me three trips to the Final Four
to go home with the trophy I wanted all along.

George O'Gorman

The New Jersey junior state cup final with Hamilton Post 313, beating the
Elizabeth Germans keeper to the far post to send the game into overtime.

5

It's a Derby Match

A soccer game is called a "derby" when the two teams are from the same town, city or region. A soccer game between two rival teams also is referred to as a derby.

During training that following Monday, there was a lot of speculation about who we would play. A lot of the seniors agreed with an article in the Oneonta Star that said we should be the No. 1 seed and probably would play NYU. The article made it sound like the only difficult decision for the NCAA selection committee was how to seed Cornell and Oneonta State. Who would be seeded No. 2 and who would be seeded No. 3? The official announcement would come out of the NCAA offices in Shawnee Mission, Kansas, at 10 a.m. Wednesday.

"We are playing Oneonta State, Billy, we are playing Oneonta State," yelled a student who I did not know on Wednesday morning. He stopped in front of me with a huge smile, grabbed both my arms, started shaking them and repeated himself: "Billy, we are playing Oneonta State on Saturday."

I was momentarily stunned because I was surprised it would be Oneonta State. As my arms vibrated from the constant shaking, I asked him, "What is your name?"

He replied, "Billy, my name is Scott."

"Hi, Scott. Nice to meet you. Where did you hear this from?"

He said, "I was just up at Binder and everyone is talking about it. They are calling it Dream Match Three."

"Scott, thank you. Nice to meet you, but I have to run or I am going to be late for my next class."

As I headed to my sociology class, I could not stop thinking about Oneonta State and that we would be playing our crosstown rival.

Hartwick had had a top 20 program since 1966. The Oneonta State University soccer program had only recently begun to produce very good teams. The rivalry and hatred was such that although the college campuses are separated by a mere mile, the soccer programs had never played until, by chance, they drew each other in the 1972 NCAA tournament. That year, the upstart Red Dragons destroyed heavily favored Hartwick 3-0. Last year, once again the teams were matched up in the NCAA Tournament. This time, higher-seeded Oneonta State had the home-field advantage, only for Hartwick to win 2-0.

From preseason on, you could feel the dislike but also great respect that Hartwick's senior players had for Oneonta State. The Red Dragons soccer roster is a United Nations of players from many different countries.

At training that afternoon, watching the facial expressions of the often-stoic Timo as he addressed the team, and Alden's follow-up comments, made me realize this was so much more than just a game. It was for bragging rights in Oneonta for the next year, a huge advantage when recruiting players. Most importantly, it was a chance to advance to the New York State final of the NCAA Tournament.

As Michael Angelotti led us through our warmup, I ran with Mooch and told him, "I love it."

Mooch gave me a puzzled look and replied, "What are you talking about; what do you love?"

I said, "Mooch, think about it, Saturday there won't be room to fit an extra body up at Elmore Field. It will be packed to the gills. When we win, we will be two wins from getting to the Final Four. For me, there is nothing more exciting than playing in a game that you have to win to keep playing and Mooch, UConn is ranked second in the country. I do not think they are that good and we will probably meet up with them in the regional final if we get that far."

Mooch said, "Billy, you're right. It will be an unbelievable atmosphere to play a soccer game in."

I said, "Mooch, for as long as I can remember, I have never played on a team where I did not expect to win the championship, from playing on the Chambersburg Little League Baseball All Star Team and expecting to get to Williamsport, to St. Anthony's High School.

"Even when I knew the team I was on was not very talented, I still always believed that somehow my team will find a way to win against teams better than us and I feel that way right now."

Mooch said, "Billy, we both came here to win a national championship. Let's do our part to give Hartwick their first national championship."

"I agree, Mooch."

You could feel the energy and excitement in the air. As we were going through our warmup, I looked around and envisioned how electric the atmosphere was going to be on Elmore Field on that Saturday.

We had a lot of question marks leading up to the game. Tim Kevill was in the hospital with the flu. Jeff Tipping and Duncan both had nagging injuries that could keep them out of the game, and Mooch was dealing with a severely bruised instep that could limit his effectiveness.

On Thursday, near the end of the training session, Timo announced the lineup so we could go over our free kicks. It looked like Duncan and Kevill both would miss the game on Saturday. Timo pushed Ron Hardy over to the right back position and put me in at the left back spot.

I thought I would be starting, but I never take anything for granted. So when Timo announced I was in the starting lineup, I could feel a surge of adrenaline shoot through my body. The first thing I thought of when I knew I was going to play left back was that I didn't think I would be doing much overlapping in the game like I did against Colgate. Oneonta State had some really dangerous attacking players.

Up front, Oneonta State usually lined up a center forward with two wingers. The team was led by Ilyasa Sykes, a tall, lanky, extremely fast player of African descent. Ilyasa led the team in scoring with 17 goals and seven assists.

Bert Bidos, a powerful, quick player with very good one-on-one skills, complemented Sykes in the attack. They were joined by either Carlos Camacho, a small, clever player who led the team in assists, or Jim Boeff, a rugged, strong, physical old-fashioned center forward with a nose for the goal. The Oneonta players up front often exchanged positions. We would match up with man-to-man marking, with Michael always the free back in his sweeper position.

Growing up as a right winger with limited playing experience on defense, I focused on four principles when I played left back:

- No. 1, I always tried to deny the player I am marking the ball.
- No. 2, if he did receive the ball, I tried to mark him so tight that he didn't have the opportunity to turn and face me, forcing him to play the ball either square or back.
- No. 3, if he did receive the ball and was able to turn and face me, I always forced him toward the touchline line and patiently waited for him to hopefully push the ball too far in front of himself, never allowing him to attack me with speed.
- No. 4, I made sure that the player I was marking never received a ball behind me. That was very effective for me and I had no desire to deviate from how I defended against the extremely talented front line of Oneonta State.

I found it difficult to concentrate in class that Friday. We had a light training session Friday afternoon, and I just wanted to get to Saturday afternoon to start the game.

Timo wanted us to be very aware defensively where Farrukh Quraishi was at all times.

Timo felt when Farrukh ran with the ball, it was important that we force him to dribble across the field and minimize his direct runs towards our goal. According to some of my teammates, Farrukh had endless energy and needed to be contained as best we could because he was one of the top players in the country.

I thought the pressure leading up to the Binghamton State game was intense. But it was nothing compared to that week. The local television station sent newscasters to our training sessions every day, and there were numerous sportswriters from many newspapers up at Elmore Field besides Jud Magrin from the Oneonta Star. It was ironic that Thom Meredith, a Hartwick alumnus who had covered soccer for the Oneonta Star with such a passion and skill the last several years, announced during the week that he was leaving to take a position with the Tampa Bay Rowdies of the NASL.

We could not walk on campus without getting stopped by what seemed like every student wishing us good luck in the game. It seemed like Oneonta and the surrounding areas were consumed with the game.

Saturday finally came and when we ran out onto Elmore Field to the tune of "Glad," chills ran through my body. A sea of bodies filled every inch of space from the track, all of the bleachers, up the hillside and into the woods. It was everything I imagined, the only difference being the number of fans from the opposing team was much greater than usual at Elmore Field.

At 1 p.m., the referee blew his whistle to start the game. Elmore Field was sun-drenched and cold. From the start, Oneonta State controlled the midfield, led by its All-American Farrukh Quraishi. Despite that, we were airtight on defense and shut down their attack in the last third of the field. Bert Bidos lined up as the right winger for Oneonta State and I did my best to deny him any touches of the ball in the first 10 minutes of the game.

Oneonta State was dominating play when, around the 13-minute mark, Steve Jameson received a ball at midfield, turned and played a through ball to the streaking Art Napolitano. Artie collected the ball and ran right towards Carl Mohammed, the last defender between Artie and the goal.

The scouting report said Mohammed often committed early to the tackle and Artie was ready. As Mohammed went down into the tackle, Artie pushed the ball past the sliding defender and managed to jump over his tackle, heading straight for goal. Jim Harrington, the talented Oneonta State keeper, came charging off his line as Artie ran into the penalty box and on a very difficult angle, he shot the ball hard and low past the outstretched arms of Harrington. The ball hit the far post and bounced into the goal. We were thrilled as we went up 1-0 in this derby match.

The Red Dragons were not deterred. Led by Farrukh, they continued to control play in the midfield. The Red Dragons dominated time of possession but produced few goal-scoring opportunities. Late in the first half, an Oneonta State defender made an errant clearance, with the ball deflecting off of Mooch and landing at the feet of Bob Isaacson, standing unmarked 12 yards from the goal. The surprised Ike could not control the ball and Oneonta State desperately cleared the ball out with what could have been our second goal of the game. The first half ended with Oneonta State dominating midfield play and time of possession, but us leading on the scoreboard.

We were physically banged up and Timo's choices at halftime to make personnel changes were limited. Tipping had to be substituted for late in the first half because his injury proved to be too painful. I thought Timo might push me into the midfield because we were getting dominated in that area of the field, but with Duncan and Kevill out and our defense playing outstanding in the first half, Timo decided to keep it intact.

The second half began similarly as the first, with Oneonta State controlling midfield but not creating good goal-scoring chances. Garth Stam, the Oneonta State coach, had made a surprise personnel change to start the game, putting talented midfielder Herb Rodriquez in the sweeper position. The Colombian-born, Elizabeth, New Jersey-raised Rodriguez was powerfully built, strong on the ball and very skillful. In the first half, he primarily stayed back in his new sweeper position. But as the second half wore on and the need for a goal grew, Rodriquez started to make runs from his sweeper position into the attack and was causing all kinds of problems for us.

We continued to shut down Oneonta State in our defensive third. But I became concerned about Rodriguez pushing into the attack more and more, and also with the ease with which the Red Dragons were getting into our last third.

As we entered the last 15 minutes of the game, Oneonta State was awarded a free kick out wide. Quraishi, with the sun behind him, struck a hard low cross along the six-yard line and Keith Van Eron was temporarily blinded by the sun, losing sight of the ball as it skidded right past him towards Ilyasa Sykes, who merely had to tap the ball into an empty net. But the ball skipped past the surprised Sykes before he could make contact. It sounded like every Hartwick fan, including me, at Elmore Field simultaneously let out a huge sigh of relief.

Time was running out for Oneonta State when they were awarded a free kick about 25 yards out. Once again, Farrukh would take the free kick. He slowly approached the ball and struck a rocket of a shot that headed to the upper seven corner of the goal. It had "goal" written all over it when the very athletic, 6-foot-1 Van Eron flew through the air and tipped the ball over the goal post for a corner kick.

It was a brilliant save by Keith. This time, you heard a collective gasp from the Oneonta State fans as everyone watching the trajectory of the ball thought it was a goal and we would be going to overtime. We defended the ensuing corner kick and played very conservatively the last few minutes. We finally heard the referee's whistle to end the game. Elmore Field erupted; our fans' cheering was deafening.

There was extreme elation and the relief we felt was so great, it was almost hard to describe. As Timo addressed the team, it was nice to see the often-unemotional Timo smiling ear to ear and basking in our victory. Alden had a huge grin on his face as he went around the locker room hugging all of the seniors.

6

St. Louis in Sight

Early that next morning, while I was up on Elmore Field doing my weekly secret training, all I could think about was the fact that we were two wins from getting to St. Louis and playing in the semifinals for the national championship. Physically, I felt so much better than the last Sunday, after the Binghamton game. I spent 1½ hours working on my technique before I headed to the cafeteria for a nice big breakfast.

After that, I spent the rest of the day in the library trying to prepare for my finals.

"Trying" was the key word because my concentration kept drifting to the NCAA Tournament. That Wednesday, Cornell would host St. Francis University, with us playing the winner. Who would be our next opponent and would we get the opportunity to avenge our loss to UConn?

Wednesday night on the AstroTurf at Schoellkopf Field, Cornell defeated St. Francis 4-2. Results from New England had UConn defeating Bridgeport 4-1 and Brown defeating Harvard 5-1. Our next game was to be Tuesday, Nov. 26, hosting Cornell; UConn would play Brown, with the New England winner coming to New York State to play the Hartwick-Cornell winner.

It snowed frequently in Oneonta and kept getting colder. To try to keep Elmore Field in as good a condition as possible, we trained at Neahwa Park. We still had classes and finals, so training didn't start until later in the afternoon. The combination of the cold, snow, and it getting darker earlier made training very challenging. It got to the point where we used what natural light we had for our technical and tactical training, and saved our fitness work for the end of each training session. If not for the little light we had coming from the newly opened portion of 1-88 highway adjacent to Neahwa Park, we would have been doing sprints in the dark on a snow-covered field.

As a team, we felt we were much better than we were when we played Cornell in the regular season. But Cornell also may have become a better team than before our 0-0 draw. In our first game, its leading scorer, Luis Portugal, had limited playing time and midfielder Abdullah Neza did not play at all. Adding those two players to the talented attacking duo of Joe Mui and David Sarachan would challenge our defense.

Timo hoped Jeff would be healthy enough to play so he could mark Joe Mui.

Timo said it was very important that defensively, we should limit the number of touches Mui and Sarachan received.

Early Tuesday morning, the Hartwick maintenance staff and a group of fans shoveled as much of the snow as possible off of Elmore Field. Cornell Coach Dan Wood was doing everything possible to get the match postponed or possibly even switched to Cornell's turf field. But Garth Stam, representing the NCAA, and Hartwick Athletic Director Dr. Roy Chipman decided the field was playable and kickoff would be at 1 p.m. as scheduled.

We had our traditional warmup in the gymnasium before we ran out on to Elmore Field. The environment was very different than our game against Oneonta State. Hartwick was on Thanksgiving break, so we did not have the great fan support we always got from our student body— and it felt like we were in Siberia. The field was frozen, with some areas still snow-covered, and it was by far the coldest environment in which I ever played a soccer game.

As we lined up to start the game, our substitutes sitting on the bench were wearing sweat suits, with parkas over them, draped with blankets. I just kept jogging in place, waiting for the referee to blow his whistle and start game. Despite the weather, I was really excited to be starting again and back in the midfield.

One minute into the game, Johnny Bluem won a ball in midfield and took several touches while making eye contact with Artie out wide on the right touchline. Artie checked back as if he was looking to receive the ball at his feet, then spun past the startled tight-marking Cornell defender. Johnny played a through ball directly behind the defender into the streaking Artie's path. Artie took one touch before serving a cross into the box and Bob Isaacson beat a slow-reacting Cornell defense to the ball and one-timed it past a surprised Jon Ross in goal for Cornell.

It was a dream start. We were up 1-0 after a little over a minute into the game. We were bursting with confidence and it showed in our play. With Mooch and Jeff much healthier than they were in the Oneonta State game, and me back in the midfield, we were clicking. We took control of the game, especially in midfield.

We were pushing for the second goal with around three minutes left in the half when Art struck a shot that had Ross beaten, only for Cornell defender Ed Hopp to block the sure goal. The rebound came out to me at the top of the box and I first-timed a shot back on goal, only to have it deflected by a Cornell defender and redirected to Artie, who flicked the ball past Ross into the back of the net before he could react. We were ecstatic. The referee's whistle ended the first half with us up 2-0.

At the locker room, our substitutes still remained covered with all of the clothing they wore on the bench, minus the blankets, and they went into the sauna to warm up.

There were not many adjustments to be made at halftime. We were all over them and in command of the game. Timo stressed the importance of not getting careless on defense and playing intelligently.

The second half started out very much how the first half ended, with us in total control. Cornell still seemed flat. We had several great opportunities early in the second half but could not finish. A third goal by us probably would have clinched this game. But against the run of play at around the 17-minute mark, Cornell was awarded a corner kick. Poor marking on the corner kick allowed Luis Portugal to head home a goal, giving Cornell life. The game instantly changed dramatically, with Cornell taking control of the midfield and displaying a level of energy not seen in the first 62 minutes of the game.

Around seven minutes later, Ike headed a Cornell free kick out of the penalty box. The ball landed at the feet of Bob Capener, who first-timed a rocket of a shot from 23 yards out perfectly into the upper left corner of the goal, tying the score at 2-2.

In a seven-minute span, our team went from total domination to fighting for our NCAA life.

The game opened up, with both teams pushing for the third goal. It was end to end, with both teams having several quality chances thwarted by Ross and Van Eron in their respective goals. The second half ended 2-2.

The rules for the NCAA tournament were that we would play a 15-minute overtime period. If the score remained tied after that, it would be followed by a second 15-minute overtime period. The rules permitted a maximum of four 15-minute overtime periods and if the score remained tied after that, whichever team had more corner kicks during the overtime periods would be declared the winner. Entering overtime, we were not overly concerned about the corner kicks because we felt there would be a winner prior to the end of 60 minutes of overtime play.

The first overtime period was a mirror image of the last 20 minutes of regulation play. We played end to end, with outstanding goalkeeping preventing goals being scored.

Early in the second overtime period, Ed Hopp cleared a shot off the goal line, then minutes later a much healthier Glenn Myernick hit a rocket that had Ross clearly beaten. But out of nowhere, Ed Hopp once again blocked a sure goal from going in. We were very disappointed at the end of the second overtime. We had two wonderful opportunities and nothing to show for it. With the weather getting colder by the minute, it was almost impossible to make any substitutions and have a player properly warmed up to enter the game.

At the start of the third overtime period, fatigue was starting to be a huge factor and the game became very stretched out, end to end. But once again, neither team could produce a goal.

Timo made us aware that we were down 3-1 on corner kicks. Through the first three OT periods, we were not concerned at all with the corner kicks, but now it was a reality that they could determine the winner.

Many players on both teams were exhausted and it was the pure desire to win that kept us going. Midway through the final period, we had several good opportunities that resulted in corner kicks, which became tied at 3-3. With around six minutes left in the game, Artie received a ball out wide and Ed Hopp came out to defend Artie. As Artie was about to attack Hopp, Timo hollered from the sidelines to get a corner kick. Artie dribbled out wide heading for the end line and as Hopp closed him down, Artie kicked the ball off the defender's shin, giving us a 4-3 advantage in corner kicks. The ensuing corner kick had Ross snatch the ball off of Ike's forehead. It was one of many outstanding saves by the Cornell keeper.

Minutes later, Ron Hardy overlapped from his left back position and kicked the ball off of Hopp, getting us another corner kick and a 5-3 advantage. The following corner kick brought a big clearance from the Cornell defense. Cornell attacker Bill Sobolewski played through, getting behind our defense, coming in on Keith Van Eron. Chasing back from my midfield position, I could not believe what I was seeing. Every touch that brought Sobolewski closer to our goal was another step closer to ending our season. As Sobolewski entered the penalty box, Van Eron exploded off his line, cutting the angle and making a brilliant save by smothering Sobolewski's shot.

With Cornell now pushing everyone up to try to get the winning goal, Ike was played through, getting behind the Cornell defense. This time it was Ross who made a brilliant save, pushing Ike's shot over the goal post and giving us a 6-3 advantage in corner kicks with only two minutes left in the final overtime period.

We took a short corner trying to kill time, but we kicked the ball over the goal line, giving Cornell a goal kick. We put everyone behind the ball defending and did not let Cornell get into our defensive third when the referee finally blew his whistle to end the game. It was a great sound to hear. We were all so exhausted and excited. We were one step closer to St. Louis. For Cornell, what a terrible way to lose a game.

I thought I had a very good game and my teammates voted me man of the match for my all-around play. Winning the game, getting to the NCAA quarterfinals and the vote of confidence from my teammates made it a great day for me. I wasn't going home for Thanksgiving, which was one of my goals when I decided to come to Hartwick.

At the same time our game was being played, up in New England, UConn beat Brown University in three overtimes. UConn would bring an 18-1-1 record into the quarterfinals, with its only loss a regular-season-ending home loss to Rhode Island. UConn was ranked fourth in the latest national poll.

I was really excited when I heard we would play UConn. The regular-season game against them was special for me because it was my first start in a Hartwick uniform and it gives us a chance to redeem ourselves for the very embarrassing 3-0 loss UConn handed us on Elmore Field.

Our team had started the season poorly, but we were just one win away from getting to the national championship semifinals at Busch Stadium. The weather for the rest of the week through game day on Sunday was expected to continue to be frigid, with more snow possible. The weather on Sunday couldn't possibly be more brutal than it was against Cornell.

In training on Wednesday, Timo went over what our tactics would be against UConn. Though Timmy Hunter was a good passer of the ball, Timo felt he would not break down our defense individually. So Timo decided we would not be concerned with eliminating Timmy Hunter via myself or another player marking him all over the field.

Although UConn was very good at keeping possession of the ball, it lacked creativity. Its most dangerous attacking player and the player we worried about the most was All-American Frantz Innocent, a skillful and quick front player.

Timo said if we could give help to the defender marking Frantz Innocent whenever he received the ball, we could limit the amount of chances they would get. Timo was meticulous with his scouting report and went over every free kick situation that UConn might get.

In particular, he mentioned a free kick UConn would take if it was within shooting distance of goal. They would have a player standing in our defensive wall, and at the last second, he would act as if he had to tell the players standing over the ball something, then would slowly walk back toward the players standing over the ball. When he got within three or four yards, they would push him the ball and as he trapped it with the sole of his foot, Timmy Hunter would run onto it and strike it, with the defenses typically not ready for the free kick.

When attacking, Timo felt that we could hurt UConn on the counter-attack and from free kicks. UConn had a lot of tall players. Timo felt that on corner kicks and free kicks out wide near our attacking goal, we could drive the free kicks hard and low, and be first to the ball.

On Thursday, we had a nice Thanksgiving dinner as a team, although it was different not being with my family and getting to eat Greek food along with traditional Thanksgiving food. The weather leading up to Sunday consisted of really cold temperatures, wind and snow, making training difficult. Rumor had it that Joe Morrone was doing everything he could to get the game moved to Storrs, Connecticut.

The minute I woke up Sunday morning I could feel the pregame jitters. This would be the most important soccer game I ever played in, and we were one win from going to the Final Four.

I headed straight for the cafeteria for a light breakfast and then went back to my dormitory room to try to relax before heading up to Binder Gymnasium. I could not sit and was pacing my dormitory room until I could not take it any longer. We were supposed to report to our locker room one hour prior to kickoff, but I headed up to Elmore Field two hours before and walked every inch of the field until it was time to get to the locker room. The field was snow-covered and bone-hard, but it did not feel as frigid as it was during the Cornell game. Finally, walking into the locker room brought me a sense of relief.

Classes were to resume the next day, with Thanksgiving break ending, and it showed when we ran out to Elmore Field to a much larger crowd than the Cornell game. Prior to the referee starting the game, I could not help but notice every UConn player was wearing training flats instead of your typical soccer cleats. I was so ready for the game to start.

Unlike our first game, which UConn dominated from start to finish, we were all over them right from the start. I was not sure if it was the weather, the importance of the game or that we were just a much-improved team from early in the season. We created quality chances but could not score.

Midway through the first half, Keith Van Eron went out for a crossed ball, uncharacteristically missed it and flattened UConn attacking player Lloyd Grant. The referee did not hesitate to blow his whistle and award UConn a penalty kick. It was eerily similar to our regular-season game when Frantz Innocent scored from a penalty kick and UConn went on to rout us. Would this be a here-we-go-again moment?

Innocent lined up over the ball. On the referee's whistle, he casually approached the ball before striking it three feet wide of the lower left corner of the goal. The miss was a huge relief for us. Minutes later, when UConn's Mike Swifford hit a rocket from 40 yards out that had goal written all over it, Van Eron stretched every inch of his body, getting his fingertip to the ball and pushing it just wide of the goal. It was a brilliant save.

We went back to controlling the game. We were awarded a free kick outside of the UConn penalty box at the 28:28 mark. Duncan took the free kick and the cross found Jeff Tipping unmarked at the far post. Tipping headed the ball past UConn's 6-foot-6 goalkeeper Ted McSherry to put us up 1-0.

Four minutes later, Timo's brilliance showed when we were awarded a corner kick. Ron Hardy went over to take the corner. He approached the ball and drilled a hard low liner that Artie got to first and headed past McSherry for a 2-0 lead.

Our confidence was growing by the minute. UConn, which had been eliminated in the New England finals the last two years and never had made it this far in the NCAA tournament, was playing without the confidence it had displayed in our regular-season meeting.

With around eight minutes to go in the half, Mike Angelotti was in a vicious collision with a UConn payer and got a nasty cut over his left eye. Our captain and sweeper had to immediately leave the game. Timo moved Ron Hardy to the sweeper position and put Timmy Kevill in at left back.

The referee's whistle ended the first half with us up 2-0. In the locker room, the doctor was stitching up the cut above Michael's eye and it looked really bad. It seemed like it did not matter what the doctor said because Michael was going to play no matter what.

Timo repeated everything we had discussed all week. Look to counter-attack, give help to whoever is marking Innocent, drive our free kicks and keep possession when we couldn't counter.

The second half began as the first half ended, with us controlling play. We had several good opportunities to get the third goal, but McSherry made two outstanding saves. When UConn kept possession, it really could not penetrate in the attacking third, and we were quick to support the defender marking Innocent whenever he received the ball.

Midway through the second half, Angelotti returned to the game with eight stitches above his eye. As the half went on, UConn was in desperation mode and started to push more players into the attack. The few times they were able to break down our defense, Van Eron was up to the task each time.

At around the five-minute mark, UConn was awarded a free kick 25 yards from goal. I lined up on the end of the wall and a UConn player was standing in front of me. As Timmy Hunter and Innocent stood over the ball, the UConn player in front of me started walking towards Hunter and Innocent shouted something.

I walked behind him, following him all the way to the ball as the UConn players shouted at the top of their lungs to the referee that I needed to give them 10 yards. I walked up to the two and waited for the referee to tell me for the third time that I had to go back and give them their 10 yards.

Before I retreated back to the wall, I could see in the UConn players' eyes that they knew we were prepared for anything they had. The ensuing free kick sailed over the goal post. That was UConn's last opportunity on goal and minutes later, the game was over.

Timo had prepared us so thoroughly for this opponent and the final score was testament to that: Hartwick 2, University of Connecticut 0.

Although there was not much handshaking between the two teams after the game, as there was a clear dislike between us, I made it a point to find Frantz Innocent to shake his hand. I think he was a great player and I wanted to wish him good luck in the pros. He told me that I played a real good game. Coming from one of the best players in the country, it made me feel really good. It was the icing on the cake. We just won our way into the Final Four, with a chance to win a national championship, and one of the best players in the country complimented me.

There was bedlam in the locker room. Everyone was jumping up and down, hollering and hugging each other. To say we were excited was an understatement. As soon as I showered, I went straight for the nearest pay phone to call my parents and let them know we won and would be going to St. Louis next week. My parents were really excited for me.

Timo is a huge reason we won that day and were going to St. Louis. He was a brilliant tactician.

7

We Could Have Been

Monday, Timo went over our schedule for the week. We would depart Oneonta at 5:30 a.m. Wednesday via Bluebird, heading to Hancock Airport in Syracuse before flying to St. Louis. Howard University had beaten Philadelphia Textile the day before and would be our opponent on Thursday evening. Kickoff was scheduled for 6:30 p.m., followed by the other semifinal pitting UCLA against two-time defending champion St. Louis University.

The Howard University soccer team was comprised of players mostly from the Caribbean region and Africa. Howard was led by Ian Bain, who many thought was the best player in the country. Not only was the Howard team athletic and skillful, but its motivation extended well past winning the 1974 NCAA men's national championship. Howard had won 17 straight games and was on a mission. History and the NCAA committee hadn't been kind to Howard University.

Leading up to its 1972 semifinal match for the national championship, defending national champion Howard was accused by the NCAA of using players who had eligibility violations. Howard held out seven players in the semifinals and lost in overtime, 2-1 to St. Louis.

To make matters worse, in January 1973 the NCAA stripped Howard of its 1971 national championship victory, stating that Howard used two players who were ineligible. The team was put on probation, thus not eligible to participate in the 1973 NCAA Tournament. Howard has waited two years to get back to this game and would be a formidable opponent for us.

Timo made one adjustment to our alignment for this game. Howard liked to play a 4-2-4 formation, so Timo decided to drop Tipping back from his defensive midfield position into the center of the defense. Johnny Bluem and Tipping would mark the two central strikers, with Michael playing behind them in his sweeper position. We would line up in a 1-4-2-3 formation. Then Timo followed with "Mooch and Billy will be in the midfield, but I want Billy to line up on the side of the field where Ian Bain is and whenever possible you mark him. Billy, I want you marking him so Mooch does not have to expend so much energy defending."

Timo's tactics made sense to me. If Ian Bain was the best player in the country, then Mooch had to be a very close second and we would need Mooch at his best when he had the ball.

On the flight to St. Louis, we were told that Dettmar Cramer would be in attendance for all of the games to look at players for the United States National Teams. Dettmar Cramer is a legendary soccer coach from West Germany who was an assistant coach under Helmut Schoen when West Germany lost to England in the 1966 World Cup final.

The United States Soccer Federation had recently hired Cramer to develop all aspects of our soccer program, from developing coaching schools to selecting and training our national teams from the youth level through the senior team. Cramer was considered to have one of the most knowledgeable soccer minds in the world. My first thought was that this could be great for Mooch. I couldn't imagine 11 better soccer players with U.S. citizenship than Mooch. Perhaps they would put him right onto the men's national team, where I feel he belonged.

It was a very exciting day for me and I could not wait to step on the field and play against Ian Bain and hugely favored Howard.

There was a steady drizzle for the Thursday night game under the lights at Busch Stadium. I couldn't help but notice how big and athletic the Howard University players were. We knew this would be our most difficult opponent of the season. Howard had scored five goals against Philadelphia Textile in its quarterfinal victory and most soccer experts said Howard was the most talented college team in the country.

Whereas UConn had one special player in Frantz Innocent, who could individually break down a defense, Howard had a player in every attacking position with that ability, with Ian Bain in the midfield orchestrating everything.

Since our early-season disastrous results, every game had seemed more important and exciting than our previous one. And the Howard game was the most exciting and important one of the season.

The pace of the game in the first few minutes was slow as the teams felt each other out. I made several runs into the attack and when we gave the ball away, there was a lot of ground I had to make up to backtrack and find Ian Bain. Although Timo didn't want me marking him all over the field early on, I decided I had to be selective when I made runs forward into the attack.

Busch Stadium is a big field and with just Mooch and I in the midfield, there was a lot of ground to cover. From Ian Bain's first few touches it was obvious he had an elegance in how he controlled the ball, as if it were on a string.

Fifteen minutes into the game, Mooch started to reveal his impeccable skills, spraying the ball from one side of the field to another, causing Howard to chase the ball much more than it may have anticipated.

The first quality opportunity of the game belonged to us. Steve Jameson took a long throw-in, which the Howard defense headed out to Mooch at the top of the box. Mooch hit a laser that had the Howard goalkeeper clearly beaten, only to whistle inches wide of the post.

Although Howard was not having much difficulty getting into our attacking third, we were very compact and organized from 25 yards and in. Howard was having a problem creating any quality chances.

I had never played in such an important game and against such a great player as Ian Bain. But as the game progressed, I could feel my confidence growing and my comfort level increasing by the minute.

The rain picked up and the tackling also picked up as the half went on. Perhaps Howard thought this would be an easy game and now realized it would be anything but easy.

We were awarded a corner kick with 20 minutes remaining in the first half. Duncan drove a perfect cross to the near post. As Howard keeper

Trevor Leibe covered the near post, Ike soared above the Howard defense at the corner of the six-yard box. Instead of heading to goal, he flicked the ball to the far post to an unmarked Jeff Tipping, standing three yards from goal. Tip emphatically headed the ball down towards the corner of the goal, which would have put us up 1-0. But out of nowhere, Trevor Leibe flew through the air and made a spectacular save. Almost immediately after, the game seemed to open up.

Minutes later, Howard attacker Ken Ilodiwge had a point-blank shot at goal. It was Keith Van Eron's turn to make a spectacular play, first blocking the shot then spinning and diving to grab the rebound as the ball was about to roll over the goal line.

We had done a good job defensively, especially in the last third, when with a little over 11 minutes left in the half, Howard was patiently knocking the ball around the perimeter of our 18-yard box. The ball eventually reached Ken Ilodiwge at the top of the D.

Johnny Bluem was positioned in front of Ilodiwge, who made several body feints and fake shot attempts, but Johnny didn't flinch from his perfect defensive positioning. Ilodiwge then chipped the ball toward the goal. Keith immediately reacted, sprinting to the corner of the goal with his arms up in the air in plenty of time to catch or tip the ball over the goal post. Inexplicably, he dropped his arms, thinking the ball was either going to go over or wide of the goal post. But the ball landed softly in the goal to put Howard up 1-0.

It was a surreal moment. A mistake by Keith, who had been spectacular for us all season and was one of the reasons we were in the semifinals. The half ended shortly thereafter.

Although giving up a goal just before halftime can be demoralizing, in this case it was not. The mood in the locker room was very positive and we felt we still would win the game. Timo and Alden repeatedly told us to be patient defensively and not dive in, and when they attacked with numbers when we won the ball, be ready to counterattack them with speed. If the counter was not on, then keep possession and make them chase the ball, very much what Timo and Alden had been talking about since preseason.

In the first half, the Howard attacking players put a lot of pressure on our defenders when they won the ball. Our defenders often bypassed Mooch and I in the midfield and played balls directly to our front players. I thought if we could do a better job of playing through the midfield, it could be a difference in the game's result.

Right from the first minute of the second half, we sensed the intensity of the game was raised to another level. Both teams' tackles were very hard. Despite the importance of the game, there were not a lot of nasty tackles, with both teams desperately wanting to get to the championship game. Play was going end to end, but neither team was having much success around the penalty box.

We were awarded a corner kick 11 minutes into the second half. Duncan served a perfect ball into the box with Ike soaring above several Howard defenders. Once again, Ike flicked the ball to the back post. Jeff Tipping came flying through the air headfirst with a spectacular diving header, burying the ball into the back of the net before Trevor Leibe could react.

All of a sudden, the game was tied and the Howard players had disbelief written all over their faces. The stadium was buzzing and the intensity of the game was growing by the minute. The Howard players began using their terrific speed to high-pressure us and looked to win the ball back immediately.

Despite the lack of space and time for us on the ball, all of the training I had done in the past summer with Ping Pong, about looking around and thinking ahead, paid off. I was so focused and aware of everyone around me that despite the pressure, I was always at least one to two plays ahead in my thoughts, knowing exactly what I was going to do with the ball well before I received it.

Midway through the second half, Howard was awarded a free kick out wide on the left side around 35 yards from goal. Sam Acquah crossed the ball into the box.

Players from both teams rose in the air to challenge for the ball. Bodies collided and the ball dropped down to the feet of an unmarked Tony

Martin, who quickly first-timed the ball into the back of the net before Keith could react.

Howard went into a more defensive posture as we pushed more players into the attack, looking to get the equalizer. We could not create any quality chances on goal, although we fought with every ounce of energy we had in our bodies before the referee blew his whistle to end the game. Score: Howard 2, Hartwick 1.

By the time I got back to the locker room I felt numb. I sat at my locker and was totally oblivious to what Timo and Alden were saying as they addressed the team. My eyes filled up with tears just as they had on the back of the team bus after our first game of the year against Montclair State University. I just sat there for what seemed like an eternity, not believing that we lost. I was the only one left in the locker room when I eventually showered and then met the team in the stands.

We watched St. Louis University beat UCLA in overtime, setting up a national championship game against Howard, with us playing UCLA in the third-place game.

The next morning, I had just finished breakfast and was relaxing in my hotel room when the phone rang.

"Hello?"

"Hey Billy, this is Charlie Lang. Listen Billy, Dettmar Cramer wants to meet you in the hotel lobby at 10."

"Charlie, why does he want to meet me?"

"Billy, he really liked the way you played and there will also be some other players there he is going to meet with."

"Charlie, are you sure about this?" "Yes, Billy. Be in the hotel lobby at 10." "OK. Thanks, Charlie."

I really was not sure what to think, but Charlie was pretty convincing. Dettmar Cramer was a world-renowned soccer coach and it felt a bit intimidating to me.

I headed for the elevator at 9:45 because I did not want to be late. When I got in the elevator and the door closed heading down, I started to feel really nervous. The elevator door opened at the lobby and I stepped out looking for Dettmar Cramer. But excluding hotel employees, the lobby was empty.

I was early, so I just stood next to the front desk getting more nervous by the minute. Waiting and waiting, I eventually asked the clerk at the front desk what time it was. He told me it was 10:05. I started to walk around the lobby thinking perhaps Cramer and the other players were somewhere right off the lobby. I did not see anything and when I turned to look up the hallway to the right of the lobby, Charlie Lang and Timmy Kevill were standing there. When we made eye contact, they burst out laughing. The joke was on me.

The third-place game against UCLA was very difficult from an emotional viewpoint. We were expected to play with passion and intensity, but our hearts were ripped out two days earlier in losing the semifinal match. I am sure every player on both teams felt the same way.

As the game wore on, it appeared we had more desire to win the game than UCLA and we won 3-1, receiving the third-place trophy. Considering how we started the season it was quite an accomplishment, although at the time the heartbreak from losing to Howard was still overwhelming.

In the championship game, Howard beat St. Louis University 2-1 in four overtimes, with Kenneth Ilodiwge getting the winning goal. Although we could have beaten Howard on Thursday night, I thought they were by far the most talented team in the country and Ian Bain was clearly the best player that I had played against.

8

I Have to Become a Much Better Player

The following Monday we had a team meeting, with Timo and Alden summarizing our season. Timo discussed at length the importance that players had to continuously look to improve their games individually and collectively as a team. He then went over our winter schedule, which would start after our Christmas break. The team would train indoors two nights a week in preparation for six indoor tournaments in the winter season, of which one was the annual Hartwick College indoor tournament.

We had four freshmen starters and three sophomore starters returning to the team. You could sense that the expectation for next year's team was to win the national championship. Besides our returning players, there were rumors swirling around that Timo had discovered two superstar attacking players from Canada who were coming to Hartwick the next year, along with a terrific right winger from the Liverpool youth team and at least three of that year's top New Jersey high school players.

I walked out of that meeting excited and nervous at the same time. Excited because it appeared we would have a very talented team the next year, with many more gifted attacking players on the team. Nervous because I knew I was going to have to improve dramatically as a player if I expected to remain in the starting lineup.

Until I left for college, I had never been away from home for more than a week at a time. I was really ready for Christmas break so I could get home and see my family and friends.

During the break, I realized that I did not give my academic studies enough attention and although I loved playing soccer more than anything else in this world, I knew I had to put much more thought and effort into my schoolwork when I returned to class.

My fears were confirmed when my fall grades revealed that I received a D for my class in American Government with Professor Kang. It made me very angry, not at Kang but at myself for receiving this grade. My father worked incredibly hard his whole adult life and paid for my education at Hartwick. I believed I let him down.

I vowed that I would never receive another grade like that again at college and schoolwork would become my first priority on a daily basis.

I was able to spend a lot of time with my best friend Denny Kinnevy. Denny is the individual responsible for getting me involved in soccer and also is the reason St. Anthony's High School was able to win the state championship. Without Denny, it would have been impossible.

During the break, excluding Christmas Day, I went to Wetzel Field and trained for a couple of hours every morning. Wetzel Field, which was two blocks from my home, is a huge baseball field. Center field seemed endless and eventually stopped with a basketball court and some park benches. Left field had a 30-foot-high fence that we often turned into a makeshift soccer goal when we practiced our shooting. We never had to worry about chasing the ball if we shot the ball too high.

We always heard rumors that Babe Ruth had played a baseball game at Wetzel Field and hit a home run that went over the park benches, over the alley behind Wetzel Field, and landed at the intersection of Chambers and Liberty Street, which is well past 550 feet from home plate. They say it was when Babe Ruth and Lou Gehrig were on a barnstorming tour across America, which was called "The Bustin' Babes" vs. the "Larrupin' Lou's."

The left-field area of Wetzel Field also had really nice grass to train on. In high school oftentimes when baseball season was over and the groundskeeper would forget to lock the equipment room, Denny and I would borrow the line chalker equipment and line a smaller version of a soccer field in left field. Denny and I then would go recruit soccer players in the neighborhood so we could have a nice seven vs. seven small-sided pickup soccer game.

Denny went to Mercer County Community College and was the leading goal scorer on a very talented junior college soccer team. We talked about how gifted our club team Hamilton Post 313 had been in the past year. We thought we could make a serious run to win the state cup in the junior division and hopefully go far in the National Cup in spring.

Post 313 was undefeated through the fall season. Unfortunately for me, there were no games scheduled during the Christmas break. Being that Oneonta is a four-hour drive from Trenton, the only games that I would be playing in would be the more difficult state cup games. Driving eight hours round trip to play a 90-minute junior cup soccer game may seem crazy to some individuals, but not to me.

We added two very talented players to our nucleus from the previous year. Tom Wieboldt, a former center forward, would play on defense for Post 313. Tom was extremely athletic, tough as nails and had a powerful shot from long distances. We were very lucky that Tony Bellinger from Willingboro, New Jersey, also joined the team.

The first time I played against Tony was at the Rider College soccer camp and I was amazed how fundamentally sound he was. He was years ahead of players his age and had to be one of the top players in the country. Tony was an extremely talented midfielder/defender who had impeccable heading technique and also was very good on the ball.

The one negative for Post 313 was that Art Napolitano decided not to play for us that year. He decided to forgo his last year of eligibility in junior ball to go directly to Trenton Extension SC, one of the premier men's teams in the Northeast.

With winter break ending, I made the four-hour trip back to Oneonta with Michael Angelotti. All we talked about for four hours was soccer. Michael had an amazing soccer brain and constantly thought outside the box. He would talk about different aspects of soccer and his viewpoints, and I would repeatedly catch myself thinking I never thought of it that way. Michael had spent a lot of time with Ping Pong and Manfred Schellscheidt, and it showed. Michael was part of the New Jersey state team that Manfred and Ping Pong brought to West Germany for a tour several years ago.

It was on this tour that numerous teams from West Germany wanted to sign and keep the hugely talented Mooch Myernick, who at the time was 15. An American player signing for a club in Europe in 1972 was unheard of; it just was not done. From a soccer perspective, Mooch would have almost certainly developed into a much greater player than he was. He was so far advanced beyond all of us, he should have been training on a daily basis with professional players.

The last time I drove to Oneonta with Michael was my senior year in high school, when I went to visit Hartwick College. At the time, we had the oil embargo and a gas shortage. On that trip, when we made it to hilly parts of central New York State, Michael would put his van in neutral going downhill to save gas. Lesson learned: Even going downhill in neutral you can surpass the speeding limit. We were stopped in Delhi, New York, and Michael was issued a speeding ticket.

The weather conditions for Oneonta in January, February and early March didn't allow for much if any outdoor training, and the soccer team moved seamlessly from outdoor season to indoor season. The team trained twice a week, Tuesdays and Thursdays, with training beginning at 9 p.m., when Binder Gymnasium became available to the team.

I remembered when I visited Hartwick my senior year in high school how intense and physical indoor training was. On that night almost a year before, I vividly remembered goalie Keith Van Eron catching All-American David D'Errico with an elbow just above the eye and giving D'Errico a nasty cut.

Our first training session was just as I thought it would be. After some technical work, we went right into scrimmaging and every touch was challenged with a lot of physical play. Since there would be only five or six indoor tournaments in the winter, excluding Hartwick's indoor tournament where we entered two teams, the competition to be selected for each tournament was very competitive. No more than 10 players would be selected for each tournament. Training two nights a week with the team was nice, but not remotely enough for me.

After our first training session on Tuesday night, Michael Angelotti asked me what my class schedule looked like on Wednesday and if I would like to train with him on Wednesday afternoon in the racquetball courts. We agreed to meet at the gym at 3 p.m.

I had never really looked inside one of Hartwick's racquetball courts. On television, they seemed to show racquetball courts with glass windows and visibility from the inside and outside of the court. But Hartwick's were wooden walls sealed off from public view. I was curious what we could accomplish with such a small area for training.

Training at 3 p.m. was perfect for me. My winter schedule was two classes Monday, Wednesday and Friday mornings, and one class every Tuesday and Thursday morning. I would have lunch, then spend a few hours on my studies before training at 3 p.m. I would have dinner at 6 p.m. and then spend a few more hours on my schoolwork, if necessary.

I met Michael at Binder and he showed me where you sign up to reserve a court. Michael had signed us up for 3-4 p.m. Individuals could sign up for a maximum of one hour.

As we crouched down and entered through the small wooden door, the court seemed even smaller than I imagined. Michael then asked, "Billy, have you ever trained in here before?"

"No Michael, I have never even been in a racquetball court before today." "Billy, this is a great place to train either by yourself or with a few other players.

"Let's stretch real good and get a good warmup before we start. What are the rules?"

"Our soccer version of racquetball is that one player serves from the back of the court versus the middle of the court. Whereas in regular racquetball you are only allowed to let the ball bounce on the ground one time and you have to strike the ball back against the wall, in our soccer version we still can only let the ball bounce on the ground one time, as long as the ball hits the ground before you have any touches with the ball. But we can have two touches to kick the ball back against the wall.

"If you receive the ball out of the air before it ever hits the ground, you are allowed an extra touch, so it is two-touch or three-touch if the ball never hits the ground."

"That's it. It seems easy enough," I said.

Michael responded with, "It is a simple game, with your first touch being very important as to how you control the ball in preparation to strike the ball against the wall with your second touch or sometimes your third touch."

Michael gave me this huge smile and told me, "You only get points when you serve, so why don't you serve first."

I went to the back of the court with the ball at my feet while Michael positioned himself on the side in the middle of the court. I did not give much thought to my first serve and struck the ball about six feet high right in the middle of the play wall.

Michael sprinted to the ball as it took a real high bounce off the ground, popping the ball up in the air with his chest. Then he volleyed a low hard shot into the corner of the play wall, which bounced off the sidewall, with me futilely chasing the ball.

On Michael's first serve, he drove the ball hard and low, hitting the far wall before ricocheting off the side wall, with me looking on hopelessly. Michael had me sprinting all over the racquetball court chasing balls one serve after the next. I rarely could get to the serves, and the few times I was able to get to the ball, I struggled to strike balls back against the wall with any power and accuracy. Michael would just bury me with his return shot.

Before I knew it, the first game ended 15-0 for Michael. I was standing there with my hands on my knees trying to control my heavy breathing when Michael laughed and asked if I wanted to call it a day. I told Michael no way, just let me get a drink, I would be right back. I thought I was in there to improve my technical skills, but realized the only benefit during that first game was the huge amount of running, which would help my fitness level.

Michael was right that it is a simple game. What he left out was that it is a simple game if you know what you are doing. I played much better the second game and we actually had some long rallies. I managed to score two points, which was a moral victory for me.

Michael was a master of every angle of the racquetball court. After running around like a chicken with no head for the last 50 minutes, the racquetball court felt a lot bigger to me than when I first walked into it. Michael asked me if I would like to train again with him that Friday afternoon and I responded immediately, "Of course."

From my experience the previous summer training at Nottingham Junior High with Ping Pong, Mooch, Michael and Kevin Welsh, I realized it was so much more beneficial for me to train with players who are much better and more experienced than me.

The thought of what I went through in preseason to make the varsity and eventually get into the starting lineup, and the realization that we would have a group of superstar blue-chip recruits coming in the fall, made me want to train harder than ever.

I settled into a nice schedule during the winter months. One or two days a week I would train with Michael. The rest of the week, I would train by myself in the racquetball courts. The one hour allowed was not enough for me. To alleviate that problem, I would sign myself up days in advance for one hour in my name, and use the name of a soccer great from around the world, such as Brazilian player Roberto Rivelino, for the second hour.

I realized that training alone in a racquetball court may be the ideal place to train individually, with the numbers of touches of the ball one can have in two hours being equal to the amount of touches you would get training with your team for weeks. You were limited only by your creativity and skill level, which would only continue to improve with more touches of the ball.

One of my favorite games to play by myself in the racquetball court was my version of two-touch soccer. While standing about seven to eight feet from the play wall, I would kick a bouncing ball gently off the wall, receive it out of the air, and with my second touch, play it back off the wall. I would repeat the process with the ball never touching the ground for as long as possible.

As I became more skillful, I added turning with the ball, using three of the walls for this training exercise. I would start as usual, kicking the ball off the front center wall. But this time, I would control the ball towards my left, where I would play the ball off the wall to my left, control the ball back towards the front center wall, play the ball off the center wall, and then control and play the ball off of the wall to my right. I would repeat the exercise going from wall to wall as long as I could keep the ball in the air.

Eventually I added into this training exercise that every time I played the ball off of one of the walls, I had to take a quick glance over my shoulder in between touches to develop my vision and get into the habit of always looking around.

Moving from wall to wall made this training exercise much more difficult, and it showed with the amount of times and frequency with which the ball would fall to the ground. The difficulty and frustration the added movement brought on only made me more determined to master control of the ball. I became better and better at this training exercise.

Although a large portion of the student body headed downtown to party during the week, I limited my going downtown to weekends. My teammates were very disciplined during the fall season about drinking during the week and reserved most of their drinking for downtown on weekends after our games.

I never really enjoyed drinking alcohol and I did not drink in high school. Being on the varsity soccer team at Hartwick was considered very special and every student knew who you were. It seemed like whenever I was in a bar, someone wanted to buy me a drink, and many could not comprehend how I did not like beer.

My standard answer was I didn't like the taste of beer. That was followed by the individual offering me a drink and saying, "You will acquire a taste for it." I never understood why I would want to drink something that I could not stand so perhaps eventually I would find the taste bearable. I tried different alcoholic drinks over the winter months but never enjoyed any of them.

Throughout the winter, Hamilton Post 313 team was winning every game rather handily in the league and breezed through the first three rounds of the State Cup. My coaches, brothers Ernie and Paul Tessein, felt it was unnecessary for me to make the trip back to Trenton for those cup games. But their scouting report indicated our quarterfinal match against the New Jersey Surfsiders could be a difficult match. I made the trip back but realized 30 minutes into the game I really could have stayed in Oneonta that weekend as we beat the Surfsiders 5-0.

This set up a semifinal match against the Passaic Sports Club the following weekend. We handled them quite easily 7-3. Denny and I scored two goals each, but we were not happy that we gave up three goals and knew if we wanted to win the State Cup, we would have to be much better on defense.

On the other side of the bracket, the Elizabeth Germans won, setting up a state cup final at Palmer Stadium on the campus of Princeton University. The Elizabeth Germans was one of the top soccer clubs in the country, with its men's team led by Manfred Schellscheidt recently winning the Open Cup in 1970 and 1972. I have very fond memories of the Elizabeth Germans. They played their home games at Farcher's Grove, where the Elizabeth German American social club has a bar and restaurant.

Hamilton Post 313 had played the Elizabeth Germans in the early rounds of the New Jersey State Cup at Farcher's Grove two years before in a game I will never forget. Not only is Farcher's Grove the most well-known soccer field in New Jersey, it's also the most difficult field to play on for several reasons. The field was 99 percent dirt, with the remaining 1% comprised more of rocks than blades of grass. This particular day, it was extremely cold and the field was frozen solid with holes, stud marks and indentations, making the basic skills of trapping, passing and dribbling extremely challenging.

The other reason that made it very difficult to play on this field was the home field fans. Two years previous, I still was playing as a traditional right winger for Hamilton Post 313 and usually played very wide, often standing on the touchline. In the first half of this game, we were attacking in the direction where, when I was standing on the touchline only a few feet away, there was a chain link fence with nowhere for fans to stand or sit anywhere on that side of the field. The first half was hard-fought because of the opposition, weather conditions and horrible field conditions. I had a fair game up to that point.

The second half, I lined up on the side of the field where the German Americans had their social club, which included a bar/restaurant and some wooden bleachers for the fans to sit on. But the majority of their fans preferred to stand a few feet from the sideline. This side of the field was lined with fans, predominately the German American ones. As the referee was about to blow his whistle to start the second half, I saw many fans standing on the touchline, right in my path.

I hear, "Hey, you little boy" before a man shouted, "Hey right winger, I'm talking to you."

I turned towards this man, who was standing five feet from me and hollering at the top of his lungs. He looked at me and said, "Did you just graduate from kindergarten?"

A group with this individual burst out laughing. Then the whole group shouted insults, making one derogatory comment after another about me.

I instantly realized that I made a huge mistake by turning toward this fan and acknowledging that I heard him. The referee blew his whistle to start the game and I quickly ran away from the group.

As the second half went on, any time I was anywhere near this group of fans, they would insult me. There really was not anything they could say that would upset me, and I was more focused and determined than ever to shut them up.

The score was 1-1 late into the second half when we were awarded a corner kick. The ball was crossed to the center of the six-yard box, where our center forward Frank Kemo went up for the header with an Elizabeth German defender. They collided and the ball came bouncing towards me as Frank lost his balance and was falling right toward the ball. I struck the ball out of the air, getting it past the Elizabeth goalkeeper—but also kicking Frank right in the mouth. There was instant jubilation that we scored the go-ahead goal, but also real concern as blood flowed out of Frank's mouth.

After Frank was tended to, I went back to my position for the kickoff.

It was quiet. It was the first time the entire second half that the group of men, who were standing at the halfway line, were not shouting insults at me.

As the referee blew his whistle to restart play, I slowly turned my head toward the one individual who started the verbal barrage and gave him a big smile before I turned away and sprinted off to finish the game. That day we earned a hard-fought 2-1 victory against a very good team. The game was a great learning experience for me in dealing with terrible playing conditions and learning never to acknowledge any opposing fan who hopes to heckle me and get me off of my game.

The great memories of that game came back to me when Paul Tessein went over the scouting report for our opponent in the State Cup final. This Elizabeth Germans team had many new players from two years before. According to the scouting report, its most dangerous attacking players were Leo Bodassian, a powerful center forward headed to Penn State that fall, and a clever midfielder in Matt Boyer, who would be going to Harvard.

The majority of their players were mostly second-generation American-born players of European descent. The report also included that they would be organized in the back and strong in the tackle.

I woke up that Saturday morning. I was really excited that we were going to be playing for the New Jersey State Cup in the afternoon. I hadn't had this feeling since the NCAA tournament and I couldn't wait to start the game. It rained off and on all morning. It was dark and overcast during our warmup.

The first half was highlighted by very tight man-to-man marking all over the field, and neither team was able to create any real quality goal-scoring chances. The Elizabeth Germans were, as I expected, very organized, disciplined and hardworking, and would be difficult to score against. The evenly played first half ended 0-0.

As the second half started, the rain picked up. The field conditions were starting to have an effect on the game. Play opened up and the flow of the game was more end to end. Midway through the second half, one of the Elizabeth Germans attackers drove a hard shot from just outside the 18-yard box, and the ball skipped off the wet turf past our goalkeeper Bobby Matthews to put them up 1-0. It was the first time all season we trailed in a game.

We felt the pressure and urgency to get an equalizer, with the huge scoreboard clock a constant reminder that we were running out of time. With 10 minutes left in the game, Paul Tessein moved me from my central midfield position up into the attack besides Denny at center forward.

With under five minutes to go, Denny slipped a pass behind the Elizabeth Germans defense and in a foot race, I barely beat my defender to the ball and struck it under the hard-approaching Elizabeth Germans goalkeeper for the equalizer. Minutes later, the referee blew his whistle to end regulation play.

You could sense that the goal deflated the Elizabeth Germans, who were minutes from hoisting the State Cup. We regained our confidence going into overtime and Denny did what he did best—score goals. He got the winning goal in overtime to make us New Jersey State Cup winners. It was a great result against a very good Elizabeth Germans team that just as easily could have won.

On Sunday, we were notified that St. Elizabeth of Baltimore was the Maryland State Cup winners and we would be playing them the next Sunday at Patterson Park in Baltimore.

Monday back at school, I asked some of my Hartwick teammates what they knew about Baltimore soccer. They said the typical player from Baltimore was usually very skillful, strong in the tackle and wouldn't back down from anyone.

Mooch offered to train with me to help me prepare for my cup game. Every afternoon, Mooch and I would head down to the lower field and spend hours on technical work. We spent a lot of time on long-distance passing, something I needed to improve. Mooch made it look effortless. His ability to consistently strike 60-yard passes that dropped right at my feet never ceased to amaze me.

As the week progressed and it was getting closer to the game, my concentration in class became more difficult as I was getting more and more excited about our regional cup match against St. Elizabeth.

On the ride back to New Jersey Friday afternoon, I thought about what I believed were significant advantages growing up in New Jersey playing youth soccer. First, New Jersey was a true melting pot of many different cultures, ethnicities and races. Different continents and countries have unique playing styles. Playing in New Jersey, we were exposed to all of those different styles.

To generalize, when we played teams in South Jersey, for the most part they were typically very American, meaning stereotypical white players from the suburbs. They usually played a physical, direct style of soccer, with aggressiveness and fast play being the priority over short passing and skillful individual play.

When we played teams in North Jersey, we often found teams that were 100 percent foreign. Many of these teams' players came from South America, and the players of Spanish descent were usually very skillful, with lots of short passing, and good dribbling skills. They tended to be clever in their play. One example being that if they were dribbling the ball and you got close to them or brushed up against them and they lost the ball, they would fall to the ground and repeatedly roll over again and again as if they were hit by a Mack truck to draw a foul.

I called this type of player "ginkers." It's not in the dictionary, but I often use it. I can't say where the term came from, but if I told someone we were going to be playing a ginker team, they knew it would be a challenging game. It wasn't just because they would be skillful, but also because they were clever and crafty. They would do whatever was necessary to disrupt your play and concentration, whether it is when you had the ball with repeated fouls or off the ball when the referee wasn't looking. Then, they would kick you or elbow you and hope you would retaliate when the referee was looking so you would get a red card.

There were also many clubs sponsored by European countries. The junior teams from Newark tended to have many players of Portuguese descent. These players tended to combine the individual play that many players of Spanish descent exhibited along with the strong fundamental skills, toughness and discipline that the European countries tended to display.

Kearny and Harrison teams usually had a roster that combined players either born in or of Scottish and Irish descent combined with local American-born players who had adapted to the playing styles of their Scottish- and Irish-born teammates. No team exemplified this more than the Kearny Scots, which had produced great soccer players, including former Hartwick College All-Americans Eddie Austin and David D'Errico, who both graduated from Hartwick College in 1974, and the highly touted Joey Ryan, a senior in high school who was expected to attend Hartwick that fall.

Of course, we had the powerful Elizabeth Germans Club, whose playing style was greatly influenced by Manfred Schellscheidt. The German American Kickers from Trenton, the Woodbridge Hungarians, ethnic soccer clubs representing Poland, Yugoslavia, Ukraine, and the list went on and on. The ability to watch and play against so many different styles of play was a great learning experience.

In New Jersey, we also were exposed to so many different types of playing surfaces. It was rare to play on a nice grass field. The norm was playing on terrible surfaces, with none more so than Farcher's Grove. The result of playing on terrible soccer fields was that the difficulty of controlling the ball in these difficult conditions actually improved our technique. When we eventually played a game on a nice grass field, it was so much easier to control the ball.

The quality, or lack thereof, of nice grass soccer fields was good for us because when we walked onto the field at Patterson Park, we were prepared for a surface that was comprised of dirt and very worn-down grass.

Five minutes into the game, it was obvious to me that St. Elizabeth's SC was a very good team. It had two players that stood out to me, one being the left winger and the other a withdrawn forward/midfielder, Sonny Askew, who was a very skillful player.

Sometimes you can watch a player touch the ball one time and know that individual player has great technique. It was obvious from Sonny's first touch that he was a very talented player.

The first half was evenly played, with neither team able to create much in the attacking third of the field. The first half ended 0-0.

As the second half wore on, both teams continued having trouble creating quality chances and we were having a very hard time controlling the midfield. With Tony Bellinger and me in midfield, I never would have believed that another junior club could neutralize us and or outplay us in the midfield. But this day, we had a difficult time making a real impact on the game. Denny and our second-leading scorer, left winger Terry Smith, were not getting the quality passes to put them in good positions in and around the penalty box.

With 10 minutes left in regulation play, we had a defensive breakdown on a corner kick and St. Elizabeth's scored the first goal of the game. Paul Tessein immediately pushed me up front alongside Denny, but unlike the Elizabeth Germans game, we couldn't get the equalizer before the referee blew his whistle to end the game.

It was a quiet bus ride back to Mercer County, and the realization that my junior career for Post 313 was officially over made me sad. Most of us had played together for four years on Post 313 and although I was very disappointed that we did not go further toward winning the National Junior Cup, we still had a lot of success for two years.

In summer 1973, Hamilton Post 313 was the first team from the United States of America to win the junior division of the prestigious Robbie International Soccer Tournament in Toronto, when we beat St. Andrew's S.C. 2-1 in overtime. Last summer, we repeated as champions of the junior division when we beat York Thistle FC with a 2-1 victory in Birchmount Stadium. Adding that to winning the New Jersey State Cup this year would make me proud of our accomplishments in the past two years, but at the moment it didn't lessen the pain of losing that day.

With the school year at Hartwick about to end, Timo held our end-of-year team meeting. He rarely showed any excitement and emotion, but at this meeting, you could sense the excitement he had for our upcoming fall season.

He reviewed the list of recruits who had committed to play for Hartwick in the fall. They included the two rumored superstars from Canada, Phil Wallis and Tommy Wilkinson; Steve Long, who was coming out of Liverpool FC's youth team; Tommy Maresca, the New Jersey High

School Player of the Year from Bloomfield, New Jersey; Esteban Reynoso from Elizabeth, New Jersey; and the highly touted Joey Ryan from Kearny, New Jersey.

In addition to this phenomenal recruiting class, Timo was waiting on the year-end grades for Angrik Stepanow, one of the three highly touted recruits from Howell, New Jersey the past year. He had to sit out our freshman season for academic reasons. Angrik was a supremely talented attacking player who despite a thin frame, had extraordinary power when striking a ball.

All of the recruits were attacking players. When Timo hinted there was a strong possibility that he would move Ron Hardy from his usual left back position to sweeper next season, my concerns magnified about where I could or would play next season.

Prior to departing for home at the end of the school year, I met with Timo. He told me with so many talented attacking players coming into the team that for me to be in the starting 11, I probably would have to compete for and win the left back position.

It was not what I wanted to hear and I realized I still had so much to prove to Timo as a player. Although I thought I made great strides in that department, it hit me like a slap in the face that he still didn't think I was talented enough to play regularly in the midfield for Hartwick. Just like the past preseason, it appeared Timo was going to hand starting positions to some of his blue-chip recruits whether they deserved them or not.

Walking back to my dorm right after meeting with Timo, I knew that if I was going to play the left back position, I really needed to work on my heading technique. I remembered a conversation I had in the racquetball courts with Michael Angelotti. He told me that when Al Miller was the Hartwick coach, the team would train with pendulum balls. He believed they still had them in storage.

I made an abrupt turn and headed back up to Binder to see Charlie Lewis, the team equipment manager. I asked Charlie if they still had some of the pendulum balls. Five minutes later, he came back and handed me one to take back to New Jersey, as long as I brought it back to school in the fall.

Regarding my heading ability: Although I was only 5-foot-3¾ inches. I could stand under the goal post, jump up and feel my hair touch the underside of the goal post, meaning my vertical jump was 2 feet 8 inches. A 32-inch vertical jump is pretty good, so if I could improve my timing and technique, I should be able to do a respectable job in the air.

The first thing I did when I got home from school was go into the backyard where we had a metal pole with an opening on the top for our clothesline and made sure that the bottom of the pendulum could fit into the opening. I adjusted the height of the ball and within 15 minutes, I had the pendulum set up perfectly to work on my heading all summer.

9

I Love the Summer

I absolutely love the summer. Not because I didn't have to go to school but because I got to spend the whole day, every day, playing soccer. Unlike many of my friends, I was very fortunate that I didn't need to get a summer job. I didn't ask my parents for much. Other than soccer shoes and occasionally some spending money to take out my on-again, off-again girlfriend Olga Pilaris, I really had no need for material things. Being able to play soccer all day far outweighed anything in my life then.

I had a driver's license but no desire to drive. My parents were fine with me not working, knowing that I spent more hours training every day than most people spent on a full-time job.

My summer schedule was like clockwork. Monday through Friday, Ping Pong came to my house at 8:45 a.m. My mother made breakfast for us. We usually left the house around 9:30 a.m. and arrived at Nottingham Junior High by 9:45 a.m. Some days it was just the two of us; other days, we were joined by Denny and/or John Pasela and Gary Kubala, two very good collegiate players from Lawrence, New Jersey.

We trained until 3:30 p.m., stopping only for a 15-minute lunch and water breaks. The weather had zero impact on our training. It didn't matter if it was 100 degrees and humid, or 75 degrees and pouring rain.

Ping Pong dropped me off at home where I showered, had dinner and relaxed for a bit before jumping on my bike at 5:30 p.m. and riding two miles to Nottingham Junior High.

Nottingham at night was pickup soccer at its best. There were two sections of nice grass divided by a cement sidewalk leading to the school, with the total area being approximately 60 yards by 40 yards. It was shirts versus skins, with discarded T-shirts serving as the goals. One night it could be seven versus seven and the next night it could be 12 versus 12.

Everybody who showed up got to play, whether they were really young, very old, great players or weak players. The more-experienced players always helped the younger ones. This is where we played our nightly small-sided games.

When large numbers of players showed up, it was tight with very limited space. Players had no choice but to develop their vision of the game. Most of the time all the players stayed until it was too dark to continue.

Back home, I turned on the back porch light and spent 15 to 20 minutes with the pendulum ball, working on my heading.

On weekends I packed a big lunch, rode my bike to Nottingham and used the great big wall at the far end of the school to practice using many of the technical games I learned on the racquetball courts. There were no pickup games on weekend nights, so I stayed at Nottingham from 9:30 a.m. to 5:30 p.m. before heading home.

Between training with Ping Pong, the nighttime pickup games and my pendulum training, I was training more than eight hours a day. I matched that on weekends by myself at Nottingham. I was in my glory. The more I trained, the better my technical skills became, and that made me want to train even more. It was a positive, self-fulfilling loop, but I also realized I was very lucky.

I was lucky because I can't imagine having better parents than I do, with my father constantly teaching me so much about life. No subject was more endearing to him than money and investing, and allowing me the opportunity to pursue my goals in soccer.

Ping Pong had become like a second father to me. It is hard to believe another amateur soccer player in the country had the good fortune to spend five or six hours a day with an individual of Ping Pong's brilliance. Many days, it was just he and I training together.

Ping Pong would pick a specific move or skill, then we'd spend hours dissecting the movement and practicing that skill. One day, Ping Pong wanted to talk about the give-and-go wall pass. His focus was twofold: 1) He'd ask me about the best way to play the pass to your teammate in order to accomplish the greatest acceleration possible, and to run past your opponent to receive the return pass; 2) What was the best way to disguise your wall pass to your teammate?

Ping Pong broke it down every way possible. For example, if our teammate to whom we would send a wall pass was on our right side, should we play the ball with our right foot versus left? Should we use the inside of our foot versus the outside? Should we attack our defender straight on before the pass, or should we change directions and dribble towards our teammate to move the defender in that direction before we play the pass?

Early in the game, we could set up an opponent for later. For example, should we play the wall pass to our teammate and give the defender the impression we want to run past him, then stop and back pedal to receive the pass and give us more space facing him? Later in the game, our opponent may be anticipating this when we plan to play a wall pass and explode past him.

Was a wall pass more effective when we received a pass and played one-touch to our teammate, accelerating past our defender? When we had possession of the ball, were we better off running at our defender at top speed to play our wall pass versus running slower before playing the ball to our teammate? Depending on my speed running towards the defender, what is the ideal distance between us when I played the wall pass?

We practiced these techniques endlessly. Ping Pong believed the only way you could be a great player was if you had total mastery of the ball. That was my goal.

We received great news when it was announced Mooch was selected to the pool of players for the USA Olympic Team and that he also would play in the Pan Am Games.

This would cause Mooch to miss part of Hartwick's preseason training and the beginning of the regular season. It also was announced that Hartwick would play in a preseason exhibition game in Delaware against Philadelphia Textile. That would be followed by the USA Olympic Team versus the Mexican Olympic Team.

Philadelphia Textile was a great team, with many of the same players that played for Philadelphia Inter SC, which knocked Trenton Extension SC out of the Amateur Cup last spring, 2-0. I marveled at how talented many of their players were. Dale Russell, John Nusum, Elson Seale, Adrian Brooks and Duval Minors were all terrific in that game and I am really excited that I would play against them the next month.

The weekend prior to heading back up to Oneonta for preseason camp, Trenton Extension was invited to play in a one-day, seven-versus-seven tournament at Farcher's Grove. It was a great way to end the summer. The Kearny Scots were entered in the tournament, and I noticed Joey Ryan was playing for them.

The first opportunity I had I introduced myself to Joey. Between games, we spent our free time together, getting to know each other a bit. We seemed to be very comfortable with each other and after watching how talented Joey was as a player, I was really looking forward to playing with him at Hartwick and hoping even more we would be in the midfield together instead of me playing left back, as Timo seems to prefer.

10

Here We Go Again

The ride back up to Oneonta with Mooch for preseason soccer camp was not nearly as anxiety-filled as the previous year, when I had driven up with my parents and did not really know if I was good enough to make the varsity. After all, Timo had repeatedly told me I should go to a different school.

This year, I knew I would be on the varsity, and with all of the training I did that summer, I was a much better player than when I left Oneonta in May. But I still had a fight on my hands to show Timo I should be in the starting 11, and at midfield.

With Mooch in one midfield position and Joey Ryan probably in another, I thought the third midfield spot would be between Zeren, Angrik, the two Canadians and myself, if Timo gave me the opportunity.

What were the Canadians' best positions, midfield or up front? That would have huge ramifications on where I would play. Zeren was an unbelievably talented player who hadn't quite adjusted to the physicality and pace of college soccer the past fall. But he also showed signs of brilliance in many indoor tournaments that past winter. Angrik was as gifted as any player on the team, excluding Mooch.

The first day of preseason was much like the last year, with fitness tests in the morning. I managed to keep my breakfast down, a huge positive considering that one year previous, I was on my knees vomiting in front of Timo.

Charlie Lang was back as our team manager and it was hard to imagine a nicer individual.

In the afternoon session after a long warmup, we played two-touch to goal for an extended period of time. I was very interested to see how good our new blue-chip recruits were, particularly our two Canadian players.

My first impression of Phil Wallis, who was a big, burly individual, was that he was an old-fashioned center forward that would compete with Artie for the center forward position. Tommy Wilkinson, small in stature, looked very skillful. They both looked like they would be good additions for our team.

In the two-touch portion of the scrimmage, Stevie Long looked average, and I was a little disappointed—until Timo took off all restrictions. My opinion of Stevie changed dramatically, as he effortlessly ran past players as if they were cones, one right after the other. It was exciting to watch Stevie beat players with his tremendous acceleration.

My first feelings about our other two highly recruited attacking players, Esteban Reynoso and Tommy Maresca, was that they couldn't be any more opposite in their styles of play. Esteban was a Colombian-born, super-skillful player who almost dared you to try to take the ball from him. Tommy was a small, compact, extremely athletic individual with blazing speed who always seemed to be trying to get control of the ball. Joey Ryan's technical ability was as impeccable as the first time I saw him play at Farchers Grove.

The following afternoon, Timo lined us up to scrimmage. The first 11 included Duncan at right back. Timo moved Jeff Tipping from his defensive midfielder position back to stopper. When Timo said, "Ron Hardy will be the sweeper," I knew I was going into the left back position.

Sure enough, Timo followed with "Greek, you go to the left back position."

I had mixed feelings because I knew my best position was in the midfield, and if I became good enough to play professionally, it most surely would be as a midfielder and not as a defender. But I also was happy just being chosen for the first 11.

Preseason was what it was supposed to be the next few days, pushing ourselves to the limit physically to get as fit as possible, competing for positions and playing time, and getting to understand the style of play of our new teammates.

Also, our bodies ached more each day, compounded by the scorching heat. It was hard for me to understand anyone going through a preseason of this level unless they truly love the game of soccer.

We had Mooch in preseason camp for the first eight days before he departed for several days of training with the Olympic team prior to its match against Mexico. He returned to Hartwick before departing for the Pan Am Games, with the United States in a group with host Mexico and Trinidad & Tobago.

As the week went on, I compared this team to the past year's squad, and I found several distinct differences, none more so than the speed and quickness we now had up front in our attacking positions with the additions of Stevie Long and Tommy Maresca.

Stevie Long would give our attack another dimension, as he went directly to the goal by beating one defender after another, and also had the unselfishness and vision to create scoring chances for teammates.

When Mooch came back from his Olympic and Pan Am Games obligations, he would be the midfield general from his central midfield position. It appears Timo handed Joey Ryan one of the other midfield spots. The third midfield position was up for grabs and the competition was intense. Zeren, Angrik and Tommy Wilkinson were vying for that position, and at times, Timo dropped Artie back into the midfield.

I had not spent one minute in the midfield during training camp and it didn't appear Timo was considering me for a spot there.

For most teams, losing a central defense comprised of Johnny Bluem and captain Michael Angelotti, both of whom were playing professionally, would be devastating. But with Jeff Tipping going into the stopper position and Ron Hardy sliding over to sweeper, we appeared, once again, to be as good in the middle of the defense as any team in the country.

Jeff had tremendous heading ability and perfect timing, and was one of those rare individuals who could hang in the air, along with being a great tackler. After one week of preseason Ron Hardy appeared as if he had played the sweeper position his whole life, showing calmness and confidence.

In goal, we were blessed with two very talented keepers in Steve Jameson, who went up front the previous year to help our anemic attack, and the very athletic and confident Keith Van Eron.

Timo appeared to be gaining a lot of confidence in Howie Charbonneau and moved him around into several positions, including converting him into a defender. Whereas the year before, Timo handed Duncan the right back position, it appeared Duncan and Howie were competing against each other for that spot.

The thought that we had three talented right backs and two probably would end up on the bench made me very confident of the team's depth and talent. Our third right back was Tim Kevill, a senior from Long Island who had played very little the past year. It appeared that Timo wouldn't let him compete for starting right back. I thought Timmy was really talented. But for whatever reason, Timo lacked confidence in him.

Our first preseason game was the next day, against Springfield University—Alden Shattuck's alma mater—in Springfield, Massachusetts.

We took two vans and Timo's car for the trip to Springfield. Timo asked Mooch to drive his car, so I jumped into it for the ride up with Mooch. Mooch entertained us with stories that only he could tell.

Midway through the trip, on an isolated portion of the highway, Mooch pulled the car next to the van Timo was driving and said, "Billy, why don't you moon the van." Without even thinking about it, I pulled my pants down and stuck my butt against the window as we went past Timo, who couldn't have been more than five feet from the window. Everyone in our car started laughing hysterically, and it appeared everyone in Timo's van also found it very funny.

Except perhaps Timo.

We arrived at the field about an hour later and began to stretch. About 10 minutes into our warmup, Timo pulled me to the side and said, "Billy, your actions in the car are not something that as a student and soccer player for Hartwick College are acceptable. I am benching you for the first half and there is a good chance you will not play at all today."

I did not have a response for him. I just nodded my head and realized I had made a huge mistake. I became really upset with myself. I had trained so hard that summer to become a better player and ensure that I would start for Hartwick. Now, I had just handed a teammate an opportunity to take my place in the starting 11.

I told myself that eventually I would get some playing time that day, and when I got that opportunity, I had better be at the top of my game.

Springfield was supposed to be similar in playing style as Cortland State. It was a typical physical education school with strong, athletic players who may lack some technical skills.

Timo inserted Howie into my left back position. Five minutes into the game, it was obvious that we were superior technically, but we had a difficult time with the high pressure applied by Springfield. Timo made numerous substitutions, but the changes did not improve the team's performance, frustrating Timo.

At halftime, Timo made it quite apparent that he was very disappointed in the team's performance. He ended his talk with, "We will start with the same 11 that started the game, except I want Billy in the left back position."

I was so excited that Timo put me back in the lineup and it showed in my play. I overlapped every opportunity I got, and received numerous perfect passes from Mooch. I felt more like a left winger than a left back. We played much better as a team in the second half. Timo made numerous substitutions throughout the second half, but kept me in for the entire half.

On the ride back to Oneonta, I was very quiet and thought about what the potential repercussions could have been for my earlier actions. If we had played a good first half, Timo probably would not have put me in the game at all. Perhaps Timo would settle for that back four for the next game. If the team had continued to play well through preseason, I may not have gotten off the bench.

I realized my very immature act could have cost me a position in the starting lineup and I would never make that mistake again. When we arrived back in Oneonta, I headed straight for Timo's office. I knocked on the door and waited for him to wave me in.

"Timo, I want to apologize to you for my very immature act on the ride up to Springfield," I said. "There is no excuse for it and as you said earlier, it is not the behavior expected from a student and soccer player at Hartwick College."

"Billy, I accept your apology." "Thank you, Timo."

On my way out, Timo said, "By the way, Billy, you had an outstanding second half today and although you are the left back, I think you will be able to contribute a lot into our attack this year."

"Thanks, Timo."

Walking back to the dorm, I thought how the day started poorly but ended on a positive note.

On Thursday morning, Aug. 28, we boarded Bluebird for Delaware to play Philadelphia Textile at 6 p.m., followed by the U.S. Olympic team's qualifying game against Mexico. Although it was only an exhibition game for us, it felt much more important. Textile would be on our regular-season schedule the next year and had Dale Russell, one of the top players in the country.

Many of our players still were competing for starting positions and varsity roster spots. I thought back to last year's ride to Cortland State University, where it felt like do or die for me to make the varsity. And though eventually I wanted to get into the midfield, I was very happy with my progress as a player and that it appeared the starting left back position was all mine.

When we arrived at the small football/soccer stadium, it already was filling up with fans. I attributed this to soccer fans coming early for the Olympic team's game against Mexico. By the time we finished our warmup the stadium was filled, making for a really nice atmosphere to play a preseason game.

The first 10 minutes of the game, Textile was all over us. We had a difficult time getting possession of the ball, let alone keeping it when we got it.

In one moment the game changed dramatically. With Textile dominating play, all of their defenders were inside our half of the field when a long clearance reached Stevie Long, who was standing out wide on the right wing just inside our half of the field. Textile's central defenders were on the halfway line, looking to catch us in an offside position. Stevie turned with the ball and effortlessly beat his defender, then raced down the field, beating the entire Textile defense into the 18-yard box before he rifled a shot off the near post. I had never seen a player with the ball outrun an entire defense for the 50 to 60 yards Stevie dribbled into the 18-yard box.

It was a very exciting moment and I realized we had a special player with the ability to change a game on his own. Stevie's solo run enabled us to relax and shifted the momentum of the game. We were in control for the rest of the first half and led 2-0 at halftime.

For the second half, Timo substituted freely, with most of our starting 11 on the bench. Philadelphia Textile kept its starting 11 in the game and scored three goals against our reserves to win 3-2.

Sitting in the stands after our game, I heard several of Textile's reserve players bashing us as if we were terrible and how they totally dominated us. The more they talked and made us out to be nothing more than an average college soccer team, the more I couldn't wait until we played them the next year.

Mooch was outstanding for the undermanned USA team against a talented Mexican team that was led by Hugo Sanchez, a phenomenal, left-footed attacking player.

With one week of double sessions left before preseason ended, the competition for playing time was intense. Whereas in the previous year I believed Timo knew who was going to start and in what positions, this year seemed very different. It appeared Timo had five or six players who definitely would start, but I'm not sure if Timo even knew what positions those players would play.

The competition for the remaining starting positions was intense and tempers were short as the week progressed. The crunching tackles we would face this season couldn't be any harder than what we were seeing every day in training. It didn't help matters that Timo juggled the lineups every day when we scrimmaged.

Friday finally arrived. At the end of our afternoon session, Timo announced that he was making his decisions for the varsity roster.

What a difference a year makes. Last year at this time, I stood helplessly with knots in my stomach, waiting to hear whether I made the varsity or was going down to the junior varsity.

I watched intently the players I thought were on the fence to make the varsity. When Timo called them up, I tried to decide, based on the player's and Timo's facial expressions, whether they were staying on the varsity or were being sent down to the junior varsity. Being the last player called up last year only prolonged the stress and pressure I felt that day.

This time, Timo called Mooch first and they talked for a few minutes before Timo turned towards me and shouted "Greek, come."

I approached Timo and all he said was, "You are playing very well. Keep it up."

With preseason coming to an end and school starting two days later, Timo gave us the weekend off. I felt so beaten up physically and drained, I decided that I would not do any secret training over the weekend, which would be the first time in over a year I would have gone two days in a row without touching a soccer ball.

For my sophomore year, I moved off campus into Depew Street. Depew Street was a duplex, and I would be living on one side along with Mooch and Artie. On the other side was Steve Jameson, Johnny Bluem, who needed a few more credits to graduate, and Tommy Maresca.

Depew Street was one small block that was off the beaten path, located in an area that appeared to be for the less fortunate. After training that Friday, I asked Mooch for his key so I could make a copy. He laughed and told me that we didn't have keys and never locked the doors, whether or not anyone was home. I thought about it for a moment and realized that in my freshman year at Hartwick, I don't think I heard of or read about any crimes in this college town.

Saturday, I moved into Depew Street and then relaxed the rest of the day. Sunday morning, I purchased my books for my classes, which were to start on Monday. I was excited about starting classes, and with so much less stress than last year, I hoped to improve my grades significantly. My Poverty and Affluence in American Society class seemed like it was going to be really interesting.

During the walk back to Depew Street, I felt much better physically than I had two days earlier after training. When I got back, I decided I would do a little bit of secret training. I changed really quick, grabbed my soccer ball and made the short walk to Neahwa Park. I spent two hours training in the exact spot I trained almost a year before to the day when I was the only Hartwick player not to play against Montclair State.

11

Something Is Missing

During the next 10 days, we settled into our fall schedule of classes, with training in the afternoon. The amount of time that had elapsed from the beginning of preseason seemed like forever and we couldn't wait to start the regular season. The fact that Timo was still constantly changing players in the lineup had many players on edge. Training continued to be combative, with a lot of players displaying short tempers.

Two days before our opening game, Mooch severely sprained his right ankle and Timo decided Mooch wouldn't play. We were ranked fifth nationally in the coaches poll and third in *The New York Times* poll run by Alex Yannis, the respected sportswriter.

Timo made a comment in the Oneonta Star that he "hopes the team understands the responsibilities that come with that ranking."

We finally got to Friday and opened up under the lights against the University of Buffalo. It took only four minutes for Stevie Long to show what a special player he was. He easily tricked two defenders, cut inside and beat Buffalo goalkeeper Matt Harbin for the first goal. Talented freshmen Joey Ryan scored the second goal at 21:43 on an assist from Artie, and the rout was on.

Buffalo scored in the last minute of the second half on only its third shot of the game to avoid a shutout. Score: Hartwick 7, Buffalo 1.

Our opponent the following afternoon was St. Francis. The Frankies from Brooklyn had watched our defeat of Buffalo and came out in an extremely defensive posture, playing a catenaccio system, packing in the defense tightly and hoping to counterattack when the opportunity presented itself. Having a coach of Italian descent in Carlo Tramontozzi, it made perfect sense from a tactical perspective.

Although everybody identifies the catenaccio system with the Italians, the defensive-oriented tactic was introduced by Austrian coach Karl Rappan in the 1930s. It became popular during the 1960s when Argentine coach Helenio Herrara used it to lead Serie A club Inter Milan to several championships. The success of Inter Milan encouraged many Italian teams to use the catenaccio system. Herrara used the same tactics when he took over the coaching duties of the Italian National Team. Catenaccio translates as "door bolt."

At 14:25, Steve Long took a pass from Zeren Ombadykow and scored the first goal of the game. Although we peppered St. Francis with many shots, we couldn't score the elusive second goal. In the last few minutes of the game, St. Francis countered us and came close to scoring the equalizer. Final score: Hartwick 1, St. Francis 0.

We won both games but I didn't think we could be happy with our performance. Buffalo was a weak team. And though we controlled the game against St. Francis, they came within inches of tying the game in the closing minutes.

In training on Monday Timo addressed all of the positives from the two games and stressed how important it was that we build on that in the next few weeks. I thought we needed regular-season games. Due to scheduling circumstances, we had two weeks before our next game at Brockport.

Once again, training had the feel of preseason, with players fighting for starting positions and playing time, with every ball contested for. With Mooch away, Timo continuously moved players around in the midfield, looking for the right combination. Unfortunately, I was not one of them.

The Brockport game couldn't come soon enough. The long layoff between games, and the fact that Brockport fouled us every opportunity it had to disrupt our rhythm, really showed in our play.

Neither team created many quality opportunities and we had difficulty stringing together a lot of passes. At the 24-minute mark of the first half,

Duncan crossed a perfect ball to me at the back of the six-yard box and I blasted the ball past the Brockport goalkeeper to put us up 1-0.

The game became even more physical. The constant fouling and off-the-ball incidents eventually led to Joey Ryan and Angrik both receiving yellow cards for retaliating after being the recipients of hard fouls.

Esteban Reynoso put on a dribbling exhibition and scored with seven minutes left to ice the game for us.

We did not play particularly well and Timo wasn't happy. Our midfield, which was technically superior to Brockport's, was outplayed and I was sure changes would be made before our next game against Colgate University.

Timo juggled lineups all week, with the midfield in constant flux. Eventually, he settled on putting Phil Wallis in as the central midfielder to play more as a defensive midfielder, and flanked him with Joey and Howie.

When we reached Saturday and our game against Colgate, we would have played only one game in three weeks. Despite all of our talent, we weren't playing well in our training sessions. We definitely needed more games.

Saturday was part of Parents Weekend. Every time I ran out onto a packed Elmore Field with "Glad" blaring, I got chills throughout my body.

Colgate came out in a defensive posture, as expected. It packed in its defense, was extremely physical and had no reservations about fouling us every opportunity it got. As the half went on, we started to create some chances. Late in the first half, Stevie Long put us up 1-0.

The second half was even more physical than the first, with numerous skirmishes and several yellow cards handed out. Long scored his second goal of the game. In the waning moments, my cross found an unmarked Randy Escobar in the box and the skillful Peruvian cleverly flicked the ball past Colgate goalkeeper Doug Bloom to make it 3-0.

The next week would be very busy for us with two away games and although I really wanted to go downtown and celebrate with the team, I decided to stay in Saturday night and study. I had a lot of reading to do for my Pushkin–Tolstoy Translation class.

Sunday, I planned to get up early and study before I headed out to the racquetball court for a couple of hours of secret training.

Although I thought I had been playing very well, I knew I needed more time to work on my technique. I also noticed several times when I had overlapped on Saturday and ended up in the midfield, I did not feel my awareness and vision of what was going on around me was as sharp as it had been.

Vision, something that Ping Pong and I constantly discussed when we trained, is one aspect of the game that I needed to improve. Perhaps my playing left back hindered my progress in this area of the game. Defenders typically have the play in front of them and rarely is anyone behind them, forcing them to always be looking around. If I stayed in the left back position, I might never have developed into the player I hoped to become.

We had a Tuesday afternoon game against UConn, followed by a Thursday evening game against Trenton State College. After we ended what UConn thought was a sure Final Four appearance for it the past November, the animosity we had for each other would show up early in that game.

The difference between Hartwick and UConn's soccer programs couldn't be more pronounced. UConn had many very talented players. But they were almost robotic in their play, seemingly orchestrated exactly where they should run to and what they should do with the ball, no matter the circumstances.

We were a team with many special players that tried to balance individualism within team play.

UConn players looked like they were entering the military, with very short hair and no facial hair. Most of our players had varieties of hair length and styles, and shaving was definitely not a mandatory exercise for us. Timo allowed us to express ourselves individually. Joe Morrone appeared to stifle the individuality of his players on and off the field.

On the bus ride to Storrs, I could not help but think about the importance that this game had for us and me on a personal level. UConn was my first start for Hartwick and that game was as vivid to me as if we played the game yesterday because it was my opportunity, and probably only chance, to show Timo I deserved to play. I have often wondered if I had played poorly in the first 20 minutes of that game, whether Timo would have yanked me and sent me down to the junior varsity the next day.

Our second game was the NCAA quarterfinals and that was a memorable victory, getting us to the Final Four. I knew whenever we played UConn it would be a special game for me. I felt my adrenaline rising as our bus entered the UConn campus.

The minute we walked onto the playing field, UConn fans sent nonstop verbal assaults our way. I guess you could say we were not feeling the love. During the warmup, you could feel the tension and pressure building as the crowd swelled.

The game started out as you would expect from two teams that really dislike each other. Both sides committed numerous hard fouls.

Seven minutes into the game, Tommy Maresca beat his defender and, from the top of the 18-yard box, hit a rocket for the first goal to put us up 1-0. It temporarily quieted the raucous crowd. Tommy had been improving every day and when he refined his technique a bit more, he would be hard for any defender in the country to mark.

The goal gave us confidence and although we controlled most of the play, we could not finish our opportunities. We led 1-0 at halftime.

The second half started out very much like the first, with us having more possession of the ball and creating more chances. But as the half went on, UConn started to get into our defensive third more and more.

With 13 minutes left in the game, Mike Swofford made a clever pass to Don Fehlinger, who beat Keith to tie the game at 1-1.

The goal boosted UConn's confidence significantly. With the crowd now thunderous every time a UConn player touched the ball, the momentum of the game changed dramatically.

Now we were under siege as UConn attacked us in waves. Keith made one superlative save after another, with the referee finally blowing his whistle to end regulation play at a very opportune time for us.

We regrouped for overtime and the game was end to end, with both teams fighting for the winning goal. Neither team could find the back of the net, and we left Storrs with a tie against the 12th-ranked Huskies.

On the bus ride back to Oneonta I sat by myself, something I had done quite often at the beginning of last year, when I was not sure what my future at Hartwick would bring. Although a tie at Storrs may be considered a good result by many, I did not feel that way. Individually, we were better than UConn, but once UConn scored, it dominated us for the remainder of regulation play.

Something was bothering me. At first, I thought it was the result that day. But then I realized that it wasn't that; it was that we really had not played remotely up to our potential all season. We had underperformed and although we were still missing Mooch, if we were to contend for a national championship, we needed to play at a much higher level. Something was missing and I was not sure what it was.

I was really excited for Mooch because the U.S.A. would be playing Mexico in front of 30,000 fans in Estadio La Bombonera. That's an environment I could only dream about playing in. I prayed that Mooch had a great game.

Wednesday, we had a light training session. Thursday, we jumped back on the Bluebird for our bus ride to play Trenton State College under the lights. Trenton State had a solid program in Division III soccer and surely would be pumped up to play the fifth-ranked team in the country.

I was excited that I would get to see my parents and brother Andy. But the thought of playing a Division III school that we were much more talented than was not quite as thrilling as playing a Top 20 Division 1 school.

Trenton State had a very talented young coach in Gary Hindley and despite the disparity in talent, I knew it would be a physically challenging game. On the bus, Timo told us that the previous night Mexico had beaten the U.S.A. 3-0 and Mooch had an own goal in the 40th minute. The U.S.A. would play Trinidad & Tobago on Friday and if the U.S.A. won or tied, it would go through to the quarterfinals.

Although we could really have used Mooch back in our lineup, I hoped the U.S.A. would win so he would get at least one more game in that environment, which could only be beneficial to him as a player.

We arrived at Trenton State. Timo put us through a very long warmup to counter the effects of sitting in a bus for four hours. It was a beautiful fall evening as we lined up to start the game.

Trenton State came out as expected, with high pressure all over the field. It was hard to relax.

At the six-minute mark, Zeren made a great pass to Artie, who dribbled around two defenders and buried the ball into the back of the net. The goal came at a good time for us, considering how we played the last 20-25 minutes in the UConn game and how we started out against Trenton State. After Artie's goal, we settled down and controlled the ball with possession primarily in our attacking half of the field.

Although I thought we played fairly well, at halftime Timo was all over us and made several changes in the midfield. It seems without Mooch around, there hadn't been a set three starting in the midfield since the beginning of preseason. I didn't know whether it was due to the fact that we weren't playing up to our potential or injuries that forced Timo to shuffle players around.

I wasn't sure what the answer was. When Mooch came back, he would go into the central midfield position and I thought Joey Ryan would play on the right side in the midfield. But I wasn't sure if Timo would play Zeren on the left side.

We were not playing particularly well in the second half when Stevie Long scored on a penalty kick late in the game to help us grind out a 2-0 victory. I had to give Trenton State credit for defending very well as a team, with excellent goalkeeping by Chris Meagher, and being quite competitive throughout the game.

After the game I spent several minutes with my family. As I was about to board the bus, my mother handed me a care package comprised of pork roll, koulourakia, spanakopita, and the latest edition of *World Soccer Magazine*. Two of my favorite things in life were *World Soccer Magazine* and spanakopita. I was in my glory and needed willpower so when we got back to Depew Street, Artie and I wouldn't eat all of the spanakopita before Mooch returned. I knew that would be a challenge.

On Friday afternoon at training, we were told that our Saturday game at Bridgeport University was cancelled due to torrential rain. We were rescheduled, weather permitting, for Nov. 13. Timo told us we would have the whole weekend off.

Friday evening, Trinidad & Tobago beat the U.S.A. 1-0, eliminating it from the Pan Am Games. Mooch would be back sometime that weekend and I could not wait to see him and hear his stories.

On Saturday and Sunday, I trained alone in the racquetball courts for several hours each day, focusing on turning with the ball and constantly looking around before I received it. After the Colgate game, when I realized I did not feel as sharp with my awareness, it put a bit of fear in me. Being alone in the racquetball court had become a place of tranquility for me. There were zero distractions, just myself, the ball and four walls to get hundreds of touches that I would never get in a typical team training session, even during Timo's training sessions, which always incorporated the ball into all aspects of practice.

Mooch walked into Depew Street late Sunday night and we spent the next several hours with him holding court, sharing stories and emphasizing what a great player this Hugo Sanchez from Mexico was.

It did not take long for Mooch's return to the lineup to be felt. Late in the first half, he sent a pinpoint cross to Esteban Reynoso for the second goal in our midweek game against Ithaca.

The final score was 2-0 and although we outplayed Ithaca significantly, it still seemed like something was missing. It could have been the combination of Mooch's long absence from the team and our numerous injuries. It did not help that Stevie Long cracked several ribs in the Ithaca game, Duncan still was bothered by a pulled thigh muscle and Randy Escobar was troubled by a knee injury.

Saturday, we were to play East Stroudsburg, which Hartwick never had beaten. The previous year, Stroudsburg beat us in the last minute. Two seasons before, it beat the Wick in the last two minutes. Training leading up to the game was tense, and I felt Timo's frustration. There was a bit of adjustment with Mooch back in the lineup.

There was the typical big crowd for our Saturday afternoon home game at Elmore Field and we came out on fire against East Stroudsburg.

Our attack was relentless, with one good opportunity created after another. At the 12-minute mark, Zeren found Artie in the box with a cross from the left side, and Artie knocked it back to Joey Ryan, who struck it first time into the back of the net for a 1-0 lead.

For the next 10 minutes, we came in waves, pounding the East Stroudsburg goal. But East Stroudsburg counterattacked and Fred Lewandowski struck a shot from 30 yards out, catching Steve Jameson off his line and tying the score at 1-1. We resumed dominating the remainder of the first half, but to no avail. At halftime, Timo was not very happy with Jamie being so far off his line that Stroudsburg scored. But he had to be happy with our attack.

The second half started out very much like the first, with us dominating the play. Midway through the half, I struck what appeared to be the go-ahead goal when the ball knuckled and dipped behind East Stroudsburg goalkeeper Paul Williamson, only to hit the bottom side of the cross bar, and was cleared off the line.

Regulation time ended with no more scores and we headed into overtime. At around the four-minute mark, Howie Charbonneau took a perfect corner kick and I timed my run, heading the ball down into the goal for what turned out to be the winning goal and our first win over East Stroudsburg.

On Monday in the *Oneonta Star*, there was a nice picture of me heading the ball into the goal, and Timo was quoted as saying that "Billy's goal was brilliant" and, "The service was perfect." It made me feel really good and my confidence grew from week to week. Although I played the whole game at left back, I felt like most of the game I was attacking and spent a lot of time in the midfield, the position I still really want to be playing.

On Monday after training, Timo pulled me aside and told me that I had had a great game on Saturday and that I had been the best player on the team so far this season. He told me to keep working really hard in training. Timo and none of my teammates are aware that every Sunday, I do my secret training in the racquetball courts for hours on end.

It's funny because when I trained by myself in the courts, I felt as if Ping Pong was with me. Everything we talked about when training together back home was so fresh in my mind, it was as if Ping Pong was right there saying, "Billy, every touch needs to be like Alabama cotton when trapping the ball. Billy, you need to constantly be looking around the field and try to be two or three plays ahead in your mind" and on and on.

We had a huge game coming up against Adelphi University, a formidable opponent, the next day. Adelphi was the defending Division II national champions. It had one of the top forwards in the country in Ron Atanasio, a great target player in Irish-born Charles O'Donnell, who was very dominant in the air, and two very strong players from Israel, defender Nimrod Dreyfuss and midfielder/defender Ronnie Schneider to go along with a very good goalkeeper in Eugene DuChateau.

Nimrod Dreyfuss crushed me in a tackle the year before and gave me the worst charley horse I ever experienced, forcing me to miss a week-and-a-half of playing time and causing me to temporarily lose my starting position.

At game time the weather was absolutely beautiful. It was one of those picture-perfect fall afternoons in the Susquehanna River Valley that belonged on a postcard. The sun was so bright that it was an extreme disadvantage for the goalkeeper facing it—and we faced the sun to start the game.

Adelphi was big and fast, and at the start of the game we had a difficult time stringing passes together. Adelphi was very conservative on defense, and when put under any pressure would knock the ball up to target player Charlie O'Donnell. I was matched up against Tommy Lang, a clever and fast right winger.

At the 17-minute mark Lang drifted into the midfield, received a pass from Nimrod Dreyfuss and played a long diagonal ball across the field to Ronnie Atanasio, who glided past two defenders and struck a curling shot inside the post that Keith Van Eron had no chance of saving. When Keith got the ball out of the net, you could see fire in his eyes. Keith was a tremendous competitor and happened to come from Long Island, so this game had even more meaning for him.

We continued to give balls away and were outplayed in the midfield, and it couldn't be solely attributed to Adelphi's pressure. Timo's frustration was showing and late in the first half, he brought on Stevie Long, who was still suffering from cracked ribs.

The first half ended with Adelphi up 1-0. Timo typically had a stoic demeanor.

But with how we played in the first half, I was not sure if he could keep his composure and not lash out at us.

This was the first time we were behind at home since our first regular-season home game last year against UConn. As Timo calmly addressed the team and made some tactical adjustments, I was amazed. I was thinking if I was the coach, I would have been all over the team, not sparing anyone because it would be hard to say anyone on our team, including Mooch, was playing well.

Going into the second half, we had the sun at our backs, meaning Adelphi goalkeeper Eugene DuChateau would have the sun in his eyes. Timo selected the 11 players that finished the first half to start the second.

We started off the second half with some urgency, stringing passes together and getting several shots on goal. We seemed to have much more energy than we did in the first half. At the four-minute mark, an Adelphi cross into our box resulted in miscommunication between two of our defenders. The ball dropped down at the feet of Ronnie Atanasio, who calmly struck the ball past a helpless Keith Van Eron for the second goal. It temporarily took the wind out of us. But several minutes later, we regained our composure, with Mooch starting to reveal his precocious skills to take over the game.

Mooch and Joey Ryan started winning the midfield battle and we created several golden opportunities—first with Art Napolitano heading one just wide, followed by Stevie Long missing a sitter in disbelief. As the half went on, we controlled the game but had a difficult time penetrating the Adelphi defense in its last third of the field.

Very late in the game, Tommy Lang received a ball out wide in the Adelphi attacking third. I sensed urgency with time dwindling down and I dove in to tackle him. But I missed the tackle. Lang dribbled around me before serving a cross into the box.

Fortunately, Keith collected the cross and moments later, the referee blew his whistle to end the game. Score: Adelphi 2, Hartwick 0.

Timo addressed the team after the game, pointing out our schizophrenic play—terrible in the first half and very dominant the last 30 minutes of the game. I hated to lose, and to lose on Elmore Field in front of our wonderful fans made it even more unbearable.

On the ride back to Depew Street with Mooch, I realized that when Tommy Lang beat me out wide late in the game, it was the first time an opposing player had beaten me all year and gotten past me. Counting our preseason tournament, this was our ninth game of the year. After thinking about that for a moment I realized that was an impressive stat, especially considering I really was a midfielder.

With the loss to Adelphi and the heart of our schedule quickly approaching, we could feel the pressure creep in. We had Lehigh Saturday in Bethlehem, Pa., followed by Cornell midweek in Ithaca on the Astro-Turf, a makeup game at Bridgeport—currently ranked 17th in the country—followed by Binghamton University at Binghamton and Penn State at home to end the regular season.

We expected to win at Lehigh, having crushed them 5-0 the previous year. But the game against Cornell would be huge. Not only was Cornell very talented, but we would play them at Schoellkopf Field, which unfortunately for us was AstroTurf, and Cornell was at its best on AstroTurf. We were not that comfortable on that type of playing surface. The winner of the Cornell game should get the No. 1 seed in New York State for the NCAA Tournament. The No. 1 seed wins the home field advantage in the NCAA Tournament.

We probably could afford to lose one of our two games against Cornell and Binghamton. But if we lost both, I believed we wouldn't qualify for the NCAA Tournament, which would be devastating for the Hartwick program and personally for me.

I came to Hartwick to win a national championship and couldn't bring myself to think that there is a possibility we would not qualify for the NCAA Tournament. After the start we had the year before, we had to fight and claw for everything just to get into the tournament. This year seemed so different until now. We were undefeated until that Tuesday, ranked in the top 10 in the country the whole year, and I realized we would have to fight for everything because no one on our schedule was going to lay down for us.

The next few weeks we were going to be very busy, so I threw myself into my schoolwork the next three days, spending a lot of time reading and trying to understand my Russian class, studying the translation of Pushkin Tolstoy.

On the bus ride to Lehigh Saturday morning, I was very excited because I would see my parents, who were driving up from Trenton. Although we destroyed Lehigh a year ago, the team was coached by Tom Fleck, considered by many to be one of the premier coaches in the country. I expected this to be a much closer game than the previous year, although I hoped I was wrong.

Lehigh's tactics were revealed right from the start of the game. The Engineers packed it in defensively, with nine players defending in front of the goalkeeper and one lone target player up front. That was how St. Francis played against us, a page out of the catenaccio system.

Although we were playing against a strong wind in the first half, we did not allow one shot on goal by the Engineers and Stevie scored a goal to put us up 1-0 at halftime.

At halftime, Timo praised our movement of the ball and Alden made the point that we had to be conscious of pushing too many players forward and leaving ourselves vulnerable to a counterattack.

With the wind now at our backs, we were relentless in the attack, creating numerous shots on goal. But outstanding goalkeeping kept us from finding the back of the net.

With 18 minutes remaining, Alden proved prophetic. Lehigh countered with a two-on-one, leaving Jamie helpless in the goal when an unmarked Tom Wilson headed in the equalizer. That was Lehigh's first shot on goal of the game. All of a sudden, the game was tied 1-1.

We attacked with a vengeance despite Lehigh repeatedly committing fouls to disrupt our rhythm. At the seven-minute mark, I was fortunate that a loose ball in the penalty box bounced my way. I found the back of the net for what would prove to be the winning goal. It was exciting for me as a left back scoring consecutive game-winning goals two Saturdays in a row with my parents watching.

After the game, I was able to spend a few minutes with my parents before boarding Bluebird for the ride back to Oneonta. I was very excited on the bus ride back but at the same time concerned, knowing the Cornell and Binghamton games would have a huge impact on our season.

Although I felt much more tired after the Lehigh game than I normally did, I still went to the racquetball courts on Sunday morning and worked on my technique for a couple of hours. I spent most of my training striking balls with my left foot and turning with the ball, always glancing over my shoulder before I received the ball coming back to me off the wall.

Monday's New York State rankings were released and we were tied with Cornell at No. 2, followed by Army and Binghamton. Adelphi was ranked No. 1 and I was thankful that Adelphi was a Division II school and had no effect on the Division I seedings for the NCAA Tournament. Oneonta State lurked a few points behind Binghamton for possibly the fourth seed of the tournament.

You could sense the seriousness of our situation and depending on our results over the next week, we could have several different outcomes, from getting the No. 1 seed, a lower seed or possibly no invitation into the tournament.

Training Monday and Tuesday was very businesslike, with an eerily quiet locker room afterwards. On the bus ride to Ithaca Wednesday, I was focused on the attacking players of Cornell. It had two very talented wingers in Joe Mui and David Sarachan, and a superb striker in Sid Nolan. Those three appeared to be the most talented players on the team, with a supporting cast of big, athletic individuals who were very aggressive in the midfield and defense in front of a good goalkeeper in Dan Mackesey.

Although last year's Final Four was played in Busch Stadium on the AstroTurf and we were comfortable knocking the ball around, it felt very different that night during our warmup. Schoellkopf Field had a track around it and the width of the field was much narrower than Busch Stadium.

Right from the kickoff you could sense there would be little time on the ball before you felt defensive pressure. Despite our not being comfortable, the game was very even when we had our first clear-cut chance on goal. Stevie Long got past an out-of-position Dan Mackesey and sent a bouncing shot towards the empty goal. But a Cornell defender came out of nowhere to clear it off the line. Minutes later, Mooch hit a rocket from 40 yards out that just went over the crossbar. The first half ended 0-0, with Cornell having slightly more possession than us.

I had a very good first half defensively, limiting David Sarachan to several touches on the ball and forcing him to play everything back. I was very focused on not letting him turn and run at me with the ball because I knew once he could run at me with the ball, he would be hard to contain.

Without us maintaining possession of the ball for long periods of time, I was not able to overlap one time in the first half.

At halftime, Timo talked about preparing for the second touch. Every time Keith Van Eron punted the ball up the field, Cornell won the battles in the air. Timo pointed out that although we probably would continue to lose the battle in the air, we needed to anticipate where the headed balls would go and win them.

The second half started out very even. Around the 10-minute mark, Cornell had a nice buildup out wide on the left side, with Joe Mui eventually serving a ball into the box that we failed to clear. The ball landed at the feet of Sid Nolan and he calmly shot the ball past a helpless Keith Van Eron.

Fifteen minutes later, another cross found Sid Nolan inexplicably unmarked in front of the goal, and once again he buried the ball into the back of the net. The second goal seemed to take the fight out of us. Cornell, now brimming with confidence, kept coming at us in waves, in what seemed like one attack after another on our goal.

With less than 10 minutes to go, Duncan took out our frustrations on a Cornell attacker, leading to a penalty kick, with Joe Mui sending Keith the wrong way and the game ending 3-0.

It was the low point of the season, and it felt very much like the previous year when we lost consecutive games to Penn State 5-1 and

UConn 3-0. This time, we had lost to Adelphi 2-0 and Cornell 3-0, with a victory over Lehigh between the two losses. Timo had little to say after the game.

We knew that if we lost to Binghamton, we most likely would play two meaningless games against Bridgeport and Penn State to end the season and be home for Thanksgiving. I love my parents very much, but the thought of being home for Thanksgiving because we didn't qualify for the NCAA Tournament almost brought tears to my eyes.

I was very disappointed in myself after the game, knowing that I had not helped the team at all in the attack. I had more touches kicking the back of Sarachan's legs then touches on the ball. Although I took him out of the game, I felt like I let the team down because we needed to create some chances in the attack and I did not contribute anything when we had the ball.

The ride back to Oneonta was eerily quiet until we pulled into the parking lot and Timo reminded us practice started at 3:30 the next afternoon.

Once again, just like the last year, we would play Binghamton for the right to get selected to play in the NCAA Tournament. For all intents and purposes, it was a playoff game.

Thursday afternoon, when I walked into the locker room, I saw players hovering around in the corner of the room reading something on the wall. I had no idea what it was. When I was close enough to the wall, I could see all of the players' names on the board and a small paragraph after each name. I still was not sure what this was. I found my name and underneath it, I read that "Billy is very limited in his play, unable to make passes of long distance on the field and is a very selfish player." Timo's signature was at the bottom of the poster.

I read the paragraph about me one more time to make sure I had read it correctly and then I sat down at my locker to change. I was livid. In my mind, I repeated the words Timo used to describe me verbatim several times to make sure I was not missing anything.

Then in my mind, I answered the accusations.

Am I unable to make long passes? Timo was correct; I was not close technically to the level that I wanted to or needed to be at, and that was a part of my game I know I needed to improve. I did not need Timo to tell me that, but he is correct.

Am I limited in my play? Yes, because I was playing the left back position. But I also needed to improve my taking players on in one-on-one situations, so that is somewhat correct.

Am I a very selfish player? I realized this was the statement that had smoke coming out of my ears. That statement was beyond comprehension. All I ever cared about was winning. Every team I had played on, all that mattered was to win, I never cared who scored the goal, the assist, just about winning. Selfish in front of the goal? Not a chance.

If someone was in a better position than me, I always gave them the ball.

I realized why Timo did not have much to say last night. I didn't bother to read the criticism, or what I assumed were criticisms, Timo wrote about each of my teammates.

During training, it appeared that most of my teammates were sharing the remarks from Timo, but I kept to myself. I felt so insulted by Timo's comment that I was a selfish player.

When training ended and I was walking into the locker room, it hit me that perhaps Timo was trying to evoke some passion and emotion in this team. Although this year's team had enough talent to win a national championship, we hadn't remotely played up to our potential this season and underperformed against the better teams on our schedule.

Although I was really bothered by Timo's selfish comment, I was very excited about our game against Binghamton, which happened to be the only team to beat Cornell that year. Once again, our fate to get into the NCAA Tournament was in our hands. A victory against Binghamton would put us in the tournament. I did not want to think about a loss.

The one-hour bus ride to Binghamton that Saturday was very quiet and it was a beautiful, sunny day. We would find out shortly if Timo's ploy would awaken this team and get us playing to our true abilities.

Seven minutes into the game, Binghamton co-captain Steve Springer received a cross from Joe Bolan and hit a rocket past Jamie for a 1-0 lead. The goal seemed to light a fire under us, and we started to play some of the best soccer of the season against a very big and athletic team.

Minutes later, Jeff Tipping was tripped in the penalty box, leading to a penalty kick for Stevie Long, who buried it to tie the game. It remained tied at halftime.

The second half brought out our true talents. With Mooch pulling the strings from his central midfield position, we were getting some great combination play, which Binghamton could not defend. Esteban Reynoso showed off his mesmerizing dribbling skills, scoring two goals in the second half and assisting Stevie Long on his second goal of the game. The final score was 4-1. It was a much-needed victory, and perhaps equally as important was the quality of our play.

The next day, the pairings for the NCAA Tournament were announced. Cornell was seeded No. 1 and would host Oneonta State. We were seeded No. 2 and would host Army. Timo said the date was to be decided, and the game must be played by Nov. 19.

We had our rescheduled makeup game against Bridgeport in Connecticut on a Thursday and were to host Penn State on a Sunday. The importance of these two matches was to build on our performance against Binghamton and prepare for our NCAA Tournament match.

The NCAA finally ruled that our first-round game would be played on Elmore Field on Wednesday, Nov. 19. As the week went on, the weather began to play havoc. Our game against Bridgeport was cancelled because its field was unplayable due to torrential rain. Also, Oneonta received enough snow that Timo decided he would rather travel to Penn State and play on its field so we could preserve Elmore Field for the Army game.

When Timo was asked why we would travel to Penn State versus just cancelling the game, he replied, "Earlier in the year, we had a 10-day layoff and it showed in our play," and he didn't want us having another long layoff before we played Army.

James Parsons, Jr.

Battling a Clemson player in the Mr. Pibb inaugural tournament
championship game. Every match we had with Clemson was
fiercely competitive.

James Parsons, Jr.

Celebrating after defeating Clemson to win the championship of the
inaugural Mr. Pibb Tournament.

Holding my brother John's dog next to our house on Depew Street.
When the rail cars behind me were moving on the nearest track
to the house, Mooch and I would play the letter game.
A creative way to work on our passing.

George O'Gorman

Standing with the great Franz Beckenbauer in the New York Cosmos
locker room.

Ed Clough

Mooch and I congratulate our teammates on another victory on Elmore Field.

Anne Dobinsky, *Binghamton Press*

My diving header gave us the first goal in a 2-0 victory over UConn in the 1976 quarterfinals to get us to the Final Four.

George O'Gorman

I am devastated after our 2-1 national semifinal loss to Indiana University in 1976.

James Parsons, Jr.

Hartwick won third place in the 1976 NCAA Tournament. I'm in the first row, fourth one in from the right, and once again, I'm not holding the trophy that I really want.

George O'Gorman

From left to right, Charles "Ping Pong" Farrauto, myself, Glenn "Mooch" Myernick, and Joe Secretario, our Trenton Extension SC manager, after our third-place victory over Clemson in 1976. This was the last time I played with Mooch as a teammate.

Ed Clough

In the wall against Penn State, protecting ourselves as best we can.

Ed Clough

My picture on the cover of the soccer program versus Penn State in my senior year.

12

The Change

Timo acknowledged there would be changes to the lineup because team captain Ron Hardy, Duncan, Steve Jameson and Khyn Ivanchukov would miss the Penn State game so they could stay in Oneonta to prepare for their final exams. Mooch would take over the sweeper position with Hardy gone.

On Saturday, we finally were able to go outside to train. After a lengthy warmup, Timo said, "This is how we are going to start against Penn State. Keith in goal, Howie at right back, Tip as the stopper, Mooch as the sweeper and Gary at left back."

When Timo said Gary at left back, I was surprised and excited because I knew Timo wouldn't drop me from the starting lineup. Then Timo said, "Joey will be the right-sided midfielder, Greek, you will be the central midfielder, and Artie will play on the left side in the midfield."

To say I was happy would be an understatement. After we had played almost the entire regular season, I finally would get the opportunity to play in the midfield. I didn't have any idea if this was a one-time opportunity for me because Ron was out or if Timo was making an alignment change.

It was a moot point because on the bus ride to Penn State, Timo called me up front to sit with him and told me he was not sure when we had everyone back what he was going to do with the lineup.

I went back to my seat and realized this game was my opportunity to get back into the midfield, hopefully permanently. I knew I had to play so well that I would make the decision for Timo. The way I look at it, Ron Hardy was a great sweeper and a great left back equally comfortable in both positions, and Mooch was just fantastic wherever he played. So Timo had a lot of flexibility with his lineup.

Now the Penn State game had even more importance for me. Midfield was where I needed to eventually play if I wanted a soccer future after college.

Knowing that I would be playing central midfield on Penn State's beautiful big grass field had me so excited, I realized I needed to calm down and focus on that role.

At Hartwick, the central midfielder runs the show, which I loved, and having Mooch and Tipping behind me was perfect. Tipping is a traditional stopper back who was great in the air with impeccable timing and equally adept at marking the opposition's top forward.

In Mooch, we had undoubtedly the best long ball passer in the country and best player, period, in my opinion. He also had the skill and speed to easily make Beckenbauer-like runs from his sweeper position into the attack. If Mooch made long runs into the attacking half of the field, it was my responsibility to cover for him and take over the sweeper position until he got back.

Penn State was still a very good team but not nearly as dynamic as they were the year before. It had lost Chris Bahr, Randy Garber and Ciro Baldino to graduation; one had been the leading scorer and the other two were the team's best and most creative midfielders.

On attack, Penn State still had two very talented wingers in Johnny Marsden and Richie Reice, who put on a dribbling clinic against us the year before. The team added Leo Bodassian from Harrison, N.J., a center forward who was one of the top recruits from last year's high school graduating class. Matt Bahr, a rock-like central defender who anchored the defense, also tackled as hard as anyone in the country.

While Timo gave us our final pregame instructions, I looked at my teammates. I realized with the tremendous pressure to qualify for the tournament now gone, the majority of the players' facial expressions gave me the impression of a confident and relaxed team.

From the referee's opening whistle, we began knocking the ball around almost at will. We strung together double-digit consecutive passes before Penn State could even get a touch of the ball. We had the Nittany Lions chasing the ball all over the field.

Mooch was initiating and directing the attacks from the back with the elegance only he possesses as a player. At times, I got caught up in watching and truly appreciating what a great player Mooch was.

At the 15-minute mark, Jeff Tipping won a crossed ball into the Penn State penalty box and headed it to an unmarked Steve Long standing in front of the goal. Stevie wasted little time in burying it for the first goal of the game.

Several minutes later, Esteban Reynoso received a ball at the top of the 18-yard line, beat three Penn State defenders that wondered how he beat all three of them in such a tight space, and calmly placed his shot past Penn State keeper Tim Dantzig for the second goal. For all intents and purposes, this game was over.

After the second goal, we tried to keep possession of the ball and conserve some energy for our upcoming game against Army. Penn State hit the post late in the first half and once in the second half, which could have changed the complexion of the game.

I was in my glory, with much of our possession flowing through me. I could not count how many give and goes I played with teammates, compliments of the endless hours training with Ping Pong during the summer to master this skill.

Keith Van Eron ended up with two saves and we seemed to build on our play from our previous game against Binghamton.

Were we finally starting to play up to our potential? And what would Timo do with the lineup when we had everyone back for the Army game? I asked myself those questions during the bus ride back to Oneonta.

On Monday, we trained on the lower field below Elmore Field. Elmore Field was a pool of water thanks to melted snow, and we hoped for lots of wind and sun to dry the field off before Wednesday's game against Army.

After training, Timo showed us films of Hartwick games against Army in 1970 and 1971, and told us this team was much more skillful than those teams. Timo's other comments were that, "They are a 90-minute team, contest every ball, don't give up on anything and are pretty good defensively and in the attack." Against common opponents of ours, Army beat Colgate 2-0 and Penn State 2-0. Its record was 11-1.

Tuesday at training, Timo announced he wasn't sure who would start up front. It depended on the fitness of Stevie Long, who had left the Penn State game with a hip pointer, and Tommy Maresca, who limped off the field with a partially hyper-extended knee.

Timo was noncommittal about the goalkeeper, but appeared to lean towards Keith.

One change Timo was sure about was music to my ears. He told us Mooch would be the sweeper, Ron Hardy would be moving over to the left back position and "Greek" would be going to the central midfield position.

I could barely hide my elation. On the outside, I fought my emotions and remained stoic. But on the inside, I felt like I was going to explode with joy. There was no other way to explain how I felt then. I had trained so hard, pretty much playing soccer 365 days a year for the last several years. Although I would have to play at a very high level if I wanted to be the permanent fixture at central midfield for Hartwick, it appeared after almost two full seasons I finally had that opportunity.

Tuesday evening, we heard that Cornell beat Oneonta State 1-0 on a penalty kick by Joe Mui. Cornell would host the New York State final the following Tuesday.

Wednesday morning, Stevie Long and Tommy Maresca passed their fitness test. They would start up front with Esteban.

As we lined up to start the game, I looked across the field. The Army players were just what I had envisioned: tall, strong and looking very fit, with closely cropped hair and no facial hair, much like the UConn players.

Although Elmore Field's conditions had improved dramatically in the previous few days, I was sure it soon would turn into a mud bath, with difficulty in playing balls on the ground.

The game started. Army players slide tackled anything that moved—the ball or the player—and it took a few minutes before we settled down and found our rhythm. It quickly became apparent we were the superior team technically, and we started controlling the ball for lengths of time, which seemed to frustrate the cadets as we started to create scoring opportunities.

At the 21-minute mark, Army keeper Don Jones came up with a sequence of saves, first against Esteban, followed by a brilliant save against Tommy. Although the playing conditions worsened by the minute, they contributed mightily to our first goal. Ron Hardy overlapped and sent in a cross, which Army defender Jaime Marenco was about to clear when he slipped to the ground and the ball struck his forearm. The referee awarded a penalty kick. To say longtime Army head coach Joe Palone was unhappy would be an understatement.

Stevie Long calmly slotted the ball into the lower left corner of the goal, giving us a one-goal lead. The goal and Coach Palone's fiery nature seemed to light a fire under Army, with every contested ball being met with bone-crunching tackles by the cadets. I received one of those tackles when the ball got stuck under my feet in the mud. I was sent airborne in what was a clean, hard tackle.

Despite the intensity of the game, we still were able to string multiple passes together, leading to good opportunities on goal. But we didn't score again for the rest of the first half and led 1-0 after 45 minutes.

At halftime, Timo emphasized the importance of us getting the ball out wide because the playing surface there was in much better condition than the middle of the field, which was getting worse by the minute. The cadets also were having trouble with the speed of Tommy and Stevie.

Timo wanted Mooch to be more conservative with his runs up the field, fearing the weather conditions could cause mistakes by our defense.

The second half started off a bit more wide open and eight minutes in Army was awarded a free kick out wide on the right. Jim Johnson sent the free kick into a crowded penalty box. Jamie sprinted off his line to collect the cross, but numerous players collided and the ball wound up in the back of the net for the tying score. It was hard to tell who the ball went off of. But that was irrelevant because a game we had dominated now was tied.

The goal seemed to reignite the fire in Army, which got more physical. There were fouls everywhere, with Mooch having to temporarily come out of the game for medical attention and Ron Hardy getting a nasty gash over his right eye that would definitely need stitches after the game.

With the game winding down, I received a ball from Mooch in the center circle, turned and split the Army defenders with a pass putting Tommy through out wide on the left. I sprinted towards our 18-yard box. Tommy beat the sweeper, who came out wide to defend him, and Tommy crossed the ball into the box, where it was headed out by an Army defender right towards me.

I turned and stretched my right foot up as high as a 5-foot-3¾ person could as Army defender Joe Oliveros ran toward me. He momentarily hesitated as my foot approached his face and in one motion, I controlled the ball down to the ground like Alabama cotton and pushed it past him. As I attempted to run around Joe, he hit me with a body block and I crumpled to the ground. Laying face first in the mud, I looked up as the referee blew his whistle to award us a penalty kick with 5:31 remaining.

The fire that Palone displayed when the first penalty kick of the game was called paled in comparison to this one. He exploded off the bench, getting face-to-face, only inches apart from referee Bill Nelson, and began a long, heated argument.

When play finally resumed, Stevie coolly struck the ball into the left-hand corner of the goal for what proved to be the winning score.

From the Army team viewpoint, my foot was up too high and should have been called a dangerous play, which would have negated the penalty kick. Timo said, "It was obvious the defender did body block Greek and the question was if Greek pushed the ball too far ahead of him."

It was a brutally physical game, but we would take a win any way we could. In the locker room after the game, Timo assessed the injuries and thanked us for the effort and heart we showed in very difficult circumstances.

Timo went over our training schedule leading up to our Tuesday game. It included a surprise trip to Ithaca on Sunday to train on Schoellkopf Field. I wasn't sure if that was NCAA-mandated that we be allowed to train on the field or if Cornell head coach Dan Wood was showing a lot of class in allowing us time on the dreaded turf.

The next several days training was very light, with many of us trying to recover from the Army game. On Sunday, we headed to Ithaca to train on Schoellkopf Field.

Timo led us through a training exercise where we focused on reading and anticipating where the headers we expected Cornell defenders to win in the air would end up. We wanted to win all of the second touches after either keeper punted the ball. We seemed relaxed and collectively felt we were better than Cornell.

Monday night while having Kraft's finest box macaroni-and-cheese dinner—which happens to be one of our favorite meals and also the most economical—on Depew Street, Artie, Mooch and I discussed the season.

Mooch strongly felt that Timo's recent alignment change made moving Ron, Mooch and myself, made us a much better team. The last few games made it appear that way. But the next night, against a Cornell team that had humiliated us only weeks earlier, would be the real test.

A quiet bus ride to Ithaca was followed by a lengthy warmup. During Timo's pre-game speech, you could sense a confident and focused team. My priorities for this game were very different than the last game we had here. Although I still had defensive responsibilities as the central midfielder, my focus was much more on our attack and establishing possession of the ball.

One minute into the game, Duncan chased down a ball played over the top and under pressure from Joe Mui, inadvertently kicked the ball out for a corner kick instead of a throw-in. Cornell's leading scorer, Mui took a perfect corner kick. Our nemesis, Sid Nolan, timed his run perfectly and adeptly headed the ball past Steve Jameson to give Cornell the lead less than two minutes into the game.

It was not the start we'd hoped for and it took us a few minutes to recover from the shock opening goal. We then started to click. With Joey playing on the right side of the midfield and Artie flanking me on the left, we started to take over the midfield and control of the game.

Early on, it became apparent that the Cornell outside backs were going to have a difficult time containing the speed of Steve Long and Tommy Maresca. We looked to get the ball to the feet of our two wingers and isolate them one on one. We began to create chances on goal. First Stevie Long had a wonderful opportunity on goal, then we followed with a barrage of shots first by Howie, then Joey Ryan and then Tommy finishing with a shot on goal, all to no avail. Cornell goalkeeper Dan Mackesey was up to the task with one outstanding save after another.

At the 36-minute mark, we were rewarded for our play. Captain Ron Hardy sent a free kick into the box, with Artie soaring above his defender and emphatically heading the ball against the crossbar. With the ball bouncing down behind the Cornell keeper, Tipping reacted first and headed the bouncing ball into the goal before Mackesey could react.

We were brimming with confidence, and the tie score did not reflect our dominance against a team that only weeks ago toyed with us. The goal seemed to give us even more momentum and it was only a matter of time before we would score the go-ahead goal.

Three minutes later, Nolan sent a long through ball to Jim Rice, who had gotten behind our defense, and as Jamey came out to cut down the angle, Rice hurried his shot and struck it weakly towards the goal. As Jameson went to collect the ball, he slipped on the turf, and we all watched helplessly as the ball bounced past him and slowly rolled into the goal.

It was a devastating sight and it took us the rest of the first half to regain our composure. At halftime we had outshot Cornell 15 to five and Mackesy had seven saves, all of which could have been goals if not for his outstanding play. For all our dominance, we committed two costly mistakes and were down 2-1.

Timo had little to say at halftime. Excluding our two mistakes, we had played an outstanding first half against a very talented Cornell team on its turf. We walked back onto the field to start the second half very confident that we would win this game.

Right from the referee's whistle to start the second half, we attacked with a vengeance and immediately took control of the game again.

As the half went on, Mooch began taking over the game. On the defensive end, he repeatedly anticipated where the Cornell passes were going and consistently won those balls, then would initiate our counter-attack either by finding one of our wingers with one of his picture-perfect diagonal passes or making one of his Beckenbauer-like runs into our attacking third.

For all of our opportunities, Mackesey was outstanding and we still were looking for our tying goal. With 10 minutes left in the game, Timo pushed Artie up front, changing our formation to a 4-2-4.

With only minutes left in the game, we were frantic to get the equalizer when a Tommy Maresca cross brought a collision between Mackesey and one of his defenders. The ball dropped down to the feet of Esteban. Reynoso one-timed the ball towards the open goal, which would have tied the score. But out of nowhere, a Cornell defender headed the ball off the goal line.

In the waning seconds, Mackesey blocked a rocket of a shot by Joey and this time Long one-timed the rebound on goal, which surely would find the back of the net. But history repeated itself and a Cornell defender flung his body in front of the shot, deflecting the ball away from goal as the referee blew his whistle to end the game.

The Cornell players displayed the elation you would expect when your goal is under siege and the referee finally blows the whistle to end the game—and you're going to play in the quarterfinals to determine who goes to the Final Four.

It was a bitter loss to swallow for us. Excluding the two costly mistakes we committed leading to the two Cornell goals, our play was outstanding. We thoroughly outplayed a terrific senior-dominated team on its Astro-Turf, a team that had embarrassed us only weeks earlier.

On the bus ride back to Oneonta, sitting by myself, staring out the window into the darkness of the night, sadness crept into me with a vengeance, with the realization that the season was over. We would not be going back to the Final Four and we would not win the national championship this year.

My thoughts then started to jump all over the place. It seemed that this very talented team of ours finally started to play up to our ability. Did

Timo's poster attack on us in the locker room light a fire under us? Did the lineup change with Ron Hardy going to left back, Mooch to sweeper and myself to central midfield make a huge difference?

The only senior player we would lose from this team to graduation would be Steve Jameson. Jamie was a great goalkeeper, often had helped the team as an attacking player when we were struggling to score goals, and was a highly respected team leader. We would definitely miss Jamie but we were very fortunate that we had another great keeper coming back in Keith Van Eron.

I hoped the recent team performances and my performances since we made the alignment changes would convince Timo I should be the starting central midfielder for Hartwick the next season.

As Bluebird pulled up to the Binder Physical Education Building and we got off the bus, I suddenly realized I would be going home for Thanksgiving after all, something I was hoping to never do when I decided to attend Hartwick.

13

Holiday Surprises

During the car ride back to Trenton the next day with Mooch and Artie, Mooch entertained us with stories about his Pan Am Games experiences in the way only he could tell a story.

Despite the pain from our loss to Cornell, it was nice to be home with my family. Thanksgiving was held at my Aunt Eve's house, where we had all of the Greek food I craved and missed through most of the school year.

Besides spanakopita, pastitsou, moussaka, baklava and lamb, my Aunt Eve also made the best tiropitas I had ever eaten. Tiropitas are Greek cheese pies made up of feta cheese, cream cheese, cottage cheese, eggs and dill, and wrapped in triangle-shaped, butter-laden phyllo.

When we returned to school to begin our three-week academic program that would end with our Christmas break, news came out that Al Miller, the coach Timo replaced at Hartwick, was leaving the Philadelphia Atoms for the Dallas Tornadoes. Miller, in his first year as a professional head coach in 1973, led the Philadelphia Atoms to the NASL championship. Trenton great Bobby Smith led the Atoms on defense.

Bobby played his high school soccer at Steinert High School before attending Rider College, where he excelled as a center forward.

Although Bobby was a center forward his whole career, when he was drafted and went to the Philadelphia Atoms, he quickly was converted to right back.

George O'Gorman, who was the head coach for the junior varsity soccer team at St. Anthony's when I attended high school there, was also the sports editor for the *Trenton Times* newspaper. O'G, as George O'Gorman was known around the state, covered the Philadelphia Atoms and the New York Cosmos for the *Times*. Many times, he gave press passes for those games to me and others. I had traveled with O'G to those games.

The press pass got me onto the field. Also, I usually had an empty camera case hanging over my shoulder so I looked more official, hoping security guards on the field wouldn't check my credentials.

I can't emphasize enough what a wonderful learning experience it was every time I had a pass and stood just five yards from the playing field.

I dreamed of playing on those fields in the not-so-distant future. It was a thing of beauty to watch Bobby Smith match up against players such as Warren Archibald and Steve David, and mark them out of the game.

What I learned from watching Bobby was that whenever he went into a tackle, he did so with every ounce of energy in his body. Every time a player attacked Bobby and tried to beat him one on one, they were met with intensity and concentration as if Bobby's life depended on it.

Bobby had so much focus and tenaciousness that opposing players often went to the other side of the field so he couldn't mark them. Add in his tremendous defensive positioning and superb heading ability, and Bobby was almost impossible to beat one on one.

The news of Miller's new job with the Dallas Tornadoes had no effect on my life—or so I thought at the time.

Brown eliminated Cornell in the quarterfinals. In the NCAA championship game, the University of San Francisco beat Final Four host Southern Illinois, Edwardsville 4-0.

On Dec. 8, I received a letter from Timo. He sent every player a summary of the season once it ended. He told me my play had been superb and that he was certainly glad that I decided to show him up. He also mentioned that I was perhaps the one person that truly felt the agony of defeat and that he was the same way in college. It ended by announcing team training in the gym at 7 p.m. on Dec. 11.

The letter gave me even more incentive to keep training harder to get better as a player, and help the team get better, so we could reach our goal of winning a national championship.

We had our first training session on the 11th. Timo and Alden went over our winter schedule. We would train as a team twice a week and participate in five or six indoor tournaments, including the one we hosted. The schedule sounded very much like the year before.

I was voted to the New York State second team, the only player selected from Hartwick or Oneonta State. There was quite an uproar in Oneonta over Mooch not being selected to either team and that Oneonta State, which had a roster filled with talented players, did not place anyone on either team.

After the news of my selection, I was up at Binder getting ready to train when Timo called me into to his office, where 15 months ago I had told a disbelieving Timo that I should be starting. He said, "Greek, the way you played this year, you should have been considered for All-American honors."

This time I was the one who was in disbelief. I left the meeting feeling like I was walking on a cloud.

That winter, I again would be very busy with soccer. One difference from the last year was that for club soccer, I would be playing for Trenton Extension SC men's team instead of Hamilton Post 313 in the juniors.

Sunday, Dec. 14, we would play in the first round of the Amateur Cup. Through a very unlucky draw, we would be playing against our archrivals, the Trenton Italians SC, considered one of the top clubs on the East Coast.

The good news was that manager Joe Secretario was able to sign Johnny Marsden and Rich Reice away from the Trenton Italians to join Trenton Extension. Sec also signed Matt Bahr, so we had a great presence from Penn State and a very talented team that could go far in the Cup.

The Trenton Italians had won the New Jersey State Cup two consecutive years and had high hopes of winning the National Amateur Cup that year. The Italians were led by Nando Vecchio, a brilliant center forward who came to the Italians after coming up through the ranks of famed Argentinian Club Boca Juniors. No one could verify whether or not Nando had played with the first team. But if he did not, then it was hard to comprehend just how talented the Boca Juniors players on the first team were.

Nando was small. But he dribbled as if the ball was on a string attached to his right foot. He ran at players at top speed, with the ball always so close to him that it was difficult for a defender to even attempt to tackle him.

Nando was supported up front by foreign-born Natale Israel, a tall, lanky, skillful front player who was a natural goal scorer. In the midfield, they had Penn State standout Ciro Baldino and two South Americans from Ecuador.

Having played against the Trenton Italians the last year in several summer tournaments, I was very aware of the two South American midfielders. One of them was very stocky and powerful, almost like an NFL fullback's body, with very tight skill. He was a dirty player who wouldn't hesitate to go over the ball in a tackle to try to break your leg.

Although it was an Amateur Cup game, many of the Trenton Italians were ex-professional players from different homelands. It's rumored that the players were paid significant cash per game played.

On defense, the Italians were led by Lilo Amari, an elegant, skillful defender born and raised in Italy. Lilo was one of the few Italians actually playing for the Trenton Italians.

Larry Keller, a very talented goalkeeper from Bucks County who attended Lehigh University, was the last line of defense for the Italians.

Playing against ginkers who were ex-professionals from overseas was a wonderful learning experience for young Americans about how to improve their play and craftiness. If you were green about the nastiness of over-the-ball tackles and off-the-ball elbows to the face, you learned very quickly. You understood early on that these players, whose careers are on the way down, wouldn't hesitate to break your leg, especially if you demonstrated you were as skillful as they or more so.

Instead of waiting until Saturday morning to go home with Mooch and Artie, I decided to leave Friday afternoon so I had an extra day to spend with my family.

Saturday morning, an unexpected snowstorm buried central New York State. Mooch and Artie were snowed in. The thought of them even attempting to drive Mooch's VW Beetle through a snowstorm made me cringe. So Sunday, we would be playing a huge game without Mooch, our best player, and Artie, our center forward and best goal scorer.

There may have been bad weather Sunday afternoon in Oneonta, but the sun was out in Trenton and the temperature was mild for mid-December. I went to the game with Denny Kinnevy, my high school teammate and leading scorer for Mercer County Community College that past season.

As we arrived at the Trenton Italians' Lincoln Field, it already was surrounded by throngs of passionate Trenton Italians fans hollering at us the minute we stepped onto the field for our warmup. It probably was a good thing I did not understand Italian because I was sure they weren't sending compliments our way. Seeing the Penn State additions to our team warming up made me feel much better about our chances against a very talented Trenton Italians team.

This game was definitely a derby match. Two teams from the same city that strongly disliked each other. The game started as I expected, with numerous hard fouls by the Trenton Italians. After several more harsh fouls from the Italians, Matt Bahr hammered Nando Vecchio in a tackle. Nando rolled over at least six or seven times to emphasize how hard he was fouled. Bahr sent a message to the Italians and after that, the game settled down with more playing and less fouling.

We were very tight in the back with Matt, Jimmy McKeown and Bobby Rostron there. I was flanked in the midfield by Timmy Murphy, whose grandfather Frank Rasimowicz owned the Trenton Extension Tavern and sponsored the team. Also playing was Barry Pellitteri, the top player on Rider College and former high school teammate of mine.

The Trenton Extension Tavern was touted as having the longest bar in New Jersey. Mr. Rasimowicz was a wonderful man and a great sponsor for the club. Timmy was one of the key players for Davis & Elkins College, a perennial powerhouse in NAIA. Timmy and Mooch grew up together and led Lawrence High School to three straight state championships before losing in their senior year.

Up front on the wings we had the two standouts from Penn State, Johnny Marsden and Richie Reice, with Denny as our center forward. In goal, we had the very talented Joey Hankins from Mercer County Community College.

All of the players for Trenton Extension were born and raised in either Mercer County, New Jersey or Bucks County, Pennsylvania, which is separated from Mercer County by the Delaware River, where George Washington crossed the river on Christmas Eve to surprise the Hessians. On the other hand, the Trenton Italians had players that were from many different countries in Europe and South America.

Midway through the first half, Johnny Marsden beat his defender, reached the end line and cut a ball back to me at the corner of the right side of the 18-yard box. I played a square ball across the top of the box to Jimmy McKeown, who beat Larry Keller with a low shot to the far corner. The half ended 1-0 and we had withstood the initial fouling and vociferous home crowd of the Trenton Italians.

Although the Italians came out with an increased intensity to start the second half, we played with a lot of composure and limited their opportunities near our goal.

Fifteen minutes into the second half Denny received a ball in the box on a clever pass from Timmy Murphy, beat two defenders and played a square ball to me, standing unmarked on the penalty spot. I first-timed the ball past a helpless Larry Keller to make the score 2-0.

Around the 75-minute mark, the Italians, desperate for a goal to get back into the game, caught us on a counterattack, with Nando running right at me at top speed. Nando gave me a body swerve, sending me the wrong way. As he ran past me, my slide tackle was late and I took him down, which was a good tactical foul on my part.

As I stood up, he walked toward me, with the referee standing on the left side of him and me on his right. He put his right arm around me as I walked away toward our goal. With his left hand, he started patting me on my left shoulder. All of a sudden, with his right hand hidden from the referee's eyesight, he grabbed my ear and squeezed it as hard as he could, trying to crush my ear. I spun and pushed him in the chest away from me.

He flopped to the ground, hollering as if I had punched a hole in his chest. He was writhing on the ground when players from the Trenton Italians started sprinting toward me, quickly followed by my teammates coming to my rescue and defusing what could easily have escalated into a riot.

After calm was restored, I was not sure if the referee was going to give me a red or yellow card.

Although the referee was only a few feet away from Nando, he could not see what he was actually doing to me. He conferred with the other referee for the longest time before deciding neither card was warranted.

It was a great ginker move by Nando and I allowed myself to lose control of my emotions momentarily. This whole time, several Italian players were holding back their stocky midfielder, who was trying to get at me. He kept pointing his finger at me while hollering in Spanish. Though my understanding of Spanish is not remotely fluent, I do know the word "*muerte*" means "death" and he directed it towards me repeatedly.

The remainder of the game I kept my radar/vision on high alert because I knew their stocky midfielder would do whatever he could to retaliate for my actions against their star player Nando Vecchio.

I looked to play one- and two-touch soccer the remainder of the game, hoping not to put myself in position to receive nasty fouls. We kept our composure the remainder of the game and did a great job of keeping possession of the ball the last few minutes, minimizing any chances the Trenton Italians could create.

When the whistle blew, I was relieved and just hoped we could get to our cars and leave Lincoln Field before any overexuberant Trenton Italians players or fans tried to do something stupid.

With the snow, the trip back to Oneonta was quite harrowing and it took two extra stressful hours to make it back. I did not walk into Depew Street until after midnight. It was our last week of classes before winter break, with my final in Cultural Anthropology scheduled for that Friday morning.

Late Wednesday morning as I walked out of the library, I heard someone calling my name. It was frigid out and everyone was covered with scarves and hats, so I had no idea where it came from. I heard my name again and kept looking around as numerous students walked past me. Someone grabbed my arm and I turned to be face-to-face with Mooch.

"Hi Mooch. What's going on?"

Mooch pulled me to the side away from the students walking by, leaned toward me and said, "Timo is leaving."

"What do you mean Timo is leaving?"

Mooch said, "Timo is going to Dallas to be Miller's assistant. I wanted to tell you before you hear rumors flying around campus, I have to get to class. We can talk about it tonight at dinner."

When I walked into my Cultural Anthropology class I was numb, and not from the cold weather. I could not concentrate for one minute in class, with all kinds of thoughts swirling through my brain. I did not ask Mooch where he received his information from; maybe he got it wrong.

I momentarily felt better, thinking the news was probably just a rumor. But when class ended and I walked out of the classroom, students I did not even know approached me and asked if the rumor that Timo was leaving was true. This rumor or fact started spreading through the campus like a wildfire, that Timo was resigning to take the assistant job for the Dallas Tornadoes.

I started the walk to the top of the campus and Binder Hall, where Timo's office was located. After a few minutes of walking I could not take it anymore. I broke into a full jog, books in hand, navigating the snow and ice on the way up and hoping somehow it was not true—though deep down, I knew it was probably a fact.

Binder's foyer was filled with people. I headed straight for Timo's office, ignoring numerous people calling my name. Although the door to Timo's office was closed, I was not thinking straight and walked right in to find Timo and our athletic director Dr. Leroy Chipman talking. I suddenly realized what I had done and was very embarrassed.

"Oh, I am very sorry Dr. Chipman. I was not paying attention. I'll come back later."

Timo quickly responded, "Billy, it's OK. You heard I am leaving."

I replied, "Well, I heard the rumor and was hoping it wasn't true but I guess it is." Timo hesitated for a moment and then replied, "It is true, I will be in Oneonta for a while before I leave for good. We will have plenty of time to talk. I have to finish up with Dr. Chipman."

"OK. Thanks, Timo."

The reality of the news deflated me. Walking out of Timo's office into the crowded foyer, I was hit with a barrage of questions from teammates and students who love Hartwick soccer. "What do you think?"

"How does this affect the soccer program?"

"Who do you think is going to be the next head coach?" "Will it be Alden?"

It was endless and I just put my replies on autopilot, responding, "I don't know" to every question as I slowly walked through the crowd and out the door.

I decided instead of waiting for Mooch and getting a ride down to Depew Street that I would walk home and collect my thoughts. We were losing one of the top soccer coaches in the country at any level.

My relationship with Timo had changed so dramatically in the last 17 months, it was almost hard to comprehend. It included him telling me to go to a different college because I was not good enough to play for Hartwick.

Also, he ordered me to help the equipment manager pick up balls—making me feel more like an equipment manager than a soccer player. I was the only player not to play against Montclair State. I told Timo I should have been starting. And the most recent one was Timo telling me I should have been considered for one of the All-American teams this year.

I worked so hard to get into this position and now he was leaving. I walked home to Depew Street. All of the questions I was asked in the Binder foyer needed to be answered, and I had no idea what the outcome would be.

We had a very lively discussion at the dinner table that night, with numerous guesses about who would be the next head coach, including Alden's chances of being named the new coach. I tossed and turned all night and got no sleep.

The next day after finishing a training session in the racquetball courts, I was approached by Betty White, who handles many administrative duties for Dr. Chipman. She asked me to meet with Chipman in his office at 4 p.m. I was a little nervous because I was not sure why he wanted to see me.

Besides his duties as athletic director, Chipman was also the head basketball coach at Hartwick. It was a perennial powerhouse in Division III basketball and Chipman was very well-known for his 1-3-1 zone defense. Many coaches from all over the country visited Chipman to better understand the nuances of his zone defense.

When I walked into Chipman's office at 4 p.m., Mooch, Joey Ryan and Ron Hardy were already there. Chipman began the meeting with, "I am the athletic director and it is my responsibility to hire the best possible coach to continue our tradition as one of the top soccer programs in Division I soccer.

"In this room we have Ron, who is the captain of the team, Mooch will represent the junior class, Billy will represent the sophomore class and Joey will represent the freshmen class. I feel that you as a group will understand and know better than I who the next soccer coach of Hartwick College should be.

"You are the selection committee and with my general screening and approval of all potential candidates, you as a group will ultimately make the selection of who we hire. We are already receiving applications from coaches. Alden will be interim coach and obviously is one of the candidates for the head coaching position. If Alden is hired as the head coach, then we will need to fill the position of the assistant coach but that selection will be made by Alden."

When we walked out of the meeting, I immediately turned to Mooch and Ron and asked, "Did I understand Dr. Chipman right? Did he say we would decide who the next head coach is?" Ron and Mooch both nodded their heads yes.

Ron replied, "We as a group will ultimately make that decision."

Alden immediately took over all of the coaching responsibilities. At the end of our indoor training session that Thursday night, Alden gathered us together and told us we were invited to participate in the first annual Mr. Pibb Super 8 Tournament. We wondered what that was. Alden said the tournament would be held March 19-21 at Southern Methodist University, and most of the top teams in the country would be there. The teams invited to the tournament were host SMU, Clemson University, St. Louis University, Penn State, Quincy College, UCLA, Southern Illinois University and Hartwick College. Excluding host SMU, all were perennial powerhouses in college soccer.

Our opening-round game would be against Southern Illinois, Edwardsville, which lost to San Francisco in the NCAA final that past season. If we won, we would play the winner of UCLA vs. Quincy College in the semifinals. Quincy College was always one of the top soccer programs in the country and was three-time defending national champion in the NAIA.

That was exciting news. It would give us the opportunity to play against some of the top teams in the country and it could not have come at a better time, as it temporarily took our mind off of Timo leaving.

The next day I took my exam for my Cultural Anthropology class and was back home in Trenton in time for dinner with my parents. We had a really nice time on Christmas, with my parents hosting the relatives for dinner. I was in my glory with lots of Greek food and getting to see my cousins, aunts and uncles.

Joe Sec had arranged to have the Mercer County Community College gymnasium open several nights each week over the Christmas break so the Trenton Extension players would have a place to train. The gym floor was a hard rubber surface, not the traditional wood basketball floor.

Late into the first training session at Mercer, I sprinted for a ball, which took a funny bounce off the bleacher stands. As I planted my left foot to change directions, I felt an extremely sharp pain shooting through my foot. I knew I had hurt myself. I sat out the remainder of the training session.

When training ended, Joe Sec took me to St. Francis Hospital, where an X-ray revealed that I had fractured the fifth metatarsal bone on my left foot. The doctor told me he was going to put me into a boot cast and I would have my foot X-rayed again in six weeks. If the fracture was healed, I would be able to start with low-impact exercises and slowly build up to jogging and finally full-time training.

It was really disappointing news for me. Trenton Extension had the next round of the amateur cup and the first round of the New Jersey State Cup coming shortly, and in all likelihood, I also would miss all of Hartwick's indoor season, including our own indoor tournament.

The only positive from all of this was that knowing I wouldn't be able to play soccer for at least two months gave me the opportunity to focus on my academics.

At first, I attended every Hartwick indoor training session to feel part of the team. But when I returned to Depew Street at night, I would get really depressed. I hadn't experienced in years not having a soccer ball at my feet every day, and I had to figure out how to deal with it. I finally did. I stopped thinking about what I was missing and instead focused on what I had to look forward to. My six-week X-ray showed that my fracture had healed 100 percent and that I was ready to pursue my short-term goals.

These goals were to be 100 percent soccer-fit for the Mr. Pibb Tournament and for us to win the championship of the inaugural event. It would enable us to showcase to the rest of the country that we were one of the best, if not the best, college soccer teams in the country.

We got bad news over the weekend: Mooch separated his shoulder in our indoor tournament and the doctor's prognosis was that it was doubtful Mooch would be ready to play in the Mr. Pibb tournament.

14

Mr. Pibb Win, Win and Win

As slow as January and February went by, March felt like a whirlwind, leading up to the Mr. Pibb Tournament. Between schoolwork, training with the team, doing extra training for my fitness and meetings with the coaching selection committee, there was not enough time in the day.

Out of all of the applications we received for the head coaching position, Jimmy Lennox, head coach for Mitchell Junior College in New London, Connecticut, appeared to be our favorite candidate, along with Alden.

Lennox had sent David Derrico and Doug Wark from Mitchell to Hartwick, and they were both All-American players. Alden ran all of the indoor and the outdoor training in preparation for the Mr. Pibb tournament and I thought he did a really good job. Mooch, told to avoid physical contact, finally trained with the team again.

The flight out to Dallas was very uneventful and we settled into our dormitory on the SMU campus. We had a team meeting that first night, in which Alden went over a scouting report he received on SIU. In the attack, SIU was led by leading scorer Tim Twellman and Greg Villa, who was supposedly a phenomenal athlete. Chris Cacciatore served many of the dangerous balls from his winger position.

Alden said Mark Moran ran the midfield and was a very good player. On defense, the Cougars were led by sophomore first-team All-American

Greg (the Face) Makowski, who was constantly looking to get into the attack, and they had a very good goalkeeper in Bob Robson.

Alden said SIU was a big, physical team, with the majority of its players coming from the St. Louis area, a hotbed of soccer. We had the utmost respect for the team and its many talented players. But I believed we could beat anyone after the way we played at the end of the season.

Friday evening as we boarded the bus for the game, Joey Ryan and I went to the back of the bus for what should have been a quiet 20-minute ride to the field. But two minutes into the ride, the bus driver stopped at another dormitory. To our surprise, the SIU team got on the bus to share the ride to the game. To say we were surprised is an understatement.

Greg Villa came to the back of the bus and sat down next to Joey and me. I couldn't help but notice that Greg had the body of an NFL corner-back, with muscles rippling everywhere. Alden's scouting report appeared to be correct about him.

Greg, Joey and I introduced ourselves and we started to have a nice, quiet conversation. My initial thought when seeing SIU board the bus was that it was going to be very awkward. But after talking with Greg for a few minutes I changed my mind.

Then out of nowhere, SIU players started singing songs and hollering chants. We were stunned as Joey turned to Greg and said, "Greg, does your team normally sing songs and do these chants on the way to games?"

Greg, who was not singing along with his teammates, just looked at us, smiled and replied, "Yes, they like to sing. But we never went to a game with the opposing team before."

We just sat in amazement for a few minutes before we continued our conversation. The bus driver had gotten lost, and a 20-minute ride became a 45-minute journey. The SIU team did not stop singing and chanting until it got off the bus.

I was amazed. I realized SIU was a supremely confident group of players, bordering on arrogant.

As we warmed up, we couldn't help but notice the field was small and bone-hard, with tremendous wind gusts. Ron Hardy won the coin toss and he elected for us to have the wind at our backs for the first half.

Alden went over the starting lineup, which included Mooch—separated shoulder and all—at sweeper. Ron Hardy was at left back and I was the central midfielder. The lineup was almost exactly how we ended the season, but Alden put in Phil Wallis as the center forward. Phil, who had not gotten a lot of playing time last season, could play in the central defense as a defensive midfielder and as a traditional center forward with great heading ability.

From the opening kickoff, we were all over SIU, with the wind appearing to get stronger by the minute. We knew we needed to take advantage of the wind while we had it. At the 20-minute mark, Zeren served a perfect corner kick and Phil Wallis buried it with a powerful header.

We came at SIU in waves. SIU rarely got the ball past midfield, but did play a ball over the top. Greg Villa, who ran like a gazelle, and Mooch, who obviously was still dealing with a painful shoulder, raced for the ball. It was two superb athletes running a 40-yard dash, with Mooch winning the race and playing the ball back to Keith Van Eron.

Several minutes later, Joey Ryan took a long throw-in and Howie Charbonneau headed the ball in for our second goal. At the 39-minute mark, Stevie Long played a beautiful through ball to Tommy Maresca, who took it to the end line and crossed it into the box to Phil Wallis, who timed his run perfectly and one-timed the ball into the back of the net to give us a 3-0 lead.

Alden began his halftime talk with, "As a team we were brilliant, we created lots of chances and we defended very well. Obviously, they will have the advantage of the wind and it is very important we try to keep possession of the ball as much as possible."

Alden then hesitated for what seemed like minutes, then turned to Mooch and said, "I am going to take you out of the game. I am not risking your health even though I know you can play through the pain.

"Ron, you will go to the sweeper position and Gary to the left back position. Time is on or side. No reason to rush."

SIU mounted an all-out attack, creating two goal-scoring opportunities in the first three minutes. Keith Van Eron responded with two brilliant saves. The wind proved to be as difficult to combat as the Cougars, and 10 minutes into the second half, Mark Moran made a beautiful pass to Greg Villa, who hit a rocket from 25 yards out to make the score 3-1.

The wind seemed to subside a bit. We started to do a much better job of getting into our rhythm and the play was much more even. SIU was desperate to get a second goal, and Greg Makowski seemed more like a left winger instead of the left back.

At the 40-minute mark, Artie was the recipient of a loose ball in the penalty box and he hammered it into the back of the net before the SIU keeper could react. That fourth goal took the wind out of SIU. Consider the game to be over. Final score: Hartwick 4, SIU 1.

The ride back to our dormitories was the complete opposite of the ride to the game. It was eerily quiet, with no conversations going on. I wondered what the SIU players would do if we started singing songs. We probably would have had an all-out riot on the bus. But we handled ourselves the way we should have, and we had to get ready for another game the next day.

When we got back to the dorm, Alden informed us that Quincy College destroyed UCLA 5-0. We knew the team would be a formidable opponent. It was important that we get some sleep.

On the bus ride to Franklin Field the following afternoon, Alden went over his scouting report for the Quincy Hawks. In the attack, they were led by Emilio John, a skillful Nigerian-born player who was supposed to be a great goal scorer but also created chances for his teammates, and Frank Vinciguerra, who Alden described as a bigger version of Tommy Maresca, with a knack for scoring goals.

On defense, they were led by Sam Bick, a big, athletic defender who possessed very good one-on-one defensive skills. This group of players had had tremendous success in the previous three years and had won three consecutive NAIA championships.

With the drought Texas had experienced, it was no surprise that the field once again was bone-hard. But the wind had calmed down and was not nearly as strong as the previous night.

Once again, we started off very quickly. On a long throw-in from Howie Charbonneau at the two-minute mark, Artie timed his jump perfectly and headed the ball past the Quincy goalkeeper for a 1-0 lead.

The game went back and forth, with Jeff Tipping dominating all balls played in the air. At the 32-minute mark, I split the Quincy defense, with Phil Wallis getting behind the last defender. Phil calmly slipped the ball past the Quincy goalkeeper to make it 2-0.

The half ended that way and we felt quite good about how the game was going. We had done a really good job on Emilio John and Vinciguerra, and were very confident we would make the finals.

We were content to play the second half in a defensive mode and not push too many players forward into the attack. As the half went on, neither team created many good chances. With time starting to run out for Quincy, it pushed Sam Bick more and more into the attack. Late in the game, we counterattacked, with Phil Wallis again able to get behind the defense, scoring his second breakaway goal of the game with five minutes left to pretty much end it. In less than 24 hours, we had beaten SIU 4-1 and Quincy College 3-0. Pretty impressive results.

We were able to see the last 15 minutes of the Clemson vs. Penn State game, which Clemson easily won 4-1. My impression was that Clemson was big, very athletic with great team speed, physical and skillful, although at times it seemed to play more individually than collectively.

We knew without a doubt Clemson would be our most difficult game in this tournament. The Clemson team was comprised mostly of players from Nigeria and Jamaica, with a few from Guyana.

Its midfield general was Clyde Watson, from Guyana. He was the one short player on the team and I would be matching up with him. I knew that whichever one of us did a better job in controlling the game probably would win the championship the next day.

I came to Hartwick to win championships and the next day I had the opportunity to win my first one of significance.

The weather couldn't have been more perfect for the first annual Mr. Pibb championship game. It was sunny with the temperature in the low 60s. The wind had continued to diminish over the weekend and wouldn't be a factor in the game.

The stadium was filled and was expected to be the largest crowd ever for a collegiate soccer game in Texas. Alden instructed us to continue to play intelligent soccer, keep our composure and not to retaliate if we received hard tackles and fouls.

Alden was prophetic in his pregame talk. Just five minutes into the game, we already were on the receiving end of numerous two-footed tackles with studs up. I knew it would not be long before Joey Ryan buried one of the Clemson players in a tackle to let them know we also could play this way.

Clemson was really talented and reminded me of the Howard University team we played in the semifinals in 1974.

At the 10-minute mark, Christian Nwokocha, one of several dangerous Clemson forwards, took a crossed ball and struck it into the side netting, giving Clemson a one-goal lead.

The goal seemed to give Clemson more confidence and they really started to knock the ball around, taking numerous long-range shots.

We survived the onslaught and slowly started to get more control of the ball. I started to get more touches and we knocked the ball around much better, making Clemson expend a lot of energy to get the ball back.

With around 10 minutes to go in the half, Phil Wallis was elbowed in the face and crumpled to the ground inside the penalty box. We were awarded a penalty kick despite a vehement argument from the Clemson defender who had accurately and forcibly placed his elbow on Phil's cheekbone.

After calm was restored, Stevie Long placed the ball on the penalty mark and calmly beat the Clemson goalie to his left side to even the score at 1-1. This gave us even more confidence and we finished out the half playing good soccer.

Despite the intensity of the game, Alden addressed the team in a calm manner, emphasizing for us not to retaliate to Clemson's fouls and overly aggressive tackling.

Five minutes into the second half, we were awarded a corner kick. Stevie Long served in the ball but a Clemson defender headed it out. With the ball coming right toward me, I was unmarked right behind the top of the D 25 yards out. I arched my back, controlled the ball with my chest, popping it up in front of me, and struck a volley out of the air. It dipped behind the goalkeeper, struck the bottom of the crossbar and went into the goal for a 2-1 lead. To say we were happy would be an understatement.

After the goal, the intensity of play became greater, with every touch and tackle challenged more aggressively than the previous one.

Clemson was attacking in numbers and being so good individually, we knew we may have needed another goal to win this game. Midway through the second half, there was a lot of confusion in our defense from a crossed ball. Keith Van Eron was screened when Taiwo Ogunjobi hammered the ball into the back of the net to even the score.

From that point on it was end to end, with both teams desperate for the next goal.

Playing against Clyde Watson made me feel like I was looking in the mirror, as our playing styles and abilities seemed so equally matched.

As the clock ticked under the 10-minute mark, Joey went on one of his maze-like dribbling exhibitions, waltzing past two Clemson defenders before hitting a rocket off the crossbar. Phil Wallis reacted first and dove through the air with a flying header to put the ball into the back of the net for a 3-2 lead.

Clemson was relentless in the last few minutes of the game, coming at us in waves, desperate to get the equalizer. In the waning seconds, Keith Van Eron was caught out of goal as the crossed ball dropped to the feet of a Clemson attacker, who calmly struck what was surely going to be the equalizer, heading for the open goal. But out of nowhere, Duncan MacDonald appeared, clearing the ball off of the goal line as the crowd was hollering 9-8-7-6-5-4-3-2-1, and the horn went off.

What an unbelievable feeling. We beat a great Clemson team and I made sure I found and shook hands with Clyde Watson, for whom I had the utmost respect. In the past college season SIU, Quincy and Clemson were ranked No. 1 in the country at one time or another—and we beat them on consecutive days. My dream of winning a national championship at Hartwick College now seemed more possible than ever.

That night we had a great time celebrating. Bernie Ross, the first-ever captain of the Hartwick College men's soccer team and one of the team's biggest fans, flew to Dallas to support us. Bernie was not only one of the nicest human beings I had ever met, but also could be unbelievably funny, especially after he had a few beers. The entire evening, Bernie had all of the players in stitches from laughing so hard, whether we were drinking Corona Gold or just water.

It was nice to see Alden having a few beers with his players because he did a tremendous job and was obviously under a lot of pressure to show he deserved to be the next head coach at Hartwick.

When the sun rose, we were still so excited about our win that several of us went outside, borrowed some bikes parked at the dormitory entrance and rode around the SMU campus until it was time to have breakfast.

15

Coaching and Educational Decisions

The lack of a head coach at Hartwick during the height of recruiting season was hurting the team's chances of getting commitments from any of the top high school players in the country. Dr. Chipman was starting to push for us to make a decision. The fact that we won the Mr. Pibb Tournament and Alden did such a wonderful job made the decision even more difficult.

Prior to the tournament, I believe we would have selected Jimmy Lennox as head coach without too much debate. But now, it was a much more difficult decision and it made me uneasy from the perspective that I really liked Alden as a coach but even more as a person.

Dr. Chipman scheduled a meeting for a Thursday afternoon to choose the new head coach. When Joey and I entered Dr. Chipman's office, Ron and Mooch were already there. Ron was a very bright and articulate individual, and he began the meeting by explaining his thoughts on the potential candidates, followed by Mooch's opinion.

Joey and I expressed our feelings. Then Dr. Chipman said, "It is time for us to make a decision."

There was a long, uncomfortable silence in the room. Had we not known Alden, it would have been much easier to just give the job to Lennox. But the fact that we all liked Alden very much as a coach and person made it much more difficult.

Dr. Chipman said if the vote was a tie, he would make the ultimate decision, but if as a committee we had a majority decision, he would abide by that outcome.

We voted to make Jimmy Lennox our next coach. There was a sense of relief that the process finally was completed. But as I left the room, I felt really bad for Alden.

Since I had come to Hartwick, Alden had worked as hard as anyone possibly could and he won the Mr. Pibb Tournament—and we gave the job to Lennox. I was so glad Dr. Chipman, and not our committee, would be relaying the news to Alden.

In the fall, I had taken a course called Theory and Analysis of Soccer, taught by Timo, and I loved the class. It was a terrific way to learn more about this great game that I loved so much and Timo's insights into the game were fantastic. It made me really think about whether I wanted to become a coach after my hopefully professional playing days were over.

Academically, Hartwick offered its students the opportunity to create a nontraditional major, for which one can receive a degree. Hartwick also offered the opportunity for one to study abroad. Since I took Timo's class, I had wrestled with the idea of creating my own major. I considered combining coaching soccer with getting a degree in Spanish.

My idea, if I decided to pursue this major, was to take off my junior year and study Spanish abroad in Madrid, Spain. I hoped Timo had connections with Real Madrid, which would enable me to train with one of its youth teams. It seemed like a win-win situation, speaking Spanish 24 hours a day and getting to train with one of the youth teams of the most famous soccer club in the world, while getting exposed to its coaching methods.

It was an exciting idea and I had been putting my paperwork together to submit to the Hartwick academic committee. But I started to get cold feet. The last time I had felt that way was when I thought about taking an extra year to train after high school before I entered Hartwick College.

I had not yet discussed my idea with Timo and was not sure how he was going to react, considering I would not be playing for the team my junior year. But that became a moot point when he resigned and went to Dallas.

I wasn't sure if I should have asked Alden for advice or discussed it with Jimmy Lennox. The deadline for me to submit my application was fast approaching. The thought of not playing with my teammates for a year really bothered me.

Would it have been fair to the team for me to take a year off, especially when we had turned the corner at the end of the past season and then won the Mr. Pibb Tournament? I expected we'd be in serious contention to win a national championship the next year.

The only people I had discussed this with were my father and my academic counselor. I felt a paralysis in trying to make a decision. So I called my father and explained everything in detail. There was silence while my father digested everything, before he replied.

"Billy, no matter what you decide, it will be a good decision. I will not tell you what to do, but most individuals would love to have the predicament you have. Think about it: You can go to Spain, learn Spanish, soak up the culture and train with a youth team of hopefully Real Madrid, which will be a fabulous experience. Or you can stay here for your junior year, further your education and with the players you have at Hartwick and Trenton Extension, contend and hopefully win a national championship or two over the next few years. This is not something you need to lose sleep over."

"Dad, after you put it that way, I guess I am very lucky not just with this decision I have to make but also that I have you as a father," I said. "Thanks Dad, love you."

"Thank you, Billy. Love you. Good night."

I felt a great sense of relief. My father had put it all in perspective for me. I decided the next day I would take a nice run around Neahwa Park and see if I could make a decision.

The next day after class, I dropped off my books at Depew Street and changed quickly into my sweatsuit. Walking out the front door, I knew that I was about to make one of the most important decisions of my life.

As I jogged through the park and enjoyed the beautiful spring weather, I thought about all of the points my father had mentioned about whether or not to go to Spain when it suddenly hit me that in the fall, if I went to Spain, I most likely would never play soccer with Mooch again as my teammate. I loved playing soccer with Mooch and I loved playing against him in training because he made me a better player. Mooch and I shared this tremendous love for the game and an insatiable will to win.

I thought about it for a few minutes, then decided I would not submit my application to study abroad. I realized that my father was 100 percent right: No matter my decision, it would be a good decision. With that, I started a very quick run back to Depew Street, feeling a great sense of relief.

16

Bicentennial Cup
and Amateur Cup

With the head coach decision made and me also deciding not to study abroad, I was able to spend all of my time focused on my schoolwork and playing for Trenton Extension.

The success we had at the Mr. Pibb Tournament set the tone for the remainder of the spring. The Penn State players fit perfectly into Trenton Extension and we were breezing through our games in the State Cup and Amateur Cup.

After getting through New Jersey in the state portion of the amateur cup we met up with Philadelphia Inter, which had won the amateur cup in 1973 and 1974. We won 2-0, beat a very difficult Casa Bianco SC out of Baltimore 2-1, and traveled to Rochester, New York to win against the Rochester Germans 2-1.

This put us into the eastern U.S. final for the right to play the western winner for the Amateur Cup. We were scheduled to play Fordham-Milan SC out of New York City on May 30.

We also reached the New Jersey State Cup final against our archrival Trenton Italians, with the State Cup final slated for June 13 at The Lawrenceville Prep School.

With the Bicentennial Tournament coming up, I was in my glory. On Friday, May 28, I was going to Yankee Stadium with Timmy Murphy and his father to watch England versus Italy.

On Sunday, we would host Fordham-Milan SC for the right to play for the United States Amateur Cup Championship. On Monday, thanks to George O'Gorman, me and my press pass would be going to New Haven to watch Brazil play Italy. I had read every word published in *World Soccer Magazine* for four years, and that gave me a fairly good knowledge of most of these national team players.

After watching a tape of the 1970 World Cup final between Brazil and Italy at the Broncos soccer camp, I fell in love with the Brazilian style of play. The technical skill, creativity and awareness of what was going on around them amazed me. It could be a weekend I never would forget.

As Mr. Murphy, Timmy and I made it to our seats in Yankee Stadium, you could feel the electricity in the air. There were huge numbers of English and Italian fans dressed in their respective team colors, singing and chanting nonstop.

I was so excited, I had to keep telling myself that although I was there to enjoy the game, I was also there to learn. Don't just watch the ball the whole time, but also look away from it and see how players made space for themselves and their teammates. Most importantly for me was to focus on the role of the central midfielders.

From the opening kickoff, it was apparent that the Italians were far superior technically, individually and collectively, although Trevor Brooking, the English central midfielder, displayed lots of skill.

The Italians struck quickly, with Francesco Graziani scoring two goals within five minutes for a 2-0 halftime lead. In the first minute of the second half, Mick Channon scored to get England back into the game. England scored twice more within seven minutes to take a 3-2 lead.

After the third England goal, the game went from a somewhat friendly international to a highly intense, nasty match. As Ping Pong had preached to me repeatedly about training my vision and looking around when playing, the same could be said for watching a game from the sidelines as a spectator.

Late in the game with the ball far up the field, I saw an Italian defender turn toward an English attacking player he had been marking and punch him right in the face, out of sight of both the referee and linesman. The game ended with the less-talented English team beating the Italian National Team 3-2.

Saturday, I spent hours at Nottingham trying to fine-tune my technical skills in preparation for Sunday's Eastern United States Amateur Cup Final.

Arriving at the Mercer County Community College soccer stadium, I noticed many of the players on Fordham-Milan were from St. Francis University and Albany State. Many were foreign-born players raised in New York City.

There was a steady rain and the forecast said it would continue all day. Frankie Selca, the skillful center forward from Albany State, lined up in the center forward position and Gregory Kourtesis, the sweeper for St. Francis University, lined up in his customary position.

The first half was even, with most of the play between the 18-yard boxes and few clear scoring opportunities for either side.

Early in the second half, Frankie Selca made space for himself, received a pass at the top of the 18-yard box, turned and fired a shot high towards the corner of the goal.

Our goalkeeper, Joey Hankins, could barely get his fingertips on the wet ball before it went in for the first goal of the game.

With Fordham-Milan being dominated by Italians and also having an Italian manager, we knew they would pack it in and revert to the catenaccio style of play for the remainder of the game.

Their goal put some urgency into our play and we started to get control of the game. We began creating good chances on goal. But each chance we had was met by the same obstacle: Fordham-Milan SC's outstanding 17-year-old high school senior goalkeeper Antonio Giordano. He was brilliant, making one spectacular save after another.

With around 15 minutes to go, Ping Pong pushed me up front from my central midfield position, alongside Artie, and we went from a 4-3-3 formation to a 4-2-4.

The move paid off almost immediately when I made a long diagonal run toward the corner flag, receiving Mooch's perfectly flighted pass as Fordham-Milan sweeper Greg Kourtesis came out to defend me. I pushed the ball through his legs, ran around him, took several more touches before picking out a teammate to pass to and crossed the ball into the six-yard box. My pass was headed back out to me and I headed the ball to Artie, who headed it to Johnny Marsden's feet. Johnny first-timed the ball into the back of the net for the tying goal.

We continued the onslaught but could not get the winner in regulation. We had expended so much energy to get the tying goal. After a five-minute break we were set to play two 15-minute halves in overtime without a golden goal rule.

We continued to dominate play in the first overtime, with Fordham-Milan keeping Frankie Selca up front as the lone attacking player and the remaining players all defending in numbers, hoping to either counterattack us or hoping to get the game to penalty kicks.

Five minutes into the second overtime period, a crossed ball by Johnny Marsden found Artie's feet a few yards behind the penalty spot. As Artie collected the ball, the wet surface caused him to start to lose his balance as he struck a shot right at goalkeeper Al Giordano. The ball skipped off the wet grass and with Giordano's reflex save, the ball inexplicably rolled right between his legs. Giordano spun around, dove back towards the goal while extending his arms as far as possible. As the ball crossed the goal line, he put his right hand on top off the ball and pulled it back on top of the goal line.

As we raised our hands for a goal, lineman Frank Lawson hesitated for what seemed like an eternity, then finally signaled goal and started running back to the halfway line.

The Fordham-Milan team was irate about the call and immediately sprinted across the field to Lawson. After surrounding him, one of the Fordham-Milan players kicked him before we could get over there and separate him from them.

We escorted Lawson, the other lineman and the referee off the field, away from the mob, with referee Roger Shott announcing, "If the West Windsor police do not get here shortly there will not be any more game."

The police arrived shortly after that and assured the referee they would stay for the remainder of the game and escort them to their respective cars after the game to avoid another incident.

The last 10 minutes were played with us killing time and keeping possession until the final whistle blew. We won a very difficult game and now we were going to be playing for the National Amateur Cup Championship at the end of June.

The next day on the train ride up to New Haven, I thought, what a great weekend. I watched the England versus Italy game on Friday. We just won the eastern half of the Amateur Cup on Sunday and would be playing for the National Amateur Cup Championship. Today, with a press pass, I would be on the field watching Brazil play Italy.

Brazil needed only a tie to win the Bicentennial Cup. But in a newspaper that day, Brazilian National team coach Oswaldo Brandao was quoted as saying he "would not even consider playing for a tie." I thought the last time these two world soccer powers played was in the 1970 World Cup final, when Brazil dominated Italy 4-1.

I took a cab from the train station to the Yale Bowl and I was a bit nervous as I entered the security gate for journalists. I finally got to the front of the line and the guard looked at my credentials, then looked up, staring at me for what seemed like forever, then looked down at my credentials again before finally saying, "OK, you can go in."

Perhaps the fact that I had a small Kodak camera on me, not a large camera that professional photographers carry on their shoulders, made the guard suspicious. When I finally walked through the gate, I was very relieved.

Although there was an area in the press box for journalists and photographers to eat before the game, I was so excited I headed straight for the field though it was 90 minutes until kickoff. I wanted to watch the players warm up and also to find out if I would be restricted as to where I could stand on the field. After walking around the field, it didn't appear there were any restrictions. If I was correct, I would be standing as close as allowed next to the Brazilian bench.

During warmups, the Brazilians were so relaxed and doing so many different tricks with the ball. It was as if the ball was an extension of their body. It seemed they could make the ball do everything they wanted except talk.

Their control was effortless and Ping Pong would have loved watching all of the traps resembling Alabama cotton with the ball just dropping dead at their feet. I spent a few minutes watching the Italians warming up and in particular Giancarlo Antognoni, the elegant, skillful midfield general who played club soccer for Fiorentina.

The warmup ended and both teams went back to their locker rooms. A few minutes later, I noticed most of the photographers were gathered near one of the tunnels leading to the field, waiting for the team introductions. So I did what any amateur photographer would do—I followed the professionals.

As the Brazilian team walked out heading towards the center circle, I tried to take pictures of them being led by Roberto Rivelino. I took several pictures and was trying to get a good picture of Zico when he stopped for me. As I was about to take the picture, I suddenly was shoved out of the way. I quickly spun around to see who pushed me and it was Fabio Capello of the Italian team. I was in his path to the lineup in the center circle and my initial reaction was that he was a real jerk. He could have just put his hand on my shoulder and made me aware that I was in his way and I would have moved.

After the national anthems of both teams, I located myself 10 feet from the end of the Brazilian team bench. I almost had to pinch myself and make sure I was not dreaming; I was standing 10 feet from the most famous soccer team in the world, getting ready to watch them play against the Italian national team. I was thinking that the Italian team should have lots of motivation after Brazil toyed with them in the 1970 World Cup final.

The game barely started when Italy was awarded a free kick out wide on the right side near the corner kick flag. The free kick was taken by Franco Causio. Brazilian goalkeeper Emerson Leao came out for the cross and misjudged it, allowing Fabio Capello to one-touch the ball into the goal to give Italy a 1-0 lead after two minutes of play.

The intensity of the game picked up after the goal. The tackles were not dirty but were extremely hard, by both teams.

At the 28-minute mark, Roberto Rivelino played a 50-yard ball with the outside of his left foot, which curled between two Italian defenders perfectly onto the path of Lula. After beating one defender, Lula played the ball back to Gil, who easily beat Dino Zoff for the tying goal.

As the half went on, Brazil was getting more control of the game. I noticed the Brazilian player Falcao, who I did not know much about, displaying impeccable technique on the ball. He was positioned in a central midfield position alongside Roberto Rivelino, the Brazilian midfield general. Falcao was getting lots of touches on the ball and almost making it look effortless despite the hard-tackling Italians.

With the first half winding down, Fabio Capello had to leave the game after a foul by Gil, then Lula was sent off after a violent foul on Pecci. This led to Italian Romeo Benetti, who was standing directly in front of the Brazilian bench, hollering at the top of his lungs at the Brazilian team.

Standing 10 feet from all of this, I wished I had an interpreter to understand what the players were hollering back and forth to each other. After calm was restored and the Italians took the free kick, the referee immediately blew his whistle for halftime. The half ended 1-1, with the Brazilians having to play a man down. I was so excited I could not wait for the second half.

During halftime, I was thinking how Roberto Rivelino went from a left winger on the 1970 World Cup-winning Brazilian team to a midfield general in 1976, often playing in a deep position in front of the Brazilian defense. It made me think of how I went from playing most of my early career as a right winger, then I moved into the midfield, and this past season for Hartwick I spent much of the time playing as a left back. Thinking about it, you never hear of it happening in the opposite direction where a player grows up as a defender, then goes into the midfield and eventually plays up front as an attacking player. It made sense.

If you grow up as a forward, you are constantly using your skills to control the ball, dribble and attack players, and look to make creative passes to break down a defense. Whether you realize it or not, you develop your vision by constantly looking around and checking the movement of players—often playing with your back to goal and the player marking you right on your backside.

99% of the time, a defender is facing the play, so he doesn't develop the habit of constantly looking around to track players, and need to think ahead of time with the question always being: What will I do if I receive the ball?

Defenders are not expected to take chances with the ball, especially in the defensive third of the field, so they cannot develop their skills to eventually move into a more attacking position. They usually do not receive passes with an opposing player right on their backside, and try to turn and face the defender as forwards and midfielders constantly do. The more I thought about it, the more it made sense to me, and I am glad that when I started in youth soccer, they put me in the right wing position.

The players came out to start the second half and I positioned myself even closer to the Brazilian bench, hoping no one would complain and make me move.

The second half started and despite Brazil playing a man down, it was controlling play. In the 48th minute, Gil received a long pass from Rivelino out wide on the right, beat the Italian defender Rocca, then almost effortlessly dribbled past Italian captain and icon Giacinto Facchetti before scoring Brazil's second goal of the game.

My first thought after seeing that goal was that Facchetti, who had been a world-class player for many years, was at the end of his international career.

The second goal invigorated the Brazilians and it was as if they were listening to samba music as they were playing, with their confidence and creativity growing with each touch. It was a thing of beauty to watch and moments later, Rivelino received a ball on the touchline right in front of me when he was confronted by an Italian defender.

In one motion he stepped down on the top of the ball with the sole of his left foot, rolled his foot down the side of the ball, slightly moving it towards the left, and then pushed the ball back to the right, exploding past the Italian defender. I had never seen that move before and I was mesmerized by it—as was the Italian defender that froze in his tracks.

I felt like a little kid at Christmas. I can never thank George O'Gorman enough for providing me with a press pass to watch my favorite team.

In the 66th minute, Roberto Bettega was given a red card and any hope the Italians had of getting back into this game was pretty much gone.

Several minutes later, Zico ran past several Italian defenders at the top of the 18-yard box and buried the ball past Dino Zoff to make the score 3-1. The rout was on.

Roberto Dinamite followed Zico's goal several minutes later to make the score 4-1. The Italians were looking just to survive the remaining minutes of the game. The final score was 4-1 and all of my focus was to get a picture with Zico.

As he came off the field, I asked him if I could have a picture with him, not really knowing how much English he understood. I used some hand gestures to further make my point.

I needed someone to take the picture and saw Falcao sitting on the end of the bench. I called his name and when he looked at me, I took his picture, then made hand motions for him to understand I wanted him to take a picture of Zico and me.

I handed the camera to Falcao, quickly put my arm around Zico and Falcao snapped the picture. I thanked them both several times and then made my way out of the stadium to find Jimmy Lennox, who had promised he would drop me off at the New Haven train station so I could make the trip back to Trenton.

I had Falcao take a picture of Zico and myself at the Bicentennial Cup. What a great way to end an unbelievable soccer weekend.

17

June Finals

The following morning Ping Pong came to the house and after breakfast, we headed to Nottingham to train. I was still so excited about the Brazilian game, I couldn't stop telling Ping Pong about it. I told him how on three occasions I noticed how when balls were coming out of the air to Brazilian players who were positioning themselves to trap the ball with their chests, the Italian defenders were looking to time the traps and win the ball.

He had discussed that aspect of the game with me on numerous occasions. The difference at the Yale Bowl was that although the Brazilian players looked as if they were arching their backs to pop up the ball, at the last second they reversed that movement and pushed the ball down towards their feet. Then they flicked it over an oncoming Italian defender who had miscalculated where the trap was going.

The beauty of this was that the time between when the ball touched the Brazilian's chest to the time when he flicked the ball with his instep over the oncoming defender was one-half second. It was done so quickly, they exploded past the oncoming defenders, who expected to challenge for a ball popped up in the air.

We discussed the mechanics of the move and the importance of the deception in making the opposing defender believe we were going to pop the ball up into the air with our first touch.

For two hours, Ping Pong served one ball after another, with me trying to execute the move with no opposition. Ping was demanding in a good way and our goal was always to strive for perfection in all technical aspects of soccer.

As I had become much more technically proficient then in the previous two years training with Ping Pong, the technical skills we worked on were much more advanced and his expectations were much loftier than when we started training together.

By the end of the week, after what must have been 1,000 touches on this move, we changed the exercise so that when Ping Pong served me the ball, he'd then run toward me, mimicking the role of the defender. I was slowly getting better at this technique, with the key word being "slowly." Though a player may get only one or two opportunities each game to execute the move, Ping Pong said I had to constantly add to my bag of tricks so I would never be predictable.

The following week, Trenton Extension teammates Timmy Murphy and Denny joined Ping Pong and I at Nottingham for training every morning. It was an exciting week and would culminate with us playing the Trenton Italians on Sunday for the New Jersey State Cup final. The game would be at a neutral site, the prestigious Lawrenceville Preparatory School.

We knew the final would be a very difficult game, physically hard and nasty at times. After watching how the Brazilian midfielders Roberto Rivelino and Falcao handled the hard, aggressive tackling of the Italian National Team, it made me realize that if my vision, awareness and thinking ahead were good and my first touch on the ball was fundamentally sound, I could avoid most of the nasty fouls and should be able to control the game. I was full of confidence going into this game, knowing I was a better player than six months before when we played the Trenton Italians.

We could sense the excitement as we approached the soccer field at the Lawrenceville Prep School campus. The weather was beautiful and the field was lined with fans. The difference between this game and our Amateur Cup game with the Italians was that this day, the fan base would be much more even for both teams, as opposed to the predominately Italian fans at Lincoln Field. We had a nice warmup and the team seemed relaxed as Ping Pong gave us our pregame talk.

Our tactics were fairly simple. We wanted to keep possession of the ball for long periods of time, making the Italians expend a lot of energy trying to win it back. We wanted to get the ball out wide to our wingers Johnny Marsden and Richie Reice to isolate them one on one against their defenders.

If we got good games from our wingers, they would get lots of crosses into the box, which should enable Artie to get good chances on goal.

On defense, Matt Bahr had to limit the number of touches Nando Vecchio got on the ball. The former Boca Juniors player was very difficult to contain once he got the ball and started running at you. Mooch was the sweeper behind Matt Bahr and Ping Pong told him to be selective with his runs into the attacking half of the field.

The game started as expected, with several hard fouls from both sides. We then began to get into our rhythm, stringing together multiple passes. But when we lost the ball, the Italians always looked to counterattack quickly up front with Nando Vecchio and the talented and sometimes-overlooked Natale Israel, a very good goal scorer.

The game flowed back and forth. At the 20-minute mark, Timmy Murphy found some space in the penalty box and beat Italians keeper Larry Keller from 18 yards out. Minutes later, the elusive Nando Vecchio beat several players in the box to tie the game at 1-1. That's how the evenly played first half ended.

Ten minutes into the second half, Johnny Marsden beat two defenders out wide and found Artie with a cross into the box. Artie volleyed the ball first time into the back of the net to give us a 2-1 lead.

The game began to seesaw back and forth. Then 15 minutes after Artie's goal, Mooch played one of his laserlike 50-yard passes, dissecting the Italians defense, with the ball landing right in stride on Reice's left instep. Richie dribbled around the last defender at the top of the 18-yard box and calmly slid the ball under the oncoming Larry Keller to make the score 3-1.

We had the Italians on the ropes. For the next five minutes we created one good chance after another, but they caught us on a counterattack and Natale Israel scored their second goal to make it 3-2.

Several minutes later with the ball at my feet in the center circle, the referee blew his whistle. There were no defenders close to me and we could not figure out why he blew the whistle. Seconds later, he gestured that the game was over. My initial thought was that there was no way we had just played 90 minutes of soccer.

Seconds later, all hell broke loose when Trenton Italians fans stormed the field, heading straight for the referee. Fans hit him with umbrellas as the referee crouched and desperately threw up his arms, trying to protect his face. Trenton Extension fans ran over and pried the referee loose from the irate Trenton Italians fans.

After what seemed like an hour, but had been just minutes, calm was restored, with the referee realizing his watch had malfunctioned and there were actually 15 minutes remaining in the game, plus any injury time to be added on.

It was reminiscent of our Fordham-Milan game, when the referee was attacked.

But this time it was an honest mistake, not a judgment call, and there was no need to wait for police to oversee the last 15 minutes of the game.

Several minutes after the game was restarted, Artie scored his second goal of the game to put us up 4-2. Minutes later, Vecchio responded with a magnificent display of dribbling before scoring his second goal of the game.

With 10 minutes left in the game, the Italians pushed everyone into the attack, looking for the equalizer. Nando was playing like a man on a mission.

We regained our composure and started knocking the ball around, using every inch of the field. It was similar to our Amateur Cup game against them, with us getting control of the ball and keeping it for long periods of time to end the game.

I kept wondering when would the referee blow his whistle to end the game. Was he adding more injury time so as to avoid any incidents after the game with the Trenton Italians fans? But he finally blew his whistle to end the game—and we were elated that we were the New Jersey State Cup champions.

Fans from both sides poured onto the field as we congratulated each other. I was looking for Nando to congratulate him on a brilliant performance. As I was walking toward him, I noticed the stocky Trenton Italians midfielder walking toward me very quickly. I scanned the crowd quickly to see if any of my teammates, particularly Mooch, were close by.

The guy was solid as a rock and after his threats at the last cup game, I really thought he was going to attack me. As I shook Nando's hand and told him he had been great, he pulled me forward and hugged me just as the hulklike figure came up behind Nando. Nando turned and said something to him in Spanish. Then the hulk turned to me and said in Spanish, "Usted es un jugador muy bueno," and extended his hand to shake mine. I was relieved and thought he was telling me I was a very good player.

I had a really good game that day and it felt great to get complimented by two very good opposing foreign players.

Even better was the fact that this guy, who probably weighed 60 to 70 pounds more than me, did not want to attack me.

We went to the Trenton Extension Tavern after the game. Timmy Murphy's grandfather Frank Rasimowicz fed us and gave us whatever we wanted to drink as we celebrated.

Frank was one tough, fiery older gentleman who did not take crap from anyone in his bar. It was obvious that Timmy took after his grandfather and they had a close relationship.

Two weeks from that day, we would be in Milwaukee to play for the National Amateur Cup Championship, and we were all really excited.

As a team, the Trenton Extension SC had not had one practice all year. We did not play in a league and, with most of our players still in college we were spread out from Oneonta, New York to State College, University Park, all the way down to Elkins, West Virginia. We all made the trek back to Trenton for cup games and were undefeated this year at 12-0. The 13th victory, by far, would be the toughest to get and by far, the most important.

No team from the greater Trenton area ever had won both the National Amateur Cup and the New Jersey State Cup.

We knew that the Milwaukee Bavarian Soccer Club would be a formidable opponent. It was led by player-coach Bob Gansler, a former Olympic player who appeared to have the same role as Ping Pong for his team.

Their top players on defense were defender Walter Ziaga, a member of the USA 1972 Olympic team, and goalkeeper John Spielmann.

On the attack, the Bavarians were led by Glen Ward, who played on the Pan American team with Mooch, and Herbert Schweinhert, a dangerous forward who spent most of his life playing in Germany. He recently returned to Milwaukee to bolster the team lineup.

Bob Spielmann led the midfield. This was the scouting report from Ping Pong on the flight to Milwaukee.

When we arrived at the hotel, we were told that the playing field was on the other side of the highway in front of the hotel. A tunnel underneath the highway led to the field. Being as excited as we were to play, most of us headed straight to the tunnel to see what the field looked like. Coming out of the tunnel, we instantly saw a beautifully manicured, very green grass field. As we walked on it, we were very happy that the field had a good width and length.

It reminded me of Penn State's field. I'd always have had good games on these types of fields and I expected the same against Milwaukee. There would be no excuses available if we didn't play a very good game. We walked every inch of the field before we headed back to the hotel for dinner, and hopefully a good night's sleep.

Waking up Sunday morning, I was very excited but also relaxed, considering that we were about to play for a national championship.

I had a good breakfast of pancakes four hours before our scheduled kickoff and then went back to the room to get packed. We had been warned that if the game didn't go into overtime, we would have time to shower and make it to the airport on time for our scheduled 6:10 p.m. departure back to New York. But if the game went into overtime, we would never make it on time.

Personally, making the flight back to New York was an afterthought. The only thing that mattered was bringing the championship back to Trenton.

Three hours later as we emerged from the tunnel, the field was filled with Milwaukee Bavarian fans. The great crowd added to the excitement.

As we lined up for the kickoff, the temperature was dramatically higher than it was in the morning. The heat could be a factor in the game.

We started the game by stringing multiple passes together and had little trouble getting into the attacking third of the field. But the Bavarians were very tight and organized in their last third, and we didn't create any chances on goal.

Although the Bavarians were the older, more experienced team, they were the ones that appeared nervous about playing in such an important game. Ours was the team playing very relaxed and confident.

Ten minutes into the game, we were awarded a corner kick. Richie Reice served the ball into the box. Artie and a Bavarian defender clashed for the ball as it came flying out to me standing on top of the 18-yard box. I took one touch, pushing it past an oncoming Milwaukee Bavarians player, and struck the ball hard and low to the right side of the goal-keeper's outstretched arms, into the corner of the goal to give us a 1-0 lead.

Instead of our goal deflating Milwaukee, it seemed to awaken them. The Bavarians showed more energy and calmness in their play.

Three minutes later, Herb Schweinhert received a pass on the corner of the 18-yard box, dribbled across the top of the 18-yard line and struck a blistering shot low and to the right past Joey Hankins to tie the game at 1-1.

As the half went on, Milwaukee's defensive tactics became apparent. Gansler knew what a great player Mooch was and every time we had possession of the ball, whether or not it was Mooch, if he pushed forward, a Bavarians forward would mark him until the Milwaukee team had regained possession. This tactic limited Mooch's ability to contribute to our attack.

They also knew we liked to keep possession of the ball, always looking to get the balls to our wingers isolated in one-on-one positions where they could turn and attack their defenders. They did an outstanding job of denying Marsden and Reice the ball and though we were dominating the midfield play, we had difficulty breaking the Bavarian defense down in the last third.

The Bavarians always looked to have seven or eight players behind the ball defensively. When they won the ball, they looked to counterattack quickly up front with Ward and Schweinhert.

The rest of the first half was even, ending at 1-1.

As Ping Pong's scouting report indicated, Schweinhert and Ward were both very good players and we would need to do a better job on them in the second half if we expected to win.

I was on my game. Early in the second half, I had not given away the ball away once despite the Milwaukee defenders getting tighter defensively on our front players as the half wore on.

Twenty minutes into the second half, Glenn Ward played a perfectly weighted through ball with Schweinhert outpacing Matt Bahr to the ball, one-timing it perfectly just inside the post to give Milwaukee a 2-1 lead.

Ping Pong's philosophy was if you're losing and need to score a goal, it really does not matter if you lose 2-1 or 3-1. With that in mind, and the fact that we were having a difficult time creating good chances, Ping Pong pushed Mooch into the midfield five minutes after the goal, and I moved up to play right behind Artie on the attack.

We were playing three versus three in the defense with zero cover. We were pushing forward in the attack, looking for the equalizer—and now battling the searing heat, the time and the stellar Bavarian defense. In the final minute, Schweinhert received a ball on a counterattack, beat his defender and crossed perfectly onto the head of Jerry Zuba, who was unmarked in the six-yard box. Zuba calmly beat Joey Hankins for the third and final goal of the game.

A minute later the referee blew his whistle to end the game. Our dream for a National Amateur Cup championship was lost. The Milwaukee Bavarians fans poured onto the field.

If there ever was a momentary consolation in losing a championship, it was that numerous Milwaukee fans approached me and told me they thought I was the best player on the field and they enjoyed watching me play. Their kind words helped me contain the tears that were waiting to pour out of me as I dejectedly walked back to the hotel to shower and quickly change for our flight home.

I knew that when I was older, I would appreciate what a huge accomplishment it was to get to the Amateur Cup final. But the first few weeks after our loss were a difficult time for me. The loss made me more determined than ever to keep improving my game to help Hartwick win a national championship.

18

Training with Ping Pong

That summer, training with Ping Pong had a few changes from the previous summer. Denny, who was going to enter Bridgeport University in the fall, started to train with us several days a week. We trained at Rider College, on the varsity soccer field. We brought a soccer net with us, put it up while we trained, took it down at the end of our session and hid it in the woods behind the goal so we did not have to carry it every time we went there.

The beauty of training at Rider was the availability (not necessarily authorized) of the facilities. The soccer field was very nice and having the net prevented us from wasting countless hours chasing balls.

Even more endearing to us was that the Rider College indoor pool was a couple hundred feet from the soccer field. Our routine was to train hard for 2 1/2 to three hours, have lunch, undress down to our soccer shorts and walk into the pool as if we belonged there with the many other students, campers, etc. We spent around 15 minutes in the water cooling off and relaxing before getting dressed and spending another 2 1/2 hours training in what often was blistering heat.

Ping Pong always tried to make our training exercises as gamelike as possible. One of his favorite shooting exercises for me as a midfielder was this: He would play a brisk square pass to me 25 yards from goal, then I would play one touch to Denny, run past an imaginary defender and first-time the return pass of my give and go with a shot on goal. We would do 30-40 passes shooting with my right foot, then the same with my left.

Ping Pong believed shooting was a lost art and we spent countless hours on different shooting exercises at Rider.

When Ping and I trained at Nottingham, we constantly worked on my technique and midfield play. Every practice included Ping putting me in front of a fence and drilling balls at me from close range. The expectation was that every trap would drop to the ground like Alabama cotton.

Every day, I worked on my Beckenbauer pirouettes. We also spent a lot of time studying the great Dutch midfielder Wim van Hanegem. How did a player as slow as van Hanegem become the best player on the field in the 1974 World Cup final?

What many people may not know is that van Hanegem had a much greater motivation against West Germany than just winning the World Cup.

Wim van Hanegem was born in Breskens, Zeeland, on Feb. 20, 1944. The van Hanegem family suffered immense tragedy that year; a carpet bombing of Breskens killed Wim's father, sister and two of his brothers, on Sept. 11, 1944.

Wim barely survived, and the loss of his family members caused him to have a tremendous hatred for the Germans.

Ping Pong and I concluded that van Hanegem was so strong on the ball that once he got it, it was nearly impossible to get it away from him. His terrific vision and ability to bend balls in any direction allowed him to dissect defenses like perhaps no other midfielder in the world.

Ping Pong said though I would never be as big or strong as van Hanegem, I could and had to become much stronger on the ball.

So we incorporated another training exercise when we had a third player to train with. With Ping Pong on my back side defending me, I tried to make space for myself before checking back for the ball. Of course, I glanced over my shoulder before I received the pass, and Ping Pong would mark me as tight as possible, often kicking the back of my legs, grabbing me, pulling on me, to simulate actual game situations, doing everything in his power to keep me from turning and facing him.

As the summer went on, I felt myself getting stronger on the ball and using my low center of gravity, making it much more difficult for defenders to get near the ball once I had possession.

Just like the previous summer, after dinner every Monday through Friday night, I rode my bike to Nottingham for our pickup games and ended the day working on my heading with the pendulum ball under the porch light. Once again it was a great summer, training seven days a week and doing exactly what I loved to do.

19

The Lennox Era Begins

Expectations were extremely high for Hartwick soccer that fall. On the ride back up to Oneonta for preseason, it hit me that if we did not win the national championship that year, the season would be considered a failure. I actually liked that pressure of expected success.

It would be our first time with Jimmy Lennox in charge as the head coach, and I was not sure what to expect. Everybody assumed that the way we ended the season with Ron at left back, Mooch at sweeper and me as central midfielder would be the way we'd line up, but there were no guarantees.

Several days before preseason, Mooch and I had a small barbecue in the backyard of Depew Street with Jimmy Harrison. Harry and Mooch had a few beers while waiting for the food to cook. A freight train slowly passed by on the railroad tracks 10 feet behind our backyard.

On numerous occasions, Mooch and I played a game where we called out a letter on the side of the train and tried to hit the letter with a kick of the soccer ball. Knowing Mooch had several beers already, I pulled back the soccer ball with the sole of my foot, hollered out, "the first O in Oswego," struck the ball and hit the letter dead on.

The ball bounced back into the yard and Mooch rolled it in front of his right foot. After patiently waiting for the right freight car, he said, "The L in Lackawanna" and nailed it.

This got Harry going and he began impersonating a play-by-play guy.

"OK, Gazonas has the ball at his feet. The train is approaching. What will he call as Myernick is waiting in the wings?"

I waited for the bigger letters to show up; not all letters were the same size on the sides of the freight cars. I called out, "M in Mohawk" and barely clipped the bottom of the M.

Harry exploded with, "Yes, Gazonas has hit his mark. Can Myernick follow this with more success?"

Mooch sized up the next set of box cars and said, "V in Valley." He hit the V dead center.

"Myernick has done it! Myernick has done it!" Harry called.

We were laughing hysterically. I tried to get my composure before I took my next kick, concentrating as best I could under these circumstances. Then the train slowed, which gave me a slight advantage and I hollered, "R in Railway" and nailed it.

We were laughing uncontrollably because we had hit letters before—but never five in a row. Mooch called a timeout to have a quick sip of his beer, lined up the ball, eyed the freight cars one after another, then said, "W in West." He drilled the ball right onto the W.

Harry was rolling on the ground and shouted out, "Under extreme pressure, Myernick has done it again."

We were laughing so hard, I had tears in my eyes. Then Harry started again. "Can Gazonas deal with this monumental pressure where mere mortals have failed in the past?"

I watched the freight cars for a letter with good size. When I saw it, I shouted out, "The first E in Erie." I struck the ball and was at least two feet wide.

Harry said, "He has missed, Gazonas has missed. It all comes down to this last strike of the ball by Glenn 'Mooch' Myernick. Can he do it?"

The last train car was approaching. Mooch, with beer can in hand, would have to act fast. We could see Mooch concentrating through the laughter. He said, "N in New York." He drilled the ball perfectly in the middle of the N.

Harry erupted with, "He has done the impossible on this warm summer day in Oneonta, New York. Myernick has done the impossible."

Our laughter was uncontrollable. Harry was one of the funniest human beings I had ever met—and he made a silly game one that I am sure we would never forget.

Several days later, Hartwick's preseason officially started and there was a tremendous excitement within the team. We were brimming with confidence because of our performances at the end of the 1975 season, including the NCAA Tournament and our success in the Mr. Pibb Tournament.

Plus, we had a new head coach in Lennox and everyone, except Steve Jameson, back for this season. We expected to be highly ranked when the preseason national rankings come out.

After the first week of training, it appeared the lineup that we had at the end of last year and during the beginning of the Mr. Pibb Tournament would remain intact, with Mooch at sweeper, Ron Hardy at left back and me at central midfield.

It was a very different feeling for me this preseason, knowing that I definitely would be starting and that I would be playing in the central midfield position, which I so coveted.

It appeared that Lennox and Alden got along really well, which was very important for the team. We were not sure how that would work out when Alden was bypassed for the head coaching position. But Alden was a true professional and actually seemed to be even more involved this season, with Lennox allowing him to do much more in practices than when Timo was the coach.

We paid attention to every word Jimmy Lennox said so we could understand his philosophy and beliefs on how the game should be played. By the end of the second week, Mooch and I were true believers in Lennox. He was a soccer purist who at all times wanted to play good, skillful, creative soccer.

With Timo as coach, we always were changing our tactics to adapt to the opposing team's strengths and weaknesses. But Lennox appeared to be the opposite. In our preseason games, our focus was 100 percent on how we wanted to play, with no alignment changes to adjust to the opponent.

My freshman year, we were not the most talented team and it made sense for Timo to adjust tactics every game. The previous year, we did not play to our potential until the end of the season. We still were making constant adjustments for the opponent until Timo made the alignment change between Mooch, Ron Hardy and me.

This year at the end of the last day of preseason practices, and prior to the first annual Mayor's Cup game during the weekend, we had a meeting in the locker room. Lennox reviewed what qualities he sought in a team captain. He wanted us to elect the captain.

I thought this was just a formality; Mooch was the obvious choice to be the captain. He was the leader on the field and off, with this charismatic way about him. Not only was I wrong, but I believe Lennox was also wrong in his thinking. It looked like Lennox had seen a ghost with his facial expression; the voting results were not what I think he had expected. Mooch and Jeff Tipping were tied.

Lennox talked some more about the qualities he wanted in a team captain—someone that has the ability, when the team was not playing well or feeling lots of pressure, to have the skill to step on the ball, calm everyone down, knock the ball around, get it back and keep possession until the team was relaxed again and playing Hartwick soccer. That pretty much described Mooch.

Jeff Tipping was a natural leader but he didn't possess the technical skills of Mooch. He had those qualities in English soccer that we so admire. Never give up, always give it your best effort, fight until the end and always encourage teammates. But Lennox wanted more from his captain.

The second vote landed Mooch the captaincy and probably taught Lennox a valuable lesson about how to select his captain.

The first game in the inaugural Mayor's Cup Tournament was on a Friday night. Although the Mayor's Cup technically was a preseason tournament, it was anything but that. If we could beat Bucknell, we were guaranteed a great opponent in the championship game because SIU Edwardsville would meet Oneonta State University in the other first-round game.

Our regular-season schedule had five hugely important and difficult games: Penn State, Philadelphia Textile, Adelphi University, Cornell and the University of Connecticut. The most important to me personally was Philadelphia Textile. Its players bad-mouthed us at the Delaware exhibition game the last preseason and again during our indoor tournament. That left a very bad taste in my mouth.

That Friday night we destroyed Bucknell University 6-1. In the nightcap, SIU and Oneonta State had a physical, hard game, which SIU won with only 20 seconds left in the first overtime on a header by Tim Holstein.

It didn't matter to us who won. Either way, it would be a very difficult game for us against a very good team and would help prepare us for the NCAA Tournament.

In the championship game, SIU was all over us to start. At the 19-minute mark, a clever cross from Timmy Twellman found Tim Holstein, who beat Keith Van Eron low to his right.

We adjusted to their physical play and did a much better job of keeping the ball on the ground and keeping possession. Late in the first half, Artie found Joey Ryan with a pass and Joey scored the equalizer. Minutes later, Angrik Stepanow scored what became the winning goal for a 2-1 lead.

Mooch was special and Jeff Tipping did a brilliant job marking the very dangerous Greg Villa out of the game. Angrik was awarded the offensive MVP of the tournament and Byron Cordero of Oneonta State won the defensive MVP honors.

We had just beaten a very good SIU team and did not have to subject ourselves to their singing on the bus this time before the game.

The regular season would start the next Saturday at home against Binghamton University. It would begin our quest for the coveted national championship.

In our home opener, we disposed of Binghamton University and its dangerous center forward Charlie Lineweaver 3-0, with two of the goals coming in the last seven minutes of the game.

Jeff Tipping did what he did best, marking the opposing center forward out of the game. It was a fair team performance. We headed up to Penn State the next weekend for the first of our very important games on the schedule.

Training during the week was hard and competitive. With 22 very good players on the roster, everyone fought to get into the starting lineup or get more playing time. We had high school All-Americans sitting on the bench who couldn't get a minute of playing time.

Lennox was a perfectionist and constantly preached for us to focus on one game at a time. We loved playing at Penn State because of its beautiful soccer field. That year, the game took on more personal significance for me because several Penn State players were my teammates on Trenton Extension SC.

I found it hard to believe that any college team in the country could beat us if we were playing on a really nice large grass field. The way we started out against Penn State confirmed my belief.

From the opening whistle, we knocked the ball around all over the field, with Penn State players rarely getting a touch. This great display of possession soccer led to two quick goals for us. We were on top of our game, controlling the first half.

But in the last minute of the first half, our defense failed to head a crossed ball out of danger. The ball landed at the feet of Penn State center forward Tim McDonald, who buried the ball into the back of the net, ending the first half at 2-1.

The goal gave Penn State momentum, but we were still very much in control of the game in the first 30 minutes of the second half. Suddenly, the game became extremely physical and nasty, with both teams committing numerous fouls.

The numerous stoppages in play disrupted our rhythm and we played rather poorly, but finished the game with a 2-1 victory. I had to take responsibility for our poor play at the end of the game because in the Hartwick style of soccer, the central midfielder was expected to control the game and dictate the rhythm of play. Fouls, nasty tackles and numerous stoppages of play were no excuse, and I knew going forward I needed to play better in these types of circumstances.

We had Brockport State coming up the following Saturday at home for Alumni Weekend, meaning Elmore Field would be overflowing with fans. It would be a great atmosphere to play in, followed by a midweek game against Colgate. But I couldn't help myself and kept thinking about our upcoming game with Philadelphia Textile.

Training was fiercely competitive all week. We destroyed Brockport 5-0, followed by a 3-0 victory over Colgate.

Now I could truly focus on our upcoming game Saturday in Philadelphia. Textile may have had the country's most talented overall first six players in its lineup. Dale Russell must have been the top forward in the country. I wondered why the Bermuda-born Russell was not playing professional soccer overseas. He often was served up front by the explosive Elson Seale, Barbados-born and raised in New Jersey, and equally skilled at creating goals and scoring.

Dave McWilliams, a goal-scoring machine, complemented Dale up front and I often viewed him as the American version of Gerd Muller, the great German center forward. McWilliams was very strong on the ball and difficult to dispossess when he shielded the ball, waiting for teammates to run off the ball for him.

In the midfield, Textile was led by Duval Minors and Adrian Brooks, two unbelievably talented and skilled foreign-born players that created havoc from their midfield positions. The first time I saw Duval Minors play was against Trenton Extension, when I was playing junior league soccer. He controlled the game and displayed impeccable skill in the midfield.

The defense was anchored by Johnny Nusum, brother of New York Cosmos goalkeeper Sam Nusum. The Bermudan-born Nusum was a powerful individual with great technique playing out of the back and often made attacking runs up the field. I would say Johnny Nusum was the second-best sweeper in the country after Mooch.

To add to the excitement of this clash, Jimmy Lennox's wife Denny was pregnant and due any day.

In the coaches poll, we moved up to second in the country; Philadelphia Textile ranked sixth. The atmosphere all week in training felt more like an upcoming NCAA Tournament game rather than a regular-season game. The seriousness and focus of our training reached an even higher level as the excitement built.

The Friday after training, we boarded Bluebird, with Joey Ryan to follow the bus driving Lennox's Trans Am in the event Lennox had to head back to Oneonta for Denny. We took the bus to Mooch's house, where the players would split up and sleep overnight there, Artie's house or my house.

The minute we arrived at Mooch's house, Mooch's mother Ruth received a phone call that Denny Lennox had gone into labor. When she told Jimmy, he thought she was joking. When Jimmy realized she was not, he jumped into his car and headed back to hopefully get to the hospital before Denny gave birth.

Denny gave birth to a beautiful, healthy girl named Courtney Lennox. Early Saturday morning, Jimmy who had been up well over 24 hours, jumped in the van of Neil and Cindy Buzzy, two of our most remarkable fans, to make the four-hour trip to Philadelphia. He arrived just as we were about to begin our warmup.

Rain had left the field very wet and soft, with more rain expected throughout the day. I had been waiting for this game for weeks and couldn't wait for the kickoff. There was a high probability that whoever controlled the midfield would win this game, and with Textile boasting about Duval Minors and Adrian Brooks, I knew it would be a great challenge for our team collectively, and myself individually.

The game started out even for 10 minutes. But it became apparent to me that Philadelphia Textile left back Ed Sheridan was going to have a difficult time containing Steve Long, and you could see our talented right winger gaining more confidence every time he touched the ball.

Midway through the first half there was a lack of communication between our defenders and Dale Russell seized the opportunity to put Textile up 1-0. The goal energized us, and we started knocking the ball around much better, playing out of our defense, through our midfield, and getting balls to the feet of our attacking players.

Our front players started to win the one-on-one confrontations, with Stevie Long leading the way with several nutmegs of Eddie Sheridan and ending with a precise pass finding the feet of Angrik Stepanow, who evened the game at 1-1.

The last 10 minutes of the first half had us all over Textile, with Artie heading a ball off the crossbar. Minutes later, another brilliant cross from Stevie Long found Angrik's head, with another header hitting the crossbar. Halftime could not come soon enough for Textile, with us having taken control of the game through dominating possession and Textile rarely threatening in its counterattacks.

Textile had five great attacking players, but it was obvious its defenders were having a difficult time with our attackers. Our domination of possession could tire them out later in the game.

Lennox's only criticism at halftime was that because we had so much success getting balls out wide to our wingers, we were not looking enough to get the ball to Esteban.

The second half started out much like the first half ended, with us controlling the ball and creating numerous opportunities on goal. But we couldn't get the go-ahead goal.

Midway through the second half, Textile won the ball in our attacking third and as Adrian Brooks was about to play the ball, Mooch called for an offside trap. All of our defenders sprinted to the halfway line as the ball was played over the top of our defense, exposing Dale Russell in an offside position.

He obviously was offside, but our defense hesitated, waiting for the referee's whistle. Dale Russell was now 10 yards past the halfway line, collecting the ball, with our defense frozen in shock that the referee did not blow his whistle.

Mooch then exploded like he was shot out of a cannon and caught up to Dale at the 18-yard line, as Keith Van Eron, who had positioned himself for a breakaway, was standing just past the six-yard box.

It was a surreal moment, with the best attacking player in college soccer versus the best defender within two yards of each other. No other players were within 20 yards.

It was as if the game went from a video to a snapshot and although it was only a few seconds, it seemed like an eternity. Dale gave several body swerves without touching the ball and Mooch maintained his defensive positioning. To the surprise of everyone, Russell dug his elegant left foot into the ground and chipped the ball so effortlessly, seeming to float in slow motion over Keith Van Eron's head into the back of the net.

It was a brilliant goal. The presence of mind and ability to score that goal in such a pressure-packed environment was an amazing act of skill, vision and intelligence by Dale Russell. I knew I would never forget that goal. So against the run of play, Textile led 2-1.

It did not take us long to get over the shock of that goal. Minutes later, I found Esteban with a pass at the top of the box and the brilliant Colombian danced around three defenders before finding the back of the net with the tying goal.

The remainder of the half, we were relentless on the attack but couldn't find the winner. When the referee blew his whistle to end regulation time, you could sense the relief on the faces of the Textile players. They were exhausted and knew if not for the brilliance of Dale Russell and several crossbars, this game would have been over.

The first of two mandatory overtime periods had us resume where we left off with one attack followed by another. Textile was listless and we were full of energy.

Midway through the first overtime period, Reynoso, with those precocious soccer skills, miskicked a pass. It deflected off a Textile defender right into the path of Tommy Maresca, who buried the ball into the back of the net to give us a 3-2 lead.

The goal took away what little energy Textile players had left. We did a great job of keeping ball possession in the second overtime. The best way to defend against Textile's great attacking players, in particular Brooks and Minors, was to make them expend all of their energy defending and chasing the ball. That's what we did.

In the last minute of the game, Joey Ryan played me a square ball and Duval Minors ran at me with what little energy he had left. I pushed the ball to my right and made it as if I was going to pass the ball, as Minors stretched his left leg to block my pass, I pushed the ball through his legs, ran around him and casually played the ball back to Joey.

Nutmegging a fantastic player like Duvall Minors was a great way for me to end the game. Seconds later the referee blew his whistle. We had earned a very important victory against a talented Philadelphia Textile team.

We stopped midway back to Oneonta to eat dinner. While the team went into the restaurant, Lennox and Mooch went next door and had a few beers to celebrate Courtney's birth. After dinner, we got back on the bus, waiting several minutes for Mooch and Jimmy to do the same, both looking much more relaxed. Alden passed out cigars to everyone and I quickly realized I couldn't stand the smell of cigar smoke.

Despite the smell, it was a great ride back to Oneonta, celebrating a very hard-fought victory and Courtney's birth.

There's a special feeling you get when you and your teammates put so much effort into a game and win. The team played really well and I had a really effective game against two of the best midfielders in the country. My confidence in our team and myself was growing. I was beaten up from the game and decided to skip secret training on Sunday.

I realized the better the team got and the more I improved as a player, the greater probability that our games would get much more physical and dirty. I most likely would get more opposing players trying to hurt me and put me out of the game.

PBS had started televising a weekly show called "Soccer Made in Germany," with Toby Charles, a Welshman, hosting the show. Mooch, Artie, Tommy and Joey Ryan, who moved into Depew Street that fall, and I watched the show religiously.

They showed weekly highlights from the Bundesliga, the first division of the men's professional soccer league in West Germany. Toby Charles was fantastic. That one night a week was very special for us.

I had received some nasty tackles and fouls the last few weeks. I made it a point that every time I watched Soccer Made In Germany, I studied how players were tackled, and tried to analyze if there was anything I could do to avoid getting hurt or at least minimize the damage.

We seemed to be on cruise control the next few weeks, disposing of University of Buffalo 6-1, University of Bridgeport 2-0, Ithaca 2-0 and

East Stroudsburg 5-1. We were ranked second in the country, trailing Clemson University.

We had a huge midweek game coming up against Adelphi University. We were ranked No. 1 in New York State, followed by Adelphi at No. 2. The winner of that game was expected to be ranked No. 1 in New York State and have the home advantage for NCAA Tournament games.

Last year, Adelphi came into Oneonta and handed us a 2-0 loss. They were a very talented team and seemed to match up against us very well. Striker Ronnie Atanasio was the player I feared most on their team.

At kickoff, there were strong winds. With the wind at our backs in the first half, we dominated play. But we could create only one very good opportunity, with Esteban rifling his shot off the goal post.

In the second half, with Adelphi having the advantage of the wind at its back, we were in a very defensive posture. Mooch orchestrated our offside trap to perfection. We repeatedly caught Ron Atanasio and Adelphi's other speedster up front, Anthony Prescott, in offside positions.

With seven minutes left in the game, Keith Van Eron was positioned far off his goal line and an Adelphi attacker chipped the ball over his head for what appeared to be the go-ahead goal. It seemed like Philadelphia Textile all over again, when Jeff Tipping appeared out of nowhere to slide toward the goal line and cleared the ball inches from the goal.

The remainder of regulation time and the two mandatory overtime periods brought few good scoring opportunities for either team. The game ended 0-0 and although it was not the result we were looking for, the tie away from home enabled us to retain the No. 1 ranking in New York State.

Cornell University was our next New York state opponent, and a tie or win against them could allow us the home field advantage throughout the NCAA Tournament leading up to the Final Four, to be played at Franklin Field at the University of Pennsylvania.

Before we got to our midweek game against Cornell, we had a home game on Saturday against Lehigh University. Lehigh was led by its standout goalkeeper Larry Keller, who also happened to be the goal-keeper for Trenton Italians SC.

Mooch was on crutches from a ligament sprain that happened against Adelphi, and Ron Hardy also would sit out our weekend game due to injury. It didn't matter. Just 25 seconds into the game we scored our first goal, led 6-1 at halftime and ended the game 8-1 victors.

A good result against a Cornell team that had beaten us the last two times we played would put us in a great position entering the NCAA Tournament.

This year, unlike my freshman and sophomore years, the regular season was really just a warmup for the NCAA Tournament. It was all preparation for the very coveted national championship trophy that had eluded Hartwick.

Cornell lost to graduation two dynamic wingers in Joey Mui and David Sarachan, but returned the dangerous Sid Nolan up front. Our rivalry with Cornell always brought physical games and we expected nothing less on Elmore Field on that Wednesday.

With a steady drizzle all day Wednesday, Elmore Field was a bit soggy by game time. Though that would hamper us a bit, not playing on Cornell's dreaded AstroTurf field should give us an advantage.

Right from the start the game was physical, marked by hard tackles and numerous fouls. Cornell goalkeeper Dan Mackesey made several excellent saves early in the game and although we had the better of the play, we had no goals to show for it.

Midway through the first half, Cornell's constant fouling had disrupted our rhythm and allowed Cornell to start to get the better of the play. It appeared that almost every 50-50 ball was met with a slide tackle from the Cornell players and bodies were flying everywhere.

I was upended twice on hard slide tackles, with the defender coming in with a straight leg studs up both times. On the second tackle, the defender left stud marks on the knee of my planted foot, and I don't know how I didn't blow out my knee. The referee did not even call a foul on the tackle, which could have ended my college and soccer career prematurely.

The half ended 0-0, and the last 15 minutes of the half reminded me of the end of our game against Penn State. Sitting on the bench in the locker room at half time, I stared at my knee and could see the stud marks indented in my skin. I felt very fortunate that I had escaped without a serious injury. I also knew that I had to be above all of the nasty tackles and fouls, and get control of the ball so we could get back to Hartwick soccer.

We began the second half doing a much better job of keeping possession of the ball. By doing so, we were able to avoid the slide tackles prevalent in the first half.

Midway through the second half, Artie struck a shot from just outside the 18-yard box and the wet surface handcuffed the usually sure-handed Dan Mackesey. The ball slipped through his hands and rolled into the goal to give us a 1-0 lead.

The goal gave us more energy. Just when it looked like we were going to get the all-important second goal, Cornell had a counterattack and forward Rick Derella first-timed a rebound off of a Keith Van Eron save and buried the ball into the back of the net to tie the game at 1-1.

The game then opened up, going back and forth. With four minutes left in the game, Khyn Ivanchukov, who replaced an injured Mooch for the game, hit a laser from 40 yards out for what proved to be the winning goal. The victory assured us of home field for the first round of the NCAA tournament.

Our next regular-season game was at home against the UConn Huskies, ranked fourth nationally. We'd quickly developed a rivalry with and real dislike for UConn. I was sure the feeling was mutual.

Friday brought a huge snowstorm that buried Elmore Field and forced the postponement of our Saturday game. Although the snow would be shoveled off the field on Saturday, Athletic Director Dr. Roy Chipman, looking to preserve Elmore Field for our NCAA tournament games, switched the match to Storrs, Connecticut, for Sunday afternoon.

We made the bus ride to Storrs minus Mooch, Ron Hardy, Jeff Tipping and Stevie Long. That was three-quarters of our starting defenders and our top winger.

Arriving at the UConn field an hour before kickoff, we found it already packed with thousands of fans, one more unruly than the next, hurling insults our way as we entered the field.

Our matchup with UConn could be repeated several weeks later, if we won the New York State region and UConn won the New England region in the NCAA Tournament. The New York State winner would host the regional game, putting us back at our favorite place to play, Elmore Field.

The best way to silence the thousands of UConn fans was to score an early goal—and we did. Five minutes into the game, Tommy Maresca found the feet of Esteban Reynoso inside the penalty box and Esteban beat the UConn keeper to give us a 1-0 lead.

Instantly it sounded more like we were at an empty cemetery than at a tension-filled soccer game. After the goal, the intensity of the game picked up dramatically with lots of fouls and players from both sides doing a lot of trash talking.

The game was fairly even when, at the 30-minute mark, Tommy Nevers was played through and had a breakaway. Keith Van Eron bolted from his goal line, cut down the angle and easily made the save.

It seemed like a lot of the first half Paul Hunter, who I thought usually played in the central defense for UConn, was matching up with me. I was not sure if that was a tactical move or just a coincidence. Late in the first half, I was dribbling the ball in the midfield and as Paul Hunter approached me, I lost my balance. As I stumbled to the ground with the ball rolling in front of me, he wildly kicked the ball, with the follow through of his foot flying inches from my face.

My history with the Hunter brothers began with older brother Timmy, who I believe did not like my kicking him when he was a senior All-American candidate and I was an unknown, small-in-stature freshman.

The half ended 1-0. Forty-five minutes to go and we could end the regular season undefeated.

Lennox's halftime speech had more to do with us keeping our composure and not letting the constant fouling disrupt our concentration and rhythm of play. UConn, for all of its very good players, still played very methodically and often lacked the creativity of an individual to break down a defense and create dangerous scoring opportunities.

UConn controlled long portions of the game in the second half. But the end result often was some long-range shooting, which wouldn't beat Keith Van Eron. The game produced numerous yellow cards. Late in the game, an altercation between Tommy Maresca and Lou Magno from UConn resulted in red cards for both players.

UConn outshot us 16-6 in the second half and 25-13 overall, but we never really felt threatened. The game ended 1-0 for us, and the animosity we had for each other was magnified.

Going into the UConn game, we were ranked tied for second nationally with Indiana University, trailing only top-ranked Clemson University—which we had beaten in the spring to win the Mr. Pibb Tournament.

The bus ride back to Oneonta was very relaxing and although we felt a sense of accomplishment in going undefeated for the regular season, the real goal was to win the Division I national championship. Anything less and we wouldn't reach our goal.

Many knowledgeable soccer fans thought that if Hartwick was going to win a national championship in the near future, this was the year because we had Mooch and a great goalkeeper in Keith Van Eron. I agreed 100 percent that Mooch was irreplaceable. But we had a lot of very talented sophomores and juniors on this team, which should make us very competitive the next year in our quest to win the national championship.

20

The Path is Set

The pairings were announced for New York State, with Hartwick getting the No. 1 seed, Adelphi University No. 2, St. Francis No. 3 and Cornell University No. 4. We would host Cornell next Tuesday, giving us a week to get rested and healthy for the tournament. Mooch, Ron Hardy and Stevie Long, who all missed the UConn game, should be back and ready for our first tournament game.

We had a very good week of training and over the weekend received good news: St. Francis upset Adelphi 2-0 in their first-round match. We appeared to match up much better with St. Francis than Adelphi, although St. Francis had some very talented players and a brilliant goalkeeper in Dragan Radovich.

We knew the Cornell game would be a physical affair and we still had that bad taste in our mouths from when they eliminated us from the tournament last year. Cornell was led on defense by its All-American candidate, goalkeeper Dan Mackesey, and their big central defender Paul Beuttenmuller.

The Cornell attack was spearheaded by leading goal scorer Sid Nolan, who I considered as good a goal scorer as anyone in the country, and the tricky Rick Derella.

Although the long time between the last regular-season game and our first NCAA Tournament game was good because our injured players got healthy, I could not wait to play the game. I counted the days until kickoff that Tuesday afternoon. It seemed like the last few days took forever.

Finally, you could sense the excitement and confidence in our locker room as Lennox and Alden gave us our pregame tactical talk. Considering the time of year, Elmore Field was in fair condition, but appeared a bit wet and soggy in the middle of the field. In our last game against Cornell, we allowed them to disrupt our rhythm of play for long periods of time with physical play. It was my responsibility to make sure that didn't happen in this game.

The sound of the opening whistle was music to my ears. We took control of the game from the beginning and did a great job of keeping possession and getting into the attacking third. In the last third, we had difficulty creating any clear-cut chances and although we dominated in time of possession, we had nothing to show for it.

Late in the first half, Rick Derella controlled an errant clearance from our defense out wide left in the 18-yard box, beat a defender and found himself with only Keith between him and the goal. Derella's shot was hard and low, heading for the near post and out of Keith's reach when Van Eron used every ounce of his God-given athletic ability to fly through the air and get a fingertip on the ball, pushing it out for a corner kick. It was a brilliant save by Keith. We all had a huge sigh of relief because we knew if Cornell took the lead, it would pack it in defensively for the remainder of the game and make it very difficult for us.

Coming out for the second half, we found an increased urgency in our attack. With Cornell focusing on denying me many touches of the ball, Mooch and I made a tactical adjustment. When we had possession of the ball, Mooch would make runs into the attack from his sweeper position and if Sid Nolan followed him, we would take the best goal scorer for Cornell 70 yards away from his goal and eliminate its most dangerous player.

I dropped back into Mooch's sweeper position and Cornell seemed confused about what to do. The tactic paid off early in the second half when after a possession with many consecutive passes, Mooch found himself with only the goalkeeper to beat. He calmly knocked the ball under the diving Mackesey for the very important first goal of the game.

The goal forced Cornell to abandon its defensive tactics. As the half went on, we dominated possession of the ball despite the center of the field becoming muddy and more difficult to play balls on the ground to feet. Although we had numerous opportunities, we could not score the elusive second goal.

Our defense was outstanding, with Keith Van Eron having to make only four saves. When the final whistle blew, we were one step closer to our goal. In the locker room after the game, we did not think about celebrating. Instead, we wanted to prepare to play St. Francis that Saturday.

Oneonta's temperature dropped dramatically late in the week. By Saturday, Elmore Field was coated with snow and the field was bone-hard frozen as we warmed up for St. Francis.

Ten minutes into the game, we could see St. Francis was going to do whatever was necessary to take Stevie Long out of the game. The Terriers' left back, Errol Sebro, repeatedly hit Steve Long with bone-crunching tackles, some fair and some called fouls. Stevie had to deal with this for the entire game.

We were all over St. Francis on attack, looking for the important first goal. But midway through the half, St. Francis caught us on a counterattack, with Clyde O'Garro beating Keith with a shot. It appeared St. Francis would go up 1-0, but I managed to clear the ball off the goal line. The remainder of the half, we peppered St. Francis goalkeeper Dragan Radovich, who came up with one great save after another. The half ended 0-0.

We scored two quick goals to start the second half, but Stevie continued to endure a physical beating from the St. Francis defenders. In my soccer career, I had never seen a player receive such harsh treatment from an opposing team. Ironically, in the waning minutes, Stevie scored to give us a 3-0 victory and a rematch with UConn for the right to go to the Final Four in Philadelphia.

There was a lot of drama involving UConn and Hartwick officials trying to make an agreement about which day we would play the quarter-final match. We wanted to play on the Wednesday before Thanksgiving and UConn pushed for a weekend game, hoping that Oneonta would get more snow and the game would have to be moved to Storrs, Connecticut.

The animosity we had for UConn was immense and grew by the minute. We ended UConn's dreams of getting to the Final Four two years before when they were by far the more talented team, and I was confident we would end their dreams again. The only loss for UConn, 18-1-2, was to Hartwick several weeks earlier.

The NCAA committee, led by regional directors Tim Schum of Binghamton State and Irv Schmid of Springfield, finally decided we would play our NCAA match on Thanksgiving.

The bad blood between the two programs did not appear to be limited to the players. In the pregame meeting between UConn officials, the New England reporters, Hartwick officials and the NCAA-appointed game chairman Tim Schum, the New Englanders' complaints about the field conditions became so unbearable, Jimmy Lennox eventually walked out of the meeting.

Ironically, the field conditions at this time were significantly better than they had been for the Cornell and St. Francis games, and those schools didn't complain about them. Perhaps UConn already was preparing its excuse in case it lost to us.

In the locker room, Tommy Maresca had the look of a caged animal waiting to get out. In our previous game, he and a UConn player received red cards, and he was dying for this game to start.

Considering it was Thanksgiving Day, we had a really nice crowd when we ran out onto Elmore Field. The temperature in Oneonta had risen a bit and the field was a bit slippery during our warmup.

Although we knew UConn as well as any team we played, we played tentatively the first few minutes of the game, and we just wanted to get everyone on the team some touches while we kept possession.

Neither team created any good chances at the start. We were awarded a corner kick at the seven-minute mark. Angrik, who had had a great season for us and did not get the credit for what a talented player he was, ran over to take the corner kick.

Elmore Field didn't have a lot of width to it. Angrik typically drove his corner kicks hard and low, with the ball usually surprising opponents with how quickly it arrived in the middle of the 18-yard box.

I lined up at the back corner of the six-yard box and Paul Hunter came over to mark me, shoving me out of the way so he could be positioned better to cover me. Most of my teammates were all at the back post, leaving lots of open space at the near post.

As Angrik approached the ball, I took one step back and sprinted past Hunter towards the corner of the six-yard box at the near post. Angrik hit a laser that could not have been more than three feet off the ground. As I approached the edge of the six-yard box, I dove head-first towards the ball, elevated several feet off the ground, and struck the ball perfectly, with the ball exploding off of my forehead and heading straight for the far post. I followed the ball, hitting the back corner of the net while I was trying to cushion my fall.

Talented UConn keeper Bob Ross watched helplessly as the ball bulged the back of the net. If I received that exact same pass 100 times, I don't think I could have executed that diving header more perfectly than I did just then.

Ten minutes later, we were awarded a free kick. Mooch served the ball into the box perfectly. Artie rose above the crowd of UConn defenders and emphatically headed the ball past Bob Ross to give us a 2-0 lead less than 20 minutes into the game. The second goal seemed to demoralize UConn, and it could not muster any good chances the remainder of the first half.

At halftime we were excited but Lennox made us focus on finishing the job, staying tight in the back and not allowing UConn to get a goal and feel they were back in the game. Alden emphasized for us to keep our composure if the game started to get nasty. We were one half away from getting back to the Final Four.

We created several good opportunities that we couldn't finish in the second half. UConn grew frustrated about the game getting away from them, resulting in numerous fouls committed against us. The highlight was when Tommy Maresca had a clear breakaway with only the keeper to beat and Paul Hunter tackled him from behind.

A scuffle broke out, but the referee decided not to hand out red cards. The teams were given a total of seven yellow cards in the second half.

With less than two minutes to go, UConn, in desperation mode, had a flurry of chances. Jim Evans had the best opportunity, from 10 yards out, but shot wide to end any hope UConn had of getting back into the game. The brilliant Keith Van Eron was called on to make just two saves in the entire game.

In the locker room after the game, we were excited that we were going back to the Final Four. But getting there wasn't our goal, which was to win the national championship.

It was very satisfying to send UConn home again, denying them the opportunity to go to the Final Four. For me, it was the last time I would play against the Hunter brothers at the collegiate level.

Although I do not care for them, they both, in their own way, were instrumental in some of the highlights of my Hartwick career. I had the utmost respect for them as soccer players and competitors.

It's funny that in soccer, or any sport, you can really dislike someone you play against but still have the utmost respect for them as players and competitors. That is how I felt about the Hunter brothers and my experiences against them have made me a better player.

21

The Light Bulb Went Off

Several days after our victory over UConn, my roommates and I were watching Soccer Made in Germany. After several bone-crunching tackles early in the highlights, it was like a light bulb went off in my brain.

The tackle in our Cornell game that left stud marks on my knee had put me on a mission to figure out the best way to avoid tackles and reduce the chances of getting seriously injured, whether through a fair tackle and/or a nasty foul.

I realized the only reason that I had not blown out my knee against the over-the-ball tackle in the Cornell game was because my planted foot slipped back because of the field conditions. If the field was dry and my planted foot stayed firm, I would have suffered a serious knee injury.

I also realized that if a millisecond before I was going to be tackled, I could lift my planted foot a couple inches off of the ground, it would produce the same result as my foot sliding back and absorbing the contact. It made perfect sense to me. Whichever foot I used to control the ball dribbling usually would be off the ground, and it was almost always the planted foot and leg that suffered the injury.

While the highlights of Soccer Made in Germany continued, Mooch, Joey, Artie and Tommy were in full conversation with comments about the game. I was totally absorbed by my discovery.

To take it further, I thought if an opposing player came at me with a straight leg at the last second, and I knew I couldn't get out of the way in time or did not see it early enough to jump over the tackle, I should not only lift my planted foot off the ground but also throw it back, which would greatly reduce the impact on contact.

I knew there never would be a solution for a player that wants to maliciously foul you from behind. But if I could reduce the chances of getting hurt from tackles coming from the side or directly in front of me, that would be very important.

The timing of lifting the planted foot off the ground was so essential and subtle, similar to the Beckenbauer Trap that Ping Pong and I worked on relentlessly.

Vision and awareness are so vital in the game of soccer. Being 100 percent aware of where the opposing defenders were around me could greatly reduce the opportunities they'd have to hurt me and try to put me out of the game.

As the season progressed, I had received more recognition as being an important part of the team, and noticed considerably more opposing players trying to intimidate me and injure me if possible. I realized that comes with the territory.

I hoped they would show a replay of that week's Soccer Made In Germany because once the light bulb went off, I was totally absorbed in the realization of what I needed to do to avoid nasty tackles and missed part of the show. That was a great week. The next week, hopefully, would see my dream realized.

22

The Final Four

The pairings were set for Saturday with Hartwick playing Indiana University in the first game at noon followed by San Francisco University against Clemson University. The battle for third place would be Sunday at noon, with the championship game scheduled to start at 2:30 p.m. at Franklin Field, on the campus of the University of Pennsylvania.

The only negative was the fact that Franklin Field was an AstroTurf field, very narrow and extremely crowned. Our team disliked the playing surface very much. I didn't feel remotely as comfortable with the ball on AstroTurf as I did on natural grass. The ball runs so much quicker on AstroTurf. That makes it much more difficult to play through balls splitting the defense without the ball either moving too fast and going over the end line, or the keeper being able to come out and collect the ball before our attacking player could get to it.

With the severe crowning of the field, playing diagonal passes out wide must always be right to feet or the ball will run over the touchline before it can be received. This surface gave Indiana a huge advantage. Its team was built around its AstroTurf stadium. Indiana is big, fast and athletic, and led by the very talented front player, Argentinian-born Angelo DiBernardo, and a very technical midfielder in Charlie Fajkus.

We had a really good week of training and the fact that my parents and Ping Pong would be at the game on Saturday made it even more special for me.

Saturday as we lined up to start, I had a really good feeling about the game. We were very confident and focused. We knew the outcome probably would be decided by which team could dictate the pace of the game. Indiana was expected to put lots of pressure on us and hoped to make the pace of the game very fast.

We would attempt to do the opposite: keep possession of the ball for long periods of time and get it out wide to our wingers to isolate them one on one against the Indiana defenders.

The game started very sloppy with lots of hard tackles, and neither team had much success in developing scoring chances. The first half seemed to be one long feeling-out period and neither team produced much excitement. We limited Indiana to three shots on goal in the first half, but we were not much more effective in creating chances for ourselves.

The game seemed to open up significantly from the beginning of the second half. First, Tommy Maresca hammered a shot past Indiana goalkeeper Cary Feld, with the ball just sailing past the crossbar. Minutes later Artie struck a direct free kick that had goal written all over it when Cary Feld dove to his right, stretched his body as far as possible, and pushed the ball wide and out of danger.

Moments later Angelo DiBernardo, who had been hampered by a double groin injury and spent the first half sitting on the bench wrapped in a blanket, turned on the magic, beating two Hartwick defenders, then calmly waiting for Keith Van Eron to come off his line to cut down the angle. DiBernardo coolly shot the ball into the right corner of the net to give Indiana a 1-0 lead.

The pro-Hartwick crowd almost immediately started chanting "Let's Go Wick," "Let's Go Wick." With Mooch telling everyone to "just settle down," we started to play with newfound urgency. Several minutes later, Stevie Long beat his defender and served a perfect cross into the box. Joey Ryan directed his header past the Indiana goalkeeper to tie the game at 1-1.

The momentum swung back our way when a minute later a Rick Spray pass found Angelo DiBernardo in the box. Angelo created a little space for himself before shooting toward the goal. Keith Van Eron dove, looking to make the fairly easy save, when the topspin of the ball and/or possibly a seam in the AstroTurf caused the ball to bounce inexplicably high over his outstretched arms and into the goal.

Indiana was jubilant and we were in shock. It was eerily similar to last year when Steve Jameson slipped on the AstroTurf against Cornell and the ball slowly rolled into the goal for the winning score in the game that eliminated us from the NCAA tournament.

Our shock lasted only a few seconds and by the time we restarted the game, we had fire in our eyes. We started pushing numbers forward into the attack. Every opportunity Mooch had to come forward, he joined in the attack.

The pressure was building on the Indiana defense when at the 18-minute mark, Indiana keeper Feld came out for a crossed ball in a very crowded penalty box, misjudging his jump for the cross with the ball deflecting towards the empty goal. I watched the ball about to cross over the goal line, getting ready to explode with joy, when out of this packed six-yard box Indiana defender George Perry reached up and punched the ball away.

The referee was standing right at the near post but must have been obstructed, thus there was no whistle signaling a penalty kick. Our pleas to the referee went in vain.

We now threw everybody into the attack, desperately trying to get the equalizer, one wave after another against a very organized and compact Indiana defense. Finally, we heard the referee's whistle that ended the game.

It was devastating to me. I just went over to the bench, buried my head in my hands and stared at the ground, feeling dazed. I truly felt we were going to win the national championship that year. My freshman year when we lost, I was very upset, but I also knew we were not the most talented team. But this team was special and in Mooch, we had the most outstanding player in the country.

When we finally got back to the locker room, just like my freshman year at Busch Stadium, I just sat there with my eyes filling up with tears, speechless and numb. I didn't hear one word that Lennox and Alden said to the team. I was in disbelief that we lost.

After leaving the locker room, I met up with my parents and Ping Pong. It was always a great feeling to see my parents, especially after being away at school for extended periods of time.

If I was really upset like I was after the game, I tried to hide my feelings from my parents so I didn't upset them. But I could see in Ping Pong's eyes that he felt the pain I was going through. Six months earlier, we both felt the agony of defeat, losing to the Milwaukee Bavarians in the Amateur Cup final and now we had lost the opportunity to play Sunday for the national championship.

After a quick lunch, we made it into the stands to watch the San Francisco vs Clemson match. I couldn't have cared less about which team we play Sunday. All I could think about was the fact that the window of opportunity to win a national championship at Hartwick was closing quickly. I had one year left to reach that goal, and many of the so-called soccer experts believed if Hartwick ever was going to win a national championship, this would have been the year.

After Sunday, we would lose Mooch, Keith Van Eron, Ron Hardy, Howie Charbonneau and Timmy Kevill to graduation. That was a huge loss in talent to make up for, let alone the unbelievable leadership skills Mooch displayed daily.

In an even match, San Francisco edged Clemson 1-0 to set up the Sunday matches. We would have our first rematch with Clemson since we beat them in the Mr. Pibb Tournament. I am sure Clemson was as devastated as us that they wouldn't be playing in the championship game.

In the locker room prior to the Clemson game, we decided we wanted to show our wonderful fans that although we lost Saturday, we still were the best team in the country.

That would be the last time, at the amateur level, that I would play with Mooch as my teammate. The thought gave me a boost of energy and I needed to redeem myself for an average performance against Indiana.

The whistle blew, but both teams just went through the motions at first before the game opened up. It did not take long to realize that

Clemson wanted to win badly, based on several hard fouls it committed several minutes into the game.

Every challenge and tackle from both sides came with 100 percent effort.

Although there were numerous highlights from the match, there was one particular play I will never forget. A ball popped up in the air equally in distance from Tommy Maresca and a Clemson defender. Both players sprinted towards the ball, then jumped in the air, challenging for the header. Tommy got to the ball first and a millisecond later, there was a violent clash of faces. Tommy went down as if George Foreman had hit him with his best punch. By the time our trainer George Mitchell got to Tommy, the surrounding area of Tommy's eye was the size of a softball. Tommy most likely would have been better off if he sustained a cut above his eye because the swelling was unlike anything I had ever seen.

This incident brought the game to an even higher level of intensity. By the time the game ended with us winning 4-3, Clemson had committed 39 fouls. So much for a meaningless game with two teams going through the motions.

The championship game was a very tight defensive game. San Francisco was not about to make the same mistake we made, which was to allow Angelo DiBernardo too much time and space with the ball. With John Brooks shadowing DiBernardo all over the field, San Francisco shut down the Indiana attack, winning 1-0 for its second consecutive national championship under the coaching of Steve Negoesco.

Long bus rides on Bluebird back to Oneonta often had me reflecting and soul searching. Our trip back after watching the championship game was no different.

The victory over a very talented Clemson team temporarily lifted my depressed state. But I couldn't escape the thought that if I had played better against Indiana, it may have gotten us to the championship game. The more I thought about it, the more it bothered me. Yes, playing on a narrow, extremely crowned AstroTurf field against a very athletic and tight-marking Indiana team was very challenging. But there was no excuse for my subpar performance.

I realized I was not good enough to help lead us to a national championship and hopefully become a professional player.

Over the winter months I would have to do more secret training than ever. Then in the summer, with Ping Pong's help, take our daily training sessions to a higher level than ever before.

Graduation would hit our team hard, but we also had many talented players returning. Goalkeeping was the one area we would definitely need help. With Keith graduating, we'd lose a superb, athletic goalkeeper. It seemed as far back as anyone can remember, Hartwick always has had a great goalkeeper.

That would be Lennox's first full year to recruit, so hopefully he would be as great a recruiter as he was a tactician and technical trainer.

As Bluebird finally pulled up to the Binder Physical Education building, the realization that I had several more weeks of school and quite a lot of schoolwork to make up from that weekend became a reality.

Mooch and Keith were headed to Orlando for the Senior Bowl. That Wednesday, we received great news from Florida that Mooch was selected the 1976 Hermann Award winner and also won the *Soccer Monthly Magazine* Player of the Year Award. Both awards were given annually to the top collegiate soccer player in North America.

Mooch was my very good friend, my roommate, my teammate and at times a mentor to me. I was ecstatic for him. Although he was blessed with unbelievable athletic ability with his speed and strength, it was his technical ability from years of relentless training and his extraordinary will to win that I believe set him apart from the other players in the country.

I thought his only real competition for either award would come from Dale Russell, who was also a special player. The New York All-State team and All-American team selections followed, with Mooch chosen for the first team of each category.

No other Hartwick player was selected to even the New York State team. And although I was a much improved player from my sophomore year when I was selected to the second team, it did not bother me at all.

What was really bothering me, and I can't shake it, was our loss to Indiana and the fact that I had a very average game. I felt like I let the team down and it affected my concentrating on my schoolwork.

The last two weeks of our December classes were a grind. Every day, I fought to stay focused and understand the material I was reading and the lectures I heard.

The only time I felt a reprieve was when I was in the racquetball courts and doing secret training. That was the only time I felt good because it was my way of making sure I never let down the Hartwick team again. It was my way of getting through the pain of the Indiana loss.

I met with Lennox the last day of classes. We discussed the team's season. Jimmy felt that I had played really well all year. Then he brought up the Final Four games.

"Greek, you know that there were a lot of professional scouts and coaches from the NASL at the games."

I replied, "Yes. I figured that would be the case."

"Greek, a lot of these coaches like you as a player but they have a real concern that you are too small to play at the professional level." There was a pause and then Jimmy finished with, "You are going to have to raise your game to another level to remove all doubts they may have about your size."

I said, "Jimmy, this is not the first time I will have to prove to a coach or coaches that they are wrong about me. I'm not sure if you're aware that Timo was reluctant to even let me try out for the varsity and I proved him wrong. I am sure I can prove other coaches wrong.

"I came to Hartwick College to win a national championship and to also hopefully become a professional soccer player. They are my goals and I am still 100 percent focused on achieving those goals." I smiled at Lennox and then told him, "Jimmy, get us a great goalkeeper and I am confident we can reach my first goal."

Lennox looked at me and replied, "I agree with you."

"Thanks, Jimmy. Have a nice holiday and wish Denny a Merry Christmas."

Finally getting home for Christmas break was a godsend. Lennox's comments about what NASL coaches said about me just made me more determined than ever to reach my goals and prove to more coaches that they were wrong about me.

Excluding Christmas Day, I went out on my own and trained every day. Depending on the weather conditions, I either would ride my bike to Nottingham and train, using the wall for hours on end, or I would walk two blocks from my house to Wetzel Field and train on the left field grass of the baseball field. Training for hours every day with the soccer ball at my feet was very therapeutic for me and I started to feel much better.

At the end of Christmas break I made myself a promise that from then until preseason late August, I would train a minimum of at least once a day so hopefully I never ever taste defeat again playing for Hartwick.

Myself, Tommy Maresca and Joey Ryan at Hancock Airport in Syracuse, getting ready to board the plane for the Final Four in 1977.

Ed Clough

Getting congratulated by my teammates after lifting the ball over the oncoming Brown University goalkeeper to put us up 2-1 in the national semifinals.

Ed Clough

Leading the team out of the tunnel onto the field at Memorial Stadium,
Berkeley, California for the 1977 national championship game. When
I stepped on to the field, I got goose bumps and chills throughout my body.
I had been waiting four years to play in this game.

Ed Clough

National championship game. Ping Pong always stressed you have to see
everything on the field to make the correct decision on the ball.

Ed Clough

A University of San Francisco player in hot pursuit of me.
Once again, I'm surveying my options on the ball.

Ed Clough

Attacking the University of San Francisco defense.

Ed Clough

Jumping for joy after Stevie Long's goal put us up 2-0 in the final.

Ed Clough

A surreal moment and finally a smile, minutes after the referee blew his whistle to end the game and we were national champions.

In the locker room with my mentor Charles "Ping Pong" Farrauto, who flew out to California to watch us win the national championship.

Ed Clough

We have the most amazing fans. Binder Gymnasium filled to the
rafters during a snow blizzard, waiting for the team to enter,
after we arrived back from California.

Ed Clough

**Hartwick College 1977 national champions.
Our final regular-season home game on Elmore Field.**

23

Dodging Death

Back at school for the winter semester, I had two classes that I really liked. Human Growth and Development was a psychology course that I really enjoyed and thought the class would be helpful with whatever I decided to do after soccer, whether coaching or in the daily rituals of life.

Dostoevsky in Translation was the other course I really took a liking to during these frigid months in Oneonta. I put a lot of time into my schoolwork.

Pretty much whatever other time I had free from classes and studying was spent up in Binder Physical Education Building, training with teammates when the gymnasium was available, practicing with the team two nights a week for indoor tournaments and tons of secret training in the racquetball courts. I was obsessed with training and tried to spend a minimum of two hours every day alone in the racquetball courts, besides training with my teammates.

As soon as the weather broke, we would get outside and prepare to defend our Mr. Pibb title in Dallas. With Trenton Extension SC, we hoped to get to the National Amateur Cup Final again and have a different result. None of our soon-to-graduate seniors should be in Dallas with us, so it would be a good measure of how good we would be next year. Most of the nation's top teams again were going to Dallas for the second annual Mr. Pibb Tournament.

Most evenings after I was done studying, I hung out with Tommy Maresca and Joey Ryan. Joey had an unbelievable stereo system and we typically hung out in his room with the volume cranked up, listening to Bruce Springsteen. Bruce was our favorite musician and we always listened to our fellow Jersey guy before every home game to get psyched for our game. Joey also loved the Rolling Stones, so we also got a fair amount of Mick and the boys. But we identified with Bruce and were so proud that we were from New Jersey.

Tommy could be very laid back at times, but also had bursts of energy and we often referred to him as "The Little Monster." It had been over two months since the Clemson game and Tommy still had some swelling around his eye.

That midweek night we were a little antsy and decided to go downtown. While Joey and Tommy had some beers at the bar, I was being my competitive self and playing foosball. I was a fair player and should have had an advantage because I rarely drank and most of my opponents drank heavily. It appeared some of the competition actually played better when they were drunk. Win or lose, I enjoyed playing foosball with and against my classmates.

Depew Street was only five blocks from downtown and depending on the time of the year, we used different modes of transportation. In the spring or early fall when the weather was nice, we often took the train downtown and walked back home later.

I was referring to the freight trains that passed behind the back of the house on Depew Street. On nice weather days, we often waited for the freight train. It often slowed as it went past our house, giving us time to jump on, hold on for several blocks and then jump off at the appropriate time.

We walked up the steps and walked over the bridge above the tracks. We were at the edge of downtown. We enjoyed it and often when we had friends over who had never ridden the train, they always were excited to ride the train downtown.

We explained the basics of jumping onto the train, but told them that when we were going to jump off the train, they must roll to cushion their fall. The speed of the train was such that those that are fairly athletic could jump off and land on their feet like a gymnast landing from a vault.

It usually was funny to watch our unknowing friends jump off of the train and roll for three or four seconds, thinking that was necessary to cushion their landing, just like we had seen on television numerous times. It was very humorous to see their facial expressions, especially when we followed them and just jumped off, landing on our feet.

If the weather was extremely cold, we usually drove downtown. This particular night, we drove downtown in Tommy's Honda Civic. When Tommy graduated from high school, his parents decided they were going to move to Florida. They purchased a new Honda Civic for Tommy to have at college so he would be able to get back and forth from Oneonta to New Jersey.

The car ride back from downtown to Depew Street entailed going over the Main Street Bridge to the light at the corner of Main and River Street, turning right onto River Street, going approximately 75 feet, making another quick right, driving another 75 feet, turning left onto Depew Street and driving past three houses to the end of the block. Our house was the last house on the right side of the street.

It was a two-minute ride, even if we got a red light at Main and River Street.

Well, this particular frigid night, snow fell as we drove over the bridge approaching River Street. The light turned yellow and Tommy floored it to beat the red light. But it changed color quicker than usual and at the last second, Tommy made a quick right turn into the gas station, then turned again abruptly, planning to drive between the two gas station islands and come out onto the River Street exit.

But the car started to slide and headed toward the gas pumps. In a millisecond, my heart started racing as I envisioned us instantly going up in flames. When we were just a few feet from the pumps, the car hit the raised island on which the pumps sit and the car flipped onto its side, changing direction and sliding for what seemed like an eternity past the other set of pumps.

When the car finally stopped, we all were momentarily in shock. Then our adrenaline kicked in. We rolled the windows down on the side of the car that was on top and began to climb out. We all looked at the car in amazement, stunned that we were not killed. Almost in unison, we all said, "We have to flip the car back over."

All three of us got on the same side of the car and lifted with every ounce of energy we had. We managed to lift it high enough that the car's weight brought it back into an upright position.

We were terrified, to say the least. Tommy got back into the car and tried to start it, but it wouldn't start. Tommy put the car in neutral, and with him steering and pushing from the side, Joey and I got behind the car, which we pushed back to Depew Street and parked in the backyard. The side of the car that hit the ground was totally crushed inward.

We went into Joey's room and sat down. Our hearts were pounding a mile a minute. It was as if we faced death and God decided to spare us. We were up the remainder of the night, thinking how lucky we were that we were not killed.

The worst part of it all is that I think Tommy forgot to renew the car insurance, which was in place from his freshman year, and he surely didn't want to tell his parents he may have totaled his car without any insurance.

That incident remained with Joey, Tommy and I for the rest of the week. Every night at dinner, the accident was all we could talk about, but also, how life could be so fleeting. The Honda Civic's small size probably was the reason we did not hit the gas pumps. A larger car most likely would have hit the island and continued into the pumps.

I always say prayers every night before I go to bed, with a standard sequence of what I pray to God for. But after the car incident, I added thanking him so much for saving us. Tommy decided that at least for the time being, he was not going to mention anything at all about the accident to his parents.

24

High Spring Hopes Lost

After the tremendous success we had with the Mr. Pibb Tournament the last spring, followed by the New Jersey State Cup final and Amateur Cup Final, I couldn't wait to get outside and start training. I loved training in the racquetball courts. But by early March and after getting through the Oneonta winters, I craved to get on grass with a soccer ball at my feet.

The Amateur Cup draw had us opening up against the Princeton SC. Compared to last year's opening-round game against the Trenton Italians, we expected an easy match and to advance to the next round.

Trenton Extension lost several players from last year's team, none more important than Mooch, who was selected first in the NASL draft by the Dallas Tornadoes and had reported to Dallas for preseason training.

We added Joey Ryan to our roster to greatly strengthen our midfield. The Princeton game was on a Sunday, so Joey, Artie and I drove to Trenton on Saturday.

Ten minutes into the game, two things stood out. One was that we were much more talented than Princeton SC. Second, Princeton had an outstanding left-footed player who was very dangerous with the ball.

We controlled the ball for long periods of time throughout the first half, but had nothing to show for it. Princeton SC started to gain confidence. The first half ended 0-0, not a big concern to us. We had been in numerous close games and knew it was only a matter of time before we scored.

Early in the second half, Princeton SC's talented left-footed player turned on the magic, and beat several of our defenders before hitting a rocket from 25 yards out into the upper corner, leaving Joey Hankins little opportunity to make the save.

We instantly turned up the intensity, pushing players forward and looking for the equalizer. With a little over 10 minutes to go, Ping Pong pushed me up just behind Artie; we were desperate to score. The Princeton SC goalkeeper made one outstanding save after another. We were in disbelief when the referee blew his whistle to end the game.

Just like that, we were out of the Amateur Cup. It was an unbelievable shock to us and the last thing we expected.

It took me a week to get over being out of the Amateur Cup. Then I focused all of my attention on Hartwick winning another Mr. Pibb championship.

The Mr. Pibb format was different that year. We were in a group with Indiana, Clemson and Quincy. Indiana would be our first opponent, followed by a rematch with Clemson.

Whichever team had the best record and/or best goal differential after two games would go directly to the championship game against the winner of the other group, which was comprised of Penn State, SMU, North Texas State and Simon Fraser, the NAIA champions from British Columbia, Canada.

We were fortunate that the weather was fairly mild in Oneonta and we were able to get in two good weeks of outdoor training before we flew to Dallas.

The Mr. Pibb Tournament and the game against Indiana had much more significance than just repaying the Hoosiers for beating us in the last year's NCAA semifinal match. In my first two years at Hartwick, we had almost always reached the championship game of every indoor tournament we played in, winning most of them. But in the last winter, our results were very disappointing and no one was sure why. The Mr. Pibb Tournament gave us the opportunity to get back to our winning ways.

As it was in the semifinal the year before, Indiana was led up front by the clever Angelo DiBernardo, with Charlie Fajkus directing play from his midfield position.

Indiana was a big, fast, athletic team, well-organized in the defense, with its attack feeding off winning balls early and then counterattacking.

There was no love lost as we lined up against Indiana. From the opening whistle, there were crunching tackles from both sides and neither team conceded an inch of playing space.

Man for man, we were a much more talented team than Indiana. But our superior technical ability often was difficult to display because of Indiana's tight man-to-man marking.

The play was mostly between the 18-yard boxes, with neither team creating many quality opportunities.

Things opened up a bit in the second half and Indiana scored the first goal of the game. Like our NCAA semifinal match, we tied the score only to have Indiana respond with another goal. Once again, the Hoosiers held on defensively and beat us 2-1.

The result was very disappointing and frustrating for me. Once again, I did not play well enough against Indiana. I did not have a poor game, but I did not do enough to dictate and control the game for us. Opponents often marked me tightly, which I could deal with. But this was two consecutive games against Indiana where I had not really controlled the game. I would address this with Ping Pong that summer.

This was Hartwick's first loss on a grass field since Timo inserted me into the central midfield position 1 1/2 years ago. As in our previous loss to Indiana on AstroTurf, I had to take a lot of the responsibility for our loss.

Clemson had destroyed Quincy 5-1 and by the time we lined up the next day for our match against Clemson, Indiana already had tied Quincy, eliminating us from reaching the championship game.

So now we were playing a meaningless game for us against a supremely talented Clemson team, which was motivated not only to reach the championship game, but also to get redemption for our last two victories against them.

In my first three years at Hartwick, excluding preseason games, I hadn't remembered playing in a game that didn't have significant importance for us.

It did not take more than two really hard Clemson fouls in the first few minutes of the game to get our juices flowing. Although the numerous fouls by both teams caused many stoppages in play, both sides created opportunities. Outstanding goalkeeping kept the game scoreless at the half.

At halftime, Lennox decided that he would substitute freely in the second half to get some of our younger players playing experience.

Clemson, knowing it needed at least a tie to reach the championship game, kept in its first 11, while Jimmy made numerous substitutions throughout the half. The second half was wide open, with Clemson having the better of the play and winning 3-1.

This was the first time since my freshman year that we had lost two consecutive games. Although we kind of conceded the second half, the thought that we went from Mr. Pibb champions to not winning a game was too much. We were a team with supreme confidence, which was being severely tested.

Although we knew that Mooch was irreplaceable, we still managed to win the Mr. Pibb Tournament the previous year with him sitting out the last two games because of injury. Before we even left Dallas, we heard the whispers again that if Hartwick ever was going to win a national championship, it would have been this past season with Mooch on the team.

Many of the so-called experts believed the remaining roster after that year's graduation wasn't talented enough to go far in the tournament, let alone win the NCAA championship—even if Lennox did find a special goalkeeper to replace Keith Van Eron.

To make matters worse, at the end of the school year Angrik Stepanow, one of our more talented attacking players, was ruled academically ineligible for the upcoming fall season. Then we were told Esteban Reynoso, our technically blessed Colombian player, was returning to Colombia to be with his family and would not be returning for the fall.

So besides losing the best player in the country in Mooch, one of the top goalkeepers in the country in Keith, two of our best defenders in Ron Hardy and the versatile Howie Charbonneau, and the underutilized Tim Kevill, we had lost two of our best attacking players, who combined for 25 goals and seven assists this past season.

I was sure many of our opponents, such as UConn, were licking their chops and thinking next year would be payback time for our recent victories over them.

The only positive in the last several months of the school year was the quality of the recruiting class Lennox got to commit to Hartwick that fall.

Bear in mind that on several occasions, we had heard a highly recruited player was a very special one, but they turned out to be average.

This particular recruiting class was led by goalkeeper Harold "Aly" Anderson from Liverpool, England; attacking midfielder John Young from Edinburgh, Scotland; a highly touted defender in Rudy Pena from Dallas, Texas; second-team high school All-American Gary McILroy from Steinert High; Peco Bosevski, Garfield, N.J.; Scott Brayton, Needham, Massachusetts; David Moore, Decatur, Georgia; and Robert Cuddy, a 20-goal scorer from Miami Dade North Community College. I hoped they were all as talented as we were led to believe.

25

Olympic Invite Declined

Artie and I received letters from the United States Olympic Committee, extending us an invitation to try out for the U.S. Men's Olympic soccer team. The tryouts were scheduled for the summer at Squaw Valley, California.

Invited players would have to pay for their transportation to Squaw Valley. The USOC would provide room and board for the one-week trial.

I was very excited about the invitation initially. Who wouldn't want to represent their country? But the idea that I would have to pay to try out for my own country's Olympic team didn't seem right to me.

I wrote a letter stating that to the Olympic soccer selection committee. I received a reply stating that if I was selected to the team, my travel expenses to participate in the tryout would be reimbursed.

I gave it some serious thought and discussed it thoroughly with my father. I understand the financial side as to why the committee would do this. But I couldn't get past the thought that I'd have to pay to try out for my own country's Olympic team. I declined the invitation.

I couldn't imagine that every top amateur player in the country would be paying to fly to California to try out. With Hartwick, I would get a lot of exposure in my senior year. If the Olympic committee believed I was one of the better players in the country, then eventually it would add me to the roster.

After my end-of-the-school-year discussion with Lennox, I knew that if I wanted to become a professional soccer player, I would have to prove many so-called soccer experts wrong.

26

My Last Summer to Train with Ping Pong

The only way I knew how to improve as a player was by doing what I had been doing the past four years: getting thousands of touches of the soccer ball every week.

Being able to train with Ping Pong and pick his brain on a daily basis during the summer gave me a tremendous edge over most of the collegiate players I competed against. The time since I met Ping Pong, going into my junior year in high school, had flown by. That would be the last summer for me to train with him.

We took our summer training to the next level. Ping demanded perfection, and an occasional bad trap or errant pass was unacceptable. He wanted and expected me to have total mastery over the ball.

The weather never was a consideration for how hard we trained. Whether it was 100 degrees with 98 percent humidity or 75 degrees with pouring rain and lightning all around us, our training never was disrupted. We were as focused as two individuals could be because we shared this unbelievable love for soccer.

Ping Pong was brilliant. We could spend days on end training on one aspect of the game, breaking it down into the smallest details to get whatever advantage was possible over an opponent.

There was one week in particular in midsummer that stood out for me. We wanted to focus on the chest trap, the various ways to use your chest to trap the balls, and the reasons why and when to use that particular trap.

We started with the most used and basic chest trap: slightly bending our knees, arching our back, receiving the ball in the middle of the chest and slightly popping the ball up into the air.

One variation from this most basic chest trap was to eliminate the arched back and either stand upright or point your chest downward, so you could receive the ball and get it down to your feet as quickly as possible.

I witnessed an ideal situation for this technique during the Bicentennial Cup. The Brazilians used this trap when the Italian defenders thought they were timing the chest trap. The Brazilians used two quick motions, one to push the ball downward and the second to flick it over the oncoming Italian players before they realized what was happening. This movement takes exact timing and precision, with no players more adept at this than the Brazilians.

The next chest trap we worked on relentlessly was the Manfred chest trap. It's named after Manfred Schellscheidt, who first demonstrated this technique at the Rider College Bronco Soccer Camp. When receiving a pass directly toward your chest, bend your knees and arch your back as far back as possible so you could pop the ball up directly behind you, spin and take off, collecting the ball in the direction it was headed.

Prior to seeing Manfred demonstrate this technique, if a ball was coming to my chest and I wanted to continue in the direction the ball was traveling, I would turn my trap to my side and then take another touch to push it in the direction I wanted to head into. The Manfred chest trap, although not very easy to master, saved seconds and touches in accelerating into the space you wanted to run into.

The last chest trap that Ping Pong thought I needed in my arsenal of skills was the Pelé chest trap. Pelé would trap the ball on the outer part of his chest right next to the shoulder, and the ball would just die and fall to his feet. The keys to this trap are cushioning the trap like catching an egg, and receiving the ball on the meatier part of your chest instead of in the middle of your sternum, which is boney and difficult to make the ball drop like Alabama cotton.

Every day, Ping Pong and I trained together, I spent a good 15 minutes in front of the chain link fence, with Ping Pong driving balls at me at various speeds and heights.

This was one of my favorite training exercises with Ping because it made receiving and trapping balls in the real game seem rather easy.

I had come a very long way from the first time Ping Pong introduced me to this exercise. Now, going into my senior year, I could make almost every pass he drove at me fall like Alabama cotton.

This exercise typically was followed by my having an imaginary defender on my back side. I then had to check back for passes from Ping Pong, making moving traps, followed by doing a Beckenbauer pirouette to make space for myself and get away from my imaginary defender.

We did this exercise hundreds of times each day, first doing my pirouettes with the inside of my right foot, then with the outside of my right foot.

Every technical training exercise I did with Ping Pong also involved improving my vision and awareness. Growing up, you rarely heard a coach emphasize looking around and if they said it, it never was reinforced.

Ping Pong always felt without great vision, you could never become a great player. His idea of vision and thinking ahead was not limited to being one play ahead. He felt I needed to think two to three plays ahead of time. He thought that as I kept improving as a player, it was only logical that teams would want to mark me tighter to eliminate or reduce my touches as much as possible.

Mastering the first touch of the ball and the ability to make space for myself after receiving the ball would allow me to control the game from my central midfield position.

Constantly working to improve my vision was not limited to only when we were attacking the opposing team. We had endless discussions about knowing where the opposing attacking players were when we were defending—especially those up front, so I could anticipate from my midfield position the passing lanes and cut out those passes.

It was a great summer that was coming to an end: Training all day with Ping Pong, followed by small-sided games at Nottingham after dinner, and ending the evening in my backyard under the porch light practicing my heading with the pendulum ball. I felt great and very confident going into my senior year—and so different than going into my first preseason at Hartwick.

27

Senior Year Preseason

I had only one real concern going into my final preseason at Hartwick. Would Harold "Aly" Anderson, the Liverpool goalkeeper, be as good as the scouting reports said he was? We had returning two solid backup goalkeepers in junior Mike Blundell and sophomore Mark Snell. But Hartwick traditionally had a very special goalkeeper, often considered one of the nation's best.

If Aly was as talented as they said, then I was very confident we could seriously contend for the national championship. It took only our first full-sided scrimmage to see that Aly was the real deal. He demonstrated catlike reflexes that had us in awe.

Among the huge number of talented recruits, John Young of Scotland also made an instant impression and looked like he would be a great addition to our team. John appeared to have the ability to almost effort-lessly beat players in one-on-one situations.

By the end of the first week of preseason, I made up my mind about who and where our first 11 should line up. With the loss of Angrik and Esteban up front, I thought it was a no-brainer for Lennox and Alden to start Steve Long out wide on the right, Artie as the center forward and Tommy Maresca out wide on the left.

In the midfield, Joey would be on the right side, I would be the central midfielder and John Young would be on the left.

Lennox had other ideas.

As preseason progressed, Lennox switched Joey Ryan to center forward and put Artie at right midfield. That made no sense to me because although both players could play and excel at either position, Artie was a better and more natural center forward and Joey's superb dribbling skills were more suited for the midfield. I had the utmost respect for Lennox, who I considered to be the best collegiate coach in the country, but this didn't make sense to me.

Coming into preseason, I expected his biggest decisions to be who would be playing on defense, considering the losses from graduation. Jeff, one of the top center backs in the country, if not the best, would be in his stopper role. Duncan would be at his customary right back position. But there were question marks for left back and sweeper.

Jim settled on Zeren early on in preseason for the sweeper position. Although Zeren never had played that position before that past spring, he seemed to adapt really well. With his flawless technique and high soccer IQ, I thought Zeren would be great back there for us. He wouldn't be making 60-yard runs with the ball upfield like Mooch did, but he had impeccable skill to lead the attack out of the back.

Left back seemed to be the most competitive spot on the team. Those vying for the spot included senior Charlie Kadupski, an athletic and hard-tackling defender who also could play anywhere in the middle of the defense; and Gary Vogel, who excelled at left back at the Mr. Pibb Tournament and was one of those rare players who came up from the junior varsity and eventually made it to the varsity. Gary had improved every year.

The other defenders vying for a starting position included senior Khyn Ivanchukov, a two-time high school All-American, more suited for one of the central defensive positions, and the highly recruited Rudy Pena. Rudy was a very gifted player but may have needed some time to adjust to the pace and physicality of college soccer.

As we finished up preseason, leading to the Mayor's Cup Tournament, there were two significant developments within the team. Lennox must have learned his lesson from the last year when he let the team vote for the captain, and it almost didn't turn out the way he expected and I believe hoped for. Jimmy and Alden took no chances this year. At the end of the week, Lennox announced I would be the captain for the upcoming season.

It truly was an honor for me to be selected captain. I was sure Jeff was disappointed he was not chosen, especially after the previous year when he was one vote from being elected captain. Jeff was a true leader and although I was very happy for myself, I felt bad for Jeff because I was sure he hoped to be named captain.

The second development was that it appeared that Lennox was handing the left back position to Rudy Pena. I had no doubt Pena would be a great player in college, possibly an All-American.

But Gary Vogel should have been named our starting left back. Gary excelled in preseason and had improved to the point that I thought if he got playing time and some exposure, he would be playing in the NASL the next summer.

Perhaps what really bothered me was that in my freshman year, Timo handed several players starting jobs; they did not have to earn their positions. I experienced the frustration and disappointment that Gary was going through.

There were two pieces to the puzzle that were wrong. Gary should have been our left back and Lennox needed to switch Artie and Joey. I went back and forth about whether I should say something to Lennox about the latter, but decided to let it play out. The next day, we would face a talented Davis & Elkins team, which finished the last year ranked ninth in the country.

In the opening game of the Mayor's Cup, Oneonta State destroyed Notre Dame 5-1, scoring two goals in the first two minutes.

In the nightcap, our game against Davis & Elkins was the complete opposite. It was a very physical game with numerous yellow cards, two red cards and few quality chances created by either team. Regulation time ended 0-0. We played two 7½-minute overtime periods to no avail and proceeded to the NASL-style shootout.

The play began with the ball at the shooter's feet 35 yards from goal. When the referee blew his whistle, the shooter had five seconds to get a shot off, with only the opposing goalkeeper in front of him. Five shooters were selected from each team. If the score was tied after the 10 players took their turns, it became sudden death, which was a terrible way to lose a game. Aly Anderson showed his brilliance on several saves and despite me missing my shooting attempt we won, allowing us to play our dreaded crosstown rival Oneonta State.

Although the Mayor's Cup was considered a preseason tournament, it was anything but when the players stepped on to the field. We were a bit disappointed in our performance against Davis & Elkins, but were excited about playing Oneonta State the next night in front of what would be a packed Damaschke Field. We knew the minute the referee blew his whistle to start the game, we would be in a war.

Every ball brought a stiff challenge and Oneonta State was all over us at the beginning of the game. Ronan Downs, Oneonta State's talented attacker, created many of the team's scoring chances. Aly Anderson, thankfully, was up to the challenge. Aly made one great save after another to hold off the initial onslaught.

We finally settled down and kept more possession of the ball. Oneonta State was a much fresher team, and it was important that we started to string multiple passes together, forcing our opponent to chase the ball and expend energy.

Late in the first half, Oneonta State goalkeeper Jim Harrington had a nasty collision with Artie and was taken off the field. The half ended 0-0.

As Lennox addressed the team at halftime, we were very tired. This was the end of our second full week of preseason and the Davis & Elkins game took a lot out of us. Lennox emphasized keeping possession for long periods of time eventually would lead to scoring opportunities.

The second half was very even. As time wound down, the game really opened up. First John Young had a great opportunity, hitting the post, followed by Artie hammering the rebound first time, with Oneonta State backup goalkeeper Mike Bednarz making an outstanding save. Finally Bednarz punched away a Jeff Tipping header.

Moments later, Keith Tozer broke through for Oneonta State and looked sure to put the Red Dragons up 1-0 when Aly Anderson exploded off his line, positioned himself perfectly and blocked Tozer's blast off his chest, deflecting the ball away from the goal.

Regulation ended 0-0 and we got ready to play our second consecutive overtime game. We were absolutely exhausted, none more so than Artie, who asked Lennox if he could move from his midfield position to center forward because he could not keep up the running necessary in the midfield.

The overtime began and continued right where the last 10 minutes left off, a flurry of end-to-end activity, with neither team getting that elusive goal. With less than two minutes left in overtime, a Tommy Maresca cross found John Young unmarked in the penalty box; he hammered another shot off the post. Artie reacted first to the rebound and headed in the winning goal for a 1-0 victory.

We were absolutely fatigued, having played 208 minutes of soccer in a little over 24 hours. The victory gave us our second consecutive Mayor's Cup championship trophy.

There is something so satisfying and special when you compete in a close game, and you are so tired, you feel you have nothing else to give of yourself but still manage to keep going until the final whistle.

The only reason we could keep pushing ourselves through these barriers was because at that point, winning the game was the only thing in your life that mattered.

When you win a game like that, it is such a special feeling. Later that night Joey, Tommy, Artie and I were basking in our victory over our crosstown rival.

I was so exhausted, I decided that Sunday would be a day of total rest for me, with no training in the racquetball courts. I could count on one hand how many times in three years that I didn't do my Sunday secret training.

The question of Aly Anderson being a great keeper was answered numerous times this weekend with one brilliant save after another.

The preseason polls came out. The coaches poll had us ranked fourth in the country. San Francisco No. 1, Indiana No. 2, Clemson No. 3 and Hartwick No. 4. But we were ranked No. 1 in the *Soccer Monthly Magazine* preseason poll.

28

It Officially Counts Now

We had one week to prepare for our regular-season opener at Binghamton on a Saturday. Physically, we were beaten up. But what was more concerning was that we hadn't scored a goal in over two full games and almost another 30 minutes of overtime.

Losing Angrik and Esteban appeared to be a much greater void to fill than the talented defenders we lost to graduation. Freshman Peco Bosevski appeared to be very technical and strong on the ball, and would be helpful in the attack. But I couldn't get past the fact that Lennox kept playing Artie in the midfield.

I thought after Artie's overtime goal, Lennox would keep him up front, but that was not to be. Jimmy put Artie back in the midfield and Joey up front in training.

Our many seniors had nervous energy prior to our kickoff against Binghamton, knowing that we were beginning what would be our last season at Hartwick. It showed in our play; we were sluggish in the first half.

The second half, we finally began to relax and started to play very good attacking soccer. The goal drought ended with us winning 3-0. Peco, filling in for the injured John Young, had a goal and one assist, and would add to our depth up front.

The defense was very tight, giving up only three shots in the second half. Our defense played pretty well, but Rudy struggled at times in his first start at left back while Gary Vogel sat on the bench. Steve Long sprained his ankle late in the game and would miss our home opener against Ithaca on Tuesday.

Heavy rains made Elmore Field almost unplayable. We switched our home game to be played at Ithaca.

Lennox made one of the two changes I was hoping for when he announced the starting lineup for the Ithaca game. He replaced Rudy Pena with Gary Vogel at left back. I was happy with the change because I thought it not only would make us better defensively but also much more physical in the back.

With John Young back in the lineup, Lennox went with Joey in the center forward position. Peco and Tommy flanked Joey on the wings.

The midfield was comprised of Artie, John Young and me. I still couldn't rationalize why Lennox, who I believe was a brilliant coach, did not see what I saw. It baffled me. But as long as we improved every week, there was not anything for me to say.

We breezed through the Ithaca game 3-0. Our sights then were set on our first difficult match of the regular season, with the very talented Penn State visiting on a Sunday.

Penn State returned nine starters from last year's 10-4-1 squad. The Nittany Lions were led by my very talented Trenton Extension SC teammates Matt Bahr on defense and Richie Reice on the attack.

Matt also was the kicker for Joe Paterno's football team. Saturday afternoon, Matt played against the University of Maryland in Penn State's 27-9 victory before jumping on the soccer bus for the ride to Oneonta.

I believed the key to this game was to minimize Richie Reice's touches on the ball. If Richie got time and space to run at Duncan, he would be very difficult to contain. My freshman year, Richie destroyed us and Penn State won 5-1. The last two years, we did a very good job of containing him and won.

Reice was complemented by a very dangerous goal scorer in Ken McDonald and a talented player in Jimmy Stamitis, who could both score and create goals for his teammates.

It seemed like it had rained for weeks in Oneonta and this Sunday afternoon was no different. The game started out with tentative play by both teams, with the first 20 minutes being more of a feeling-out period.

Around the 24-minute mark, we received a free kick on the edge of the box. I stood over the ball, with Artie standing slightly behind me on my right side. After the referee's whistle, I faked as if I was going to roll the ball into Artie's path, and Penn State players in the wall sprinted toward the ball. The referee lectured the Penn State players about encroaching the 10 yards and marched them back to the proper distance.

This time, I rolled the ball into Artie's path and he hit a laser that had upper corner written all over it. Penn State goalkeeper Dan Gallagher took one step to his right and then jumped through the air with his body fully extended. His fingertips barely reached the ball, but he managed to push it around the post for a corner kick. It was a brilliant save.

Moments later on the ensuing corner kick, he leaped up and caught the ball inches from Tommy Maresca's forehead. He held the ball all the way to the ground.

Minutes later, Gallagher made another outstanding save, this time on a Tipping header, followed by an even more difficult save on a header by Artie. We could have been up three or four to nothing right now, but had nothing to show for it.

Penn State created several good scoring opportunities in the last few minutes of the half, but Aly was his sure self, stopping two goal-scoring chances. The first half ended 0-0.

Three minutes into the second half, a Duncan corner kick found Jeff Tipping's head. With Gallagher moving toward his near post, Jeff directed his header to the back post. The Penn State keeper had no chance to recover and make the save. Tip's header put us up 1-0.

As the half went on, with Penn State in need of a goal, it started to push more players into the attack. The game opened up quite a bit.

Duncan had done a very good job on Richie Reice up to this point. But at around the 12-minute mark, Reice beat Duncan and a second defender, and dribbled in toward goal with no one in his path. Aly sprung off his line like a cat and managed to smother the ball at Reice's feet for a huge save.

Penn State had us on our heels and minutes later, Kenny MacDonald whistled a shot inches wide of the right post. In the waning moments, a poorly executed offside trap had Stamitis played through, with only Aly to beat, when the ball became stuck in the mud and he over-ran it.

There was some relief when the referee blew his whistle to end the game. We beat a very good Penn State team, with Aly getting another shutout.

I made my way over to Mr. Walter Bahr, who I have gotten to know from our Trenton Extension games. Matt's father was a soccer icon in this country and Mr. Bahr has always been willing to dispense his wisdom to me whenever I had questions for him.

That year for the NCAA Tournament, the New York State winner would play the Mid-Atlantic region winner instead of the New England winner. There was a high probability that the Mid-Atlantic winner would be either Penn State or Philadelphia Textile. So we could meet this team again for the right to go to the Final Four.

The last few weeks, we trained in horrible conditions. That dramatically affected the quality of our training sessions and was really starting to bother Lennox. The lower field was total mud. Neahwa Park was saturated and if we trained on Elmore, we would destroy the field for our home games.

Lennox reached out to Oneonta officials about having the opportunity to train on Damaschke Field, but they turned us down. During his post-game interview with the local press after our Penn State game, I overheard Jimmy tell reporters that the lack of quality training was affecting our play and that is why we had been inconsistent.

Jimmy started walking away, then turned back to the reporters and said angrily, "We are the fourth-ranked team in the country and we have nowhere to train. As a last resort, we have gone to Corning Glass and used their fields, but the grass is very high and it is very hilly."

Lennox in many ways is like Ping Pong. They are both soccer purists who want and expect perfection. I loved it. I would not want it any other way.

Pelé's farewell game with the Cosmos was scheduled for Saturday, Oct. 1, 1977 at Giants Stadium in New Jersey. Lennox had been trying to get our scheduled game at Brockport for that day changed to Sunday so all could go see Pelé's last game as a professional. Brockport declined to switch the date. We were all a bit disappointed.

I had been in the Cosmos locker room numerous times, thanks to a press pass supplied by George O'Gorman. But Pelé always had so many people around him, I had never wanted to bother him for a photo with me. I really regretted that. He was one of my idols and the greatest soccer player of all time.

Brockport typically had a big, unruly crowd for our games up there. Its passionate fans often threw out insults, among other things, in our direction.

The minute we stepped on the field we knew the constant rain of the past few weeks was not limited to Oneonta. The field was so wet, every step felt like we were sinking into the ground.

Despite the extremely muddy field conditions, we were in total control of the game right from the kickoff. The only problem was that we couldn't finish our chances. The half ended at 0-0.

The second half started out very much like the first, with us in total control but unable to score. Our frustration was building. Although it was obvious we were a much better team than Brockport, we couldn't get that elusive first goal.

With seven minutes remaining in a 0-0 game, I beat their offside trap and clearly was through, with only goalkeeper Chris Djernes to beat.

Chris sprinted off of his goal line and confronted me at the top of the 18-yard box. I dipped my left shoulder as if I were going to my left, then pushed the ball past him with the outside of my right foot. The Brockport goalie slipped to the ground as I calmly went around him.

I looked up at the empty goal and shot the ball wide of the net. I was in disbelief. It was an opportunity that was much easier to make than miss, and the field conditions would not be an acceptable excuse. There were none. I simply missed an empty goal. The game ended 0-0.

The tie put the first blemish on what had been an undefeated, untied season. On the bus ride back, all I could think about was how I could have missed such an easy opportunity. To make matters worse, we had missed Pelé's farewell game.

The only bright spot on the long bus ride back to Oneonta was that Bobby Smith was playing in Pelé's farewell game, which was televised around the world. Every youth soccer player out of Mercer County was unbelievably proud of Bobby. We all hoped to follow in Bobby's footsteps someday and play in the NASL.

We followed our Brockport game with a rather poor performance against Colgate University. We were down 1-0 with 15 minutes to go after Glenn Goodmon hit a rocket of a free kick into the upper right corner, beating Aly Anderson. It was the first goal Aly and our team had given up in almost seven full games.

After the goal, we all dug down deep. Tommy Maresca tied the game at the 82-minute mark and then followed that goal with the game winner with one minute remaining.

Excluding the last 15 minutes of the game, we were outplayed by a much less-talented team. I am an optimist by nature and although we performed poorly for most of the game, we turned it on when it counted the most.

Our team was extremely talented and we had two important intangibles. One, we were an unselfish group of players. We didn't care who scored the goal or who got the assist. Two, we cared only about winning. As a group, we had the will-to-win quality that all great championship teams possess.

We had lots of injuries, with none hurting the team's performance more than Stevie Long's absence. And despite the abysmal training conditions, I was very confident that we were the best team in the country. Now if Jimmy Lennox would switch Joey and Artie back to what I consider their best positions, I wouldn't expect anyone in the country to beat us.

As we prepared to host 14th-ranked Philadelphia Textile for our Homecoming weekend, it was hard not to notice the performance of our crosstown rivals. Since our victory over Oneonta State in the Mayor's Cup, the Red Dragons had been destroying their opponents. They had been led in the attack by Keith Tozer, who had been a goal-scoring machine.

The addition of several very talented freshmen to its returning squad may make Oneonta State a very difficult opponent to get past come tournament time, as it seemed to improve every week. It may have been the most talented group Oneonta State had since my freshman year.

In addition to us, Cornell, Adelphi, Oneonta State, Long Island University and St. Francis were fighting for tournament berths. That year, getting out of New York State could be more difficult than winning a quarterfinal match against the Mid-Atlantic region winner.

It would be hard to live up to the last year's epic game against Philadelphia Textile. To this day, many fans still talk about that game, held in Philadelphia, as one of the greatest college soccer games ever played in the city.

I would be hard-pressed to think of a greater individual matchup than the one the year before between Mooch and Dale Russell. Despite graduation hurting both teams, Textile still boasted three of the top players in the country: Dave MacWilliams up front, All-American Adrian Brooks in the midfield and John Nusum in the sweeper position, playing in front of a very good goalkeeper in Dave Treschek.

As we lined up for the opening kickoff, the atmosphere was electric in front of a capacity Homecoming crowd against Textile.

The game started conservatively, with very tight man-to-man marking all over the field. Neither team created a quality chance on goal until nine minutes remained in the half. Steve Long beat his defender out wide before serving a perfect cross into the path of Peco Bosevski, who first-timed the ball inches over the crossbar.

Only minutes later, Textile's Kevin Salanon was played through with only Aly to beat. Aly sprinted off his line, cut the angle and was able to dive to his left and push the ball over the goal line. The first half ended 0-0, with both defenses shutting down the opposing attacks.

At halftime, Lennox emphasized that we needed to look to counter-attack with speed whenever we won the ball, and if the opportunity to counter was not on, we needed to do a better job of keeping possession of the ball, have patience and let them chase it.

We did a much better job of dictating the tempo of the game when the second half began. We started stringing 10, 12, 15 consecutive passes, and our long periods of possession started to wear down the Textile players.

At the 17-minute mark, we were awarded a free kick at the corner of the 18-yard box. I took my customary position on the ball with Artie positioned for me to roll the ball into his path, giving him a better opportunity to strike the ball past the wall.

On the referee's whistle, I rolled the ball towards Artie. As all of the Textile players in the wall rushed toward Artie, he faked the shot and played the ball back to me. Stevie Long was standing unmarked on the six-yard box and I found his head with my cross. Stevie headed the ball past Treschek for the first goal of the game.

We continued to control the game in the second half, with Textile managing only two shots on goal. Final score: 1-0. It was our best performance that season, and against a very good opponent that we may have to play again to book a trip to Berkeley, California.

Having Stevie Long healthy and match-fit after missing several weeks would be a huge factor in reaching our goal of winning the national championship.

Lennox and Alden were very happy with our performance, especially after how we played against Colgate. In the second half we did a great job of keeping possession of the ball. The ability of our team to keep the ball for long periods of time forced the Textile players, and none more so than Adrian Brooks, to expend so much energy defensively that when they did get the ball, they were ineffective because they were so tired.

The second benefit of long periods of possession and being patient was that it enabled us to get the ball to our wingers in good positions, where Tommy and Stevie had enough space to turn and face their defenders instead of receiving balls with the defenders right on their backsides, not allowing them to turn.

29

Finally, the Right Lineup

Despite a very good performance that Saturday, we still produced only one goal. We had scored only four goals in our last four games, and our goal production had to improve significantly if we were going to be victorious for five consecutive NCAA Tournament games and hoist the trophy in California.

Lennox and Alden had to know this and in training the following Monday, Lennox finally changed the lineup. Jimmy switched Artie to the center forward position and Joey was dropped back into the midfield. To say I was thrilled would be an understatement. I had been waiting for this change since preseason.

Artie was a natural goal scorer who hadn't scored a goal since the Mayor's Cup. This change should give Artie many more goal-scoring opportunities in front of the goal, where he typically was deadly.

Dropping Joey back into the midfield allowed him many more opportunities to use his dribbling skills, running at players instead of always receiving balls up front with a defender on his backside. Perhaps even more important to the team was the fact that Joey was a fierce tackler. Through fair tackles and sometimes hard fouls, Joey often could be an intimidating and disruptive force to the opposing team.

Joey had that rare ability of not only being very skilled with the ball, but also extremely hard in the tackle. Mooch and Joey always had been my favorite teammates to play alongside.

Why did Lennox play Artie in the midfield to begin with? Rumors started to circulate within the team that in preseason, Artie approached Jimmy and told him his chances of getting drafted and playing in the NASL would improve significantly if he played in the midfield instead of as an attacking player up front.

There are very few North Americans playing up front in the NASL. Most NASL teams played their mandatory two North American citizens in the defense or the goal.

If this rumor was a fact, I respected Lennox for trying to help one of his players position himself for the professional league. But at the same time, he wasn't doing what was best for the team. He also was hurting Joey's chances to get drafted the next year into the NASL.

This rumor was the only logical reason that I could think of as to why Lennox would play Artie in the midfield that season. Last season was different because we had the luxury of Esteban and Angrik up front.

Whatever the truth was doesn't matter. I felt this was the last piece of the puzzle to put our best team on the field, and that was all that mattered to me.

The results of the adjusted lineup were apparent rather quickly. In our midweek game, we scored two first-half goals at Albany State and coasted to a 3-0 victory led by two Stevie Long goals.

On the same day, Oneonta State's first game since getting into the coaches poll top 20 rankings produced a 2-2 tie in New York against St. Francis University.

That Friday, we made the trip to Bridgeport University in what most likely would be the last time I would play against my best friend Denny Kinnevy.

The rain was so torrential, we were told the game was cancelled and we were to board the bus to make the trip back to Oneonta.

But somewhere in the next 30 minutes, the officials changed their minds and we drove to the field, arriving at a monsoonlike environment. The weather was reminiscent of our game against Brockport, with the only difference being the playing surface was not as soft as Brockport's. The first half of play was very challenging. The weather conditions made it difficult for us to string multiple passes together and probe the Bridgeport defense for openings. We managed to create several good opportunities, but to no avail. The best chances in the first half came from Bridgeport when twice our defenders slipped down and Bridgeport players got behind our defense, only to have Aly display his catlike reflexes twice to keep Bridgeport off the scoreboard. The first half ended 0-0.

In the second half, the rain subsided a bit and we took control of the game. We started to keep the ball for long periods of time, eventually leading to what could be described only as a textbook goal.

Joey beat his opponent in the midfield, played the ball out wide to Stevie Long, who beat his defender, then dribbled to the touchline before serving a perfect cross to Artie. He first-timed the ball past helpless Bridgeport goalkeeper Eric Swallow.

The one goal was all we needed to close out the game. The significance of this game was that Artie finally scored his first goal of the regular season. The thought of Artie playing up front and Stevie Long's ankle finally starting to feel better had me really excited. Barring any serious injuries, you could sense that our attack was only going to get better as the season progressed.

We had a week between games, which gave us time to get healthier. The team had Saturday off, and after I spent a late night downtown drinking a little bit of blackberry brandy with what seemed like every college student from Hartwick, the light training session Lennox had for us on Sunday was appropriate.

I rarely ever drank, but after our training session I still felt the effects of the blackberry brandy. So I headed over to the racquetball courts for some secret training and perhaps more importantly, to sweat out every-thing that was still inside me.

After a much-needed shower, I grabbed a late lunch in the cafeteria and then spent the next several hours in the library trying to get ahead on my academic studies.

On my walk home down to Depew Street, I thought how my college soccer career would be over one way or another in the next few months. It was almost hard to believe. Dec. 4 was the preferred date for me to play my last college game. That was the date for the national championship game.

Lennox decided that we would start practicing on Elmore Field despite the possibility we could really damage it for our home games. The quality of our training sessions immediately improved dramatically.

Although Lennox was set in his lineup, with few substitutes playing in most games, the reserves train as hard or harder than the first team, still fighting, hoping to get playing time. I always felt the amount of depth we had on this team in the last few years was an important contributing factor to its success.

We had high school All-Americans who couldn't get five minutes of playing time, yet every day they trained as hard as possible to take away a first teamer's job.

I never had to worry about complacency. Every day, I trained like I still had something to prove, and I hoped to improve a little bit each day.

I've often thought about how I felt when I walked to the back of the bus after we played at Montclair State in my first college soccer game, and I was the only player on the team not to get into the game. That feeling never left me and drove me every day, whether on Elmore Field for a team training session, secret training in the racquetball courts or training with Ping Pong.

There were numerous connections between the Hartwick and East Stroudsburg University soccer programs. The legendary Dr. John McKeown had led the East Stroudsburg men's soccer program for 25 years. He was the head coach when Jimmy Lennox played for East Stroudsburg. The two assistants on this year's Stroudsburg team were ex-Hartwick players, former All-American Eddy Austin and Jeff Marshall.

Stroudsburg's leading goal scorer was Dave Munson, one of Oneonta High School's greatest players ever, if not the most talented player to graduate from the local high school. On defense, Stroudsburg was led by Joe Donahue, a high school teammate of Tommy Maresca's at Bloomfield High School.

On Saturday, our Parents Weekend match against East Stroudsburg University had a special meaning for two of my teammates. Jeff Tipping's and Duncan Macdonald's parents made the trip from England to see their sons play in their last Parents Weekend game of their storied careers at Hartwick.

Jeff and Duncan were glowing with happiness that their parents were in attendance. We all wanted to put on a great performance for them.

Right from the kickoff we were all over East Stroudsburg, creating one quality chance after another. If East Stroudsburg keeper Paul Williamson wasn't making one outstanding save after another, our shots were hitting the crossbar or being cleared off the line by Stroudsburg defenders. We thoroughly dominated the first half, but walked into our locker room at halftime disappointed with the 0-0 score.

The second half began where the first half ended, a siege of attacks on the East Stroudsburg goal with nothing to show for it.

The frustration was mounting well into the second half. It was starting to feel like my freshman year when we totally controlled the game only to lose against the run of play.

Finally at the 17-minute mark, my corner kick found the head of Tommy Maresca and his header somehow skidded past the until-then-brilliant Paul Williamson into the goal.

Four minutes later, East Stroudsburg's Joe Donahue made a run up the field from his sweeper position and ended up cracking a first-time shot towards the far post. It had tying goal written all over it until Aly stretched his body well beyond the normal limits of a human being to fingertip the ball around the post for a corner kick. It was a brilliant save.

With 37 seconds to go, Joey Ryan took a long throw-in from Rudy Pena, beat two defenders, and hit a punishing low drive that found the back of the net for a 2-0 victory over our outmanned opponent.

We received great news later in the day when we found out that Adelphi University was beaten by St. Francis University 1-0. This was a damaging blow to Adelphi's hopes of getting into the tournament.

Our upcoming midweek game with Adelphi took on even more importance for Adelphi. It most likely would need a victory against us to get back into the top four of the state. A draw for us should have been sufficient to keep us at the top of the state polls.

Adelphi had given us lots of trouble in my first three years at Hartwick. Our record against them was two ties and a loss. Adelphi was always very talented and athletic, and seemed to match up very well against us and never were in awe of us, like some of our opponents.

The last two New York State teams I would want to play at tournament time were Oneonta State, because of the sheer emotion that such a rivalry brings, and Adelphi. I believed we were the best team in the country. But we preferred an easy path to the Final Four before we matched up against Clemson, followed by either San Francisco or the Midwest winner.

Clemson had been pounding teams and beat No. 1 St. Louis University 3-1 that weekend. The second-ranked Clemson Tigers surely would move to No. 1 in the national rankings.

It was a beautiful sun-drenched fall day as we lined up to start the game against a desperate Adelphi team. The importance of the game showed immediately in its play; they were all over us. Adelphi was high-pressuring us all over the field. If not for some outstanding saves by Aly Anderson, we easily could have been down 2-0 just 20 minutes into the game.

As the half went on, we started to settle down, keeping more possession of the ball. But we still had a difficult time breaking down Adelphi's defense in our attacking third of the field. We were fortunate when the referee blew his whistle for halftime that the score was the 0-0.

Lennox and Alden addressed the team at halftime and neither was the least bit happy with our play. Keeping good possession of the ball usually brought us good results. Lennox once again emphasized that we had to do a better job of counterattacking quickly when the opportunity presented itself, and when we couldn't attack with speed, keep the ball and make Adelphi chase it. That was an indirect way of Lennox telling me that I needed to get more of the ball and have more influence dictating the tempo of the game.

We came out on fire to start the second half, with Tommy Maresca drilling a rocket right at Adelphi keeper Billy Phillips. Several minutes later, Artie drilled a shot low, heading into the corner, when Phillips extended himself fully and somehow made the save. We were in total control of the game.

Midway through the second half, Joey Ryan whistled a shot inches wide of the goal post and followed that up with another shot that grazed the top of the goal post.

We were all over Adelphi and at the 21-minute mark, John Young cut out a pass and played the ball to Joey in the midfield to start a counterattack. Joey beat one defender and split the Adelphi defense with a perfect pass that put Stevie Long through with just the goalkeeper to beat. Stevie calmly drilled the ball past Billy Phillips to put us up 1-0.

Moments later, Ron Atanasio beat two defenders and Aly Anderson made a rare mistake and got caught off his line. Atanasio shot the ball towards the empty goal. Jeff Tipping sprinted back and punched the ball away inches before crossing the goal line. The referee called for a penalty kick.

Adelphi's Nimrod Dreyfuss stood over the ball like the Hulk waiting for the referee to blow his whistle. The referee finally did so and Nimrod slowly approached the ball. He hit a laser that went wide to the left of the goal. Players on both teams were stunned.

The miss re-energized us and we once again created quality chances despite some very hard fouls by Adelphi to disrupt our play.

As the game wound down, it appeared we finally were going to beat Adelphi. A harmless Adelphi cross into the box had Aly Anderson coming off his line to collect the ball. But he collided with Hartwick defender Khyn Ivanchukov, and the ball rolled right to Nimrod Dreyfuss, who casually kicked the ball into the empty net. Seconds later, the referee blew his whistle to end regulation time. Lack of communication had cost us dearly.

Overtime did not produce any real quality chances for either team and the game ended 1-1. It was an acceptable result for us, but at the same time disappointing because we let victory get away from us.

We had what should be our easiest game of the season that Saturday against Syracuse. It also would be the last regular-season home game for the seniors. The following week, we would have a huge game against Cornell that could decide the No. 1 seed for New York State and a final regular-season game at UConn. Then we would start the REAL season, the NCAA Tournament.

The day after the Adelphi game, I received a letter from Timo Liekoski and the Dallas Tornadoes. They wanted to know that if they chose me in the upcoming NASL draft, would I be willing to leave school early to be available for preseason. I had gotten a lot of recognition this season and knew I needed to get some advice from Lennox.

After training the following day, I walked into Lennox's office and told him I needed some advice.

Jimmy asked, "Greek, what do you want to talk about?"

"Jimmy, I received a letter from Timo asking if they drafted me would I leave school early to attend their preseason. I have to make a decision whether to leave school in January or stay for the winter semester."

Lennox replied, "Greek, there are a lot of teams that are interested in you. I have gotten numerous calls from NASL coaches about you. You are one of the best players in the country. What is really important for you is that you go to a team that wants to play skillful soccer and not a more traditional English team, which plays a lot of long balls and you get whiplash in the midfield."

"Thanks Jim," I said. "I just wanted to make sure I would be getting drafted before I take a leave of absence from school."

Jim said, "All right Greek. See you tomorrow at training." "Thanks again, Jim."

That night I called my father and discussed the different scenarios with him. He was fine with me leaving school as long as I made sure I graduated in the near future.

I had wrestled with what to do for a while, and I always felt better after I spoke to my father. I had two required sociology classes that I was taking, Sociological Statistics and Sociological Methods. Completing these classes would fulfill all of my required classes for a degree in sociology.

I then could take independent studies for the remaining 18 credits I would need to graduate. I could do these independent studies from anywhere, so I would not have to come back to Hartwick to get my degree.

Running out on to Elmore Field with Glad blaring gave me a momentary feeling of sadness, knowing this match against Syracuse was the last regular-season game I ever would play on Elmore Field.

Syracuse was no match for us and early in the first half, we exploded for four goals in five minutes. At the 27-minute mark, John Springer put the Orangemen on the board, beating Aly from 20 yards out to make it 4-1.

Minutes later, we scored again on a diving header by Artie to regain a four-goal lead. With 10 minutes to go in the half, Aly Anderson had a terrible collision with a Syracuse attacker and was knocked out. It was irrelevant to us that Syracuse scored on the play to make the score 5-2.

Aly's health was all that mattered and after a few scary moments, he was able to walk off the field. The half ended 5-2 and we all rushed into the locker room to check on Aly's status. He looked fine, with George Mitchell attending to him. We were told he suffered a mild concussion and should be ready for our huge match Wednesday in Ithaca. Knowing that Aly would be fine was a great relief for all of us.

Lennox made it clear that early in the second half, he would make lots of substitutions. I thought that was a great idea. Our substitutes worked so hard every day in training and got very little playing time.

I also knew that my playing time would be cut short and there was one thing I always wanted to do on Elmore Field, but never felt comfortable or had the opportunity to do. I had always wanted to do a rainbow in a real game. With us totally in control of this game, I knew it was now or never.

Early in the second half, I overlapped around Stevie Long and ended up near the corner flag with the ball at my feet. I dribbled towards the goal as a Syracuse defender was sprinting out of the 18-yard box to confront me. I rolled the ball up the back of my right heel with the inside of my left foot, then flicked the ball over my head and the oncoming defender's head. I sprinted around the Syracuse player and as I collected the ball coming to the ground, I was momentarily startled that it actually worked.

I had my sights on Artie making a near-post run and drove the ball to the near post, only to have the Syracuse defender head the ball out of bounds for a corner kick.

In my whole soccer career, I had never tried a rainbow in a real game. This was the perfect situation. We were winning by three goals against an inferior team and even if I lost the ball, Syracuse was still almost 120 yards away from our goal. That was the highlight of the game for me and a moment I always would cherish, even if it did not lead to a goal.

The second half was much tighter defensively for both teams and although our substitutes were outstanding, the second half remained scoreless. Final score was 5-2. On Monday, the new national and state rankings came out. Clemson was No. 1 nationally and Hartwick was No. 2. New York State rankings had us No. 1, LIU No. 2, Cornell No. 3, and St. Francis No. 4. Oneonta State was No. 5 and Adelphi was at No. 7.

The slim chance that Oneonta State had of moving up in the rankings to the No. 4 spot or better to get an NCAA Tournament bid vanished the following Monday afternoon when Cortland State upset the Red Dragons, 2-0. It was a devastating loss for our crosstown rivals.

Our upcoming midweek game at Cornell had the feel of an NCAA Tournament game. A loss would not end our season but probably would result in our dropping in the rankings to where our first-round game would be at Cornell or LIU.

Hartwick's last regular-season loss was almost two years before to the day at Schoellkopf Field. Since that 3-0 embarrassment, we were undefeated in our last 26 regular-season games.

If we won that game, we would be assured of playing all of our NCAA Tournament games on natural grass. That was a much more pleasant thought than our struggles on AstroTurf.

Once again, Cornell's offense would be led by the always-dangerous Sid Nolan and the defense would be anchored by Paul Beutenmiller.

We started the game playing very conservatively and tight in the back. We knew Cornell would be very aggressive to start the game and we wanted to absorb its pressure, looking for the right opportunities to counterattack.

Late into the first half, Cornell had seven shots on goal, although none were very threatening to Aly. We had none at that point. But with four minutes remaining in the first half, Duncan found space outside on the right, overlapping Stevie Long and dribbling to the end line before sending in a perfect cross that found Joey Ryan. He blasted the ball past Cornell keeper Chris Ward.

As the half wound down, Aly sprinted out towards the corner flag for a long through ball and was beaten to it by a Cornell player who first-timed the ball towards an empty goal. We all watched helplessly as the ball sailed inches wide of the goal post.

That was a rare mistake by Aly and almost very costly.

We went into halftime feeling very good about this game. Once again, the prevailing theme from Lennox and Alden was that we had to do a better job of keeping possession of the ball. Lennox also mentioned that Cornell's outside backs were marking our wingers very tightly all over the field and there would be opportunities for Tommy and Stevie Long to drag their defenders into poor positions, making space for our outside midfielders to attack those open spaces.

In the second half, we did a much better job of keeping possession of the ball and limited Cornell's chances on goal. At the 18-minute mark, Tommy Maresca made a run across the field, leaving a gaping hole in the Cornell defense. Joey Ryan sprinted into the space created by Tommy and I played Joey through with a diagonal ball. Joey collected the ball and took several touches before his cross was met by a great diving header by Artie to give us a 2-0 lead.

As we jogged back to the center circle after the goal, I could not help but think that this was exactly what Lennox had talked about at halftime.

It was a great goal and it deflated the Cornell players. Final score, 2-0. To finally win a game on AstroTurf was very rewarding to us. Jeff Tipping had a great game containing the very talented Sid Nolan. It was a very good result against an outstanding Cornell team.

That Saturday would mark our final regular-season game. We would be playing in Storrs, Connecticut against UConn. The game had a much different feel than all of our previous games against them in my four years at Hartwick.

In the past, all of the games had such importance—none more so than the two NCAA quarterfinal games to get to the Final Four and the first game I ever started for Hartwick against UConn, which gave me the opportunity to prove myself to Timo.

I often wonder if I had played poorly in that game, would Timo ever have given me another opportunity in a Hartwick uniform. I honestly doubt it. A poor performance in that game most likely would have earned me a one-way ticket to the junior varsity.

This would be the first time I would not be playing against one of the Hunter brothers. I loved playing against them. There was something special when you matched up with an opponent that was so talented and driven that only your best would keep you competitive against them.

Whenever I played against Tim or Paul Hunter, I knew that I had to be 100 percent ready physically, technically, mentally and emotionally. Anything less and I knew that I would have a very hard time competing against them.

This was an off-year for UConn, which was 9-8. There really was no way UConn would get an NCAA invite even it beat us. But Joe Morrone had a lot of influence in New England. It would be nice to put the nail in the coffin so UConn didn't get selected for the NCAA Tournament.

We didn't care for them and they had a strong dislike for us. Their 10,000-plus fans on Saturday afternoon confirmed their feelings towards us the minute we arrived at the field.

The only thing UConn had beaten Hartwick at since our regular-season loss my freshman year was recruiting the highly touted freshman Erhardt Kapp The talented New York defender decided to attend UConn instead of Hartwick. We really wanted him with us and were disappointed that he chose UConn.

Scouting reports say Erhardt has played really well this year. The UConn team was very different than the last few years, not nearly as talented. On the attack, it was led by four-year starter and co-captain Tommy Nevers, who had 34 career goals, and Medrick Innocent, the very skillful younger brother of UConn great Frantz Innocent.

Bob Ross, UConn's veteran goalkeeper, was injured in the season opener and had not played since. According to the scouting report, goalkeeping had been a real problem for the team this season.

Ten minutes into the game, Artie found Gary Vogel overlapping from his left back position into the penalty box. The ever-improving Vogel beat UConn keeper Paul Wynstanley to the far post.

Despite a great environment with a huge crowd, we didn't appear to have our normal intensity. Perhaps subconsciously we wanted to make sure we didn't get hurt just before the NCAA Tournament starts, and it was showing in our play.

Late in the first half, Medrick Innocent split Zeren and Gary with a great through ball to Tommy Nevers, and Nevers beat Aly to tie the game at 1-1.

The second half, we started to keep possession of the ball for long periods of time and it seemed to take the crowd out of the game. Although UConn was desperate for a win, it created few quality chances.

With six minutes remaining in the game, we received a free kick 25 yards from the UConn goal. I stood over the ball with Artie to my right, waiting for the referee to get the UConn wall 10 yards from the ball. On the referee's whistle, I rolled the ball into Artie's path; seconds later, his shot bulged the back of the net.

The goal silenced the 10,000 Huskies fans and was pure joy to our few hundred fans who made the trip from Oneonta.

The game ended 2-1. The victory was our 28th consecutive regular-season game without a loss. Despite that feat, the bus ride back from Storrs was very quiet. Every player on the team knew that everything we had accomplished in the past two years would be meaningless if we didn't win the national championship. Anything less would be unacceptable.

30

The Real Season Starts Now

The NCAA Tournament bids were not expected to be announced until Thursday. Lennox made it clear that he hoped to play our first-round game that Saturday.

That was his plan until early in the week, when seven of our players contracted the flu. Aly was so sick that he was in the infirmary on intravenous feeding. For two days, everything I tried to eat or drink had come out of me.

I was told we had 12 players at training that day and then Rudy Pena had to leave. It wasn't the ideal way for the team and me to prepare for the tournament.

By the third day I was feeling better. I had oatmeal for breakfast and did not have to run to the bathroom. I headed to the first class I would be attending that week. After my morning classes, I went to the cafeteria and had chicken noodle soup, toast and a lot of water.

That season my weight had fluctuated between 130 and 132 pounds, although in the program it lists me at 5-foot-5 and 133 pounds. In the game program, I always wanted to appear as if I was taller and heavier than I was.

Arriving at Binder for training, the first thing I did was head to the scales. It said 125 pounds. I thought it was a mistake. I stepped down, readjusted the settings and then got back on the scale. It still said 125 pounds. I got off the scale and moved the settings much higher. I did not want anyone to see that I was down to 125.

I changed and headed for Elmore Field. It was so good to get back on the soccer field. Having the ball at my feet after being in bed for two days made me feel great.

Despite not keeping any food down the prior two days, I was surprised how good I felt physically.

Thursday came with the announcement of the pairings. We were seeded No. 1 and our first-round opponent would be St. Francis. LIU ended up with the two seed and would host Cornell. Oneonta State and Adelphi University weren't selected and I shed no tears for those programs.

We set our sights on St. Francis. Forwards Steve Long and Tommy Maresca, midfielder John Young, and keepers Aly Anderson and Mike Blundell were still flu-ridden and according to Lennox, doubtful for Sunday's first-round game.

Sal Scalici led the St. Francis attack with eight goals and three assists. In the defense, St. Francis was led by returning first-team All-American goalkeeper Dragan Radovich.

The previous year in the NCAA Tournament, the St. Francis team kicked Stevie Long all over the field. I had never seen one player repeatedly kicked and be able to endure the physical beating he received.

Many tackles were fair, bone-crunching tackles but there also were some nasty fouls, and the referee gave little protection to Stevie. From the opening whistle in the last year's game it was obvious that St. Francis left back Errol Sebro would do whatever he could to intimidate Stevie. How Stevie managed to stay in the game and endure the brutal tackles was hard to imagine.

This is one aspect of the game where we would have to do a much better job. We needed to protect our attacking players so they had opportunities to break down the opposing defenses.

Sunday morning in the locker room, it was great to see everyone on the team suiting up and expected to play. Aly looked like he was still a bit under the weather, but emphatically told Lennox that he was fine to play.

Whenever the weather was brutal outside, we always warmed up as a team in Binder gymnasium prior to heading out to Elmore Field. I think it was a huge advantage and that day, more than ever, should be helpful.

After last-minute instructions from Lennox and Alden, we headed out to a frigid, snow-covered, bone-hard Elmore Field. It was so cold, I felt sorry for our substitutes, even if they would be in sweat suits, with parkas on top and wrapped in sleeping bags.

As we lined up waiting for the referee's whistle to start the game, you could not help but notice the difference in the body language of our players and the St. Francis players. They appeared very stiff, like they were frozen and did not want to be out there. On the other hand, we were thoroughly warmed up and getting ready to play in weather conditions we were familiar with.

Ninety seconds into the game, Artie elevated above a St. Francis defender, heading the ball past a beaten Radovich only to see his header bounce off the post and go out of bounds for a goal kick.

We were all over St. Francis and a minute later, Duncan struck a corner kick to the near post, where Radovich and defender Alfred Carrabotta had some miscommunication. With neither making more than a half-hearted attempt to get to the ball, Tommy Maresca snuck in between the two and headed home the first goal of the game.

Minutes later, Gary Vogel overlapped on the left side, crossing the ball into the box. St. Francis defender Alimu Sillah went to clear the ball and inexplicably missed it. The ball ended up at Artie's feet with only Dragan Radovich between him and the goal. Artie drilled the ball past Radovich to put us up 2-0 six minutes into the game.

St. Francis was desperate to get back into the game and put some pressure on our defense. Minutes later, Jeff Tipping cleared a crossed ball out of our box. As the clearance headed to Errol Sebro in the midfield, Joey sprinted towards Errol to put immediate pressure on the St. Francis defender. Errol's first touch was not perfect and the hard playing surface caused the ball to bounce high into the air.

Joey continued running towards Errol, then while sliding, put his studs up going right through the bouncing ball, with his follow through going right into Errol's groin. Errol collapsed to the ground, writhing in pain, rolling around in agony on the frozen surface of Elmore Field.

The referee wasted no time in giving Joey a yellow card. It appeared to me that Joey was sending Errol and St. Francis a message that we also could play a physical game, and would not stand by and watch our attacking players get kicked like last year without retaliating.

A little over 10 minutes into the game, Duncan overlapped Stevie Long and received a through ball out wide on the right. Duncan made his way to the end line before his cross found the head of an unmarked Napolitano. Artie's header went over the outstretched fingertips of Radovitch and floated just under the cross bar to give us a 3-0 lead.

For all intents and purposes, the game was over. St. Francis mounted its first attack on goal at the 23-minute mark when Aly came up with his first save of the game, against Clyde O'Garro.

Fifty seconds later, Duncan once again was overlapping out wide on the right side. He made his way to the touchline before cutting the ball back to Stevie Long, standing at the top of the 18-yard box. Long calmly received the ball, then drove a low, hard shot to the near post, beating the St. Francis goalkeeper for goal No. 4.

At this point Lennox had some of the subs begin to warm up to replace players that had battled the flu. Peco Bosevski came on for Tommy and the talented freshman wasted no time in getting goal No. 5.

With us up by five goals, the quality of our play began to deteriorate. The half ended 5-0. In the locker room, Lennox hammered at us that we needed to keep playing good, focused quality soccer, keep our composure and not do anything silly if the game started to get nasty.

At 37 seconds into the second half, our defense sprinted up to play an offside trap when Sal Scalici played a through ball for Errol Sebro. Errol appeared to be in an offside position and as we hesitated, waiting for the referee's whistle, Errol continued down the field. The whistle never came. Errol was boring in on Aly and buried a hard low shot past him.

The goal had no real significance other than to end Aly's shutout. After the kickoff, we must have put 20 consecutive passes together. Any momentary thought St. Francis had about getting back into the game evaporated, with its players chasing the ball as we played keep away.

St. Francis was dying to get out of the frozen tundra of Oneonta and into its heated bus back to New York City. The final score was 5-1. It was a good start for us, especially considering the impact the flu had on our preparation for this game.

One down and four more games to go. After the game, St. Francis Coach Carlo Tramontozzi was quoted as saying, "We will never win this thing because we always have to come up here and play in these conditions."

The schedule for the rest of the tournament looked favorable for us. That Wednesday, Cornell would play LIU down in New York City, with us hosting the winner either Saturday or Sunday. That gave us a week to get healthier and prepare for the New York State final.

When we beat the winner of Cornell-LIU, we should have another week off before we would play in the quarterfinals at the Mid-Atlantic region winner. The quarterfinal game should be on a grass field and the finals in Berkeley, California, also would be played on a grass field. It had been over two years since we lost an NCAA regular-season or NCAA Tournament game on a grass field.

Our team was very confident and focused. We knew that we couldn't look ahead to our potential semifinal matchup against Clemson, which crushed George Washington University 4-0 in their first-round game.

Wednesday, Lennox went down to New York and watched Cornell beat LIU 2-1. Lennox addressed the team before training on Thursday. His message was very clear.

"Our last two regular-season games had us playing very lackadaisical. Against Cornell, they dominated us in the second half and we won because we took our chances.

"We are going to do everything possible to keep Cornell from knocking long balls from the back to their front players. In transition, we are going to pressure the ball when we lose it and immediately try to win it back. They have one outstanding player in Sid Nolan and it will be Tip's job to shut him down."

Training was very intense, with Lennox and Alden constantly on the first team to high-pressure the ball as soon as we lost possession. Lennox had hoped we could play the game on Saturday so the majority of the student body could attend before going home for Thanksgiving break. Dan Wood pushed for Sunday and the NCAA committee decided on a Sunday afternoon kickoff.

The weather conditions in Oneonta had warmed up and we were expecting a fair amount of rain before the Sunday kickoff, meaning Elmore was going to go from bone-hard and frozen against St. Francis to muddy against Cornell.

Thursday night. I studied until 2 a.m. preparing for my two finals. Completing the two exams Friday morning brought me a great sense of relief that I could give all of my attention to our match against Cornell.

The weather forecast was correct and Sunday afternoon, Elmore Field had many extremely muddy areas. Running out onto Elmore Field, my only real concern was Sid Nolan. He had been a real problem for us over the years. The fact that Jeff Tipping, who I considered the best stopper back in the country, was marking him made me feel better.

Despite the less-than-perfect field conditions, we had a dream start. Less than two minutes into the game, a Tommy Maresca pass found an unmarked Joey Ryan standing 25 yards from the goal. Joey received the ball, turned and rifled a shot, surprising slow-reacting Cornell goalkeeper Chris Ward as the ball sailed into the goal for the first goal of the game.

We implemented Lennox's tactics to the letter. We established control of the game with our short passing game and when we lost the ball, in most cases, we were able to quickly win it back.

Lennox's tactics appeared to be working. We continued to control the ball for long periods of time but could not get a second goal before half-time. I think Cornell was happy to get off the field down only 1-0.

Lennox was very pleased with our first-half performance. We did exactly what he preached all week. We kept very good possession of the ball and when we lost it, we were able to win it back most times right away. Then we made Cornell expend a lot of energy chasing the ball again.

Early in the second half, we realized that the Cornell right back could not contain Tommy "The Little Monster" Maresca. Tommy had great speed, but sometimes he got in this moment in time where he had an extra gear and just sprinted past players as if they were standing still. This was one of those moments. Tommy was bursting with confidence and energy.

We repeatedly got the ball to Tommy out wide so we could isolate him against the Cornell defender, who physically was just not fast enough to stay with Tommy. Neither the defender nor the muddy conditions could slow down Tommy.

Fourteen minutes into the second half, Tommy beat his defender again, dribbled around the keeper and struck the ball towards the goal. The ball deflected off of a Cornell defender heading for the empty net when it stopped dead in the mud on the goal line. Another Cornell defender came across and cleared it out of danger.

The clearance and avoiding a two-goal deficit seemed to energize Cornell. With a newfound energy, Cornell started to attack our defense for the first time all game. Minutes later, Sid Nolan played a beautiful through ball that found Ricky Derella behind our defense, and Derella beat Aly Anderson for the goal to tie the game at 1-1.

The goal really fired up Cornell. We had dominated Cornell until the last few minutes, and now Cornell thought it could win the game.

As we lined up to restart the game, there was no finger pointing or negative comments amongst us. We won as a team and lost as a team. We had been involved in so many important games in the last few years, the goal did not phase us one bit. We knew we were the best team in the country and we would prove it.

We immediately started knocking the ball around again, looking to isolate our wingers. Five minutes later, Gary Vogel overlapped, was played through and just had the keeper to beat when he was tripped from behind.

John Young placed the ball on the penalty spot and calmly beat the Cornell keeper to put us back on top 2-1. As the half wore on, Cornell now had to push more players forward to try to get the equalizer. But it was the Tommy Maresca show once again.

Tommy was relentless in his attacks on the Cornell goal, only for goalkeeper Chris Ward to repeatedly deny him with one outstanding save after another. Finally in the last minute of the game, Stevie Long served a cross into the box and Tommy Maresca's header finally beat the Cornell keeper for goal No. 3.

The final score was 3-1. We would be spending another Thanksgiving in Oneonta, and for a good reason: We were still alive in the tournament. Two down, three games to go.

Getting changed in the locker room after the game, I couldn't help hearing reporters interview Timo and Lennox. Timo was there scouting for the Dallas Tornadoes. The first comment I heard our ex-Hartwick head coach make was, "The Wick has a shot at the national title. This team definitely has the tools to get to the final."

When an *Oneonta Star* reporter asked Timo what else he thought, he replied, "All they need is a little luck. They say you make your own luck, but I think some of it is inherited. One break and they could go all the way."

Then it was Lennox's turn to get interviewed. He said, "Our midfield has played really well the last two matches. We have been controlling play and doing pretty much what we want to. The defense has also been doing a great job."

Lennox then was asked what he thought Hartwick's chances were of reaching the finals. He tersely replied, "It looks very good."

I liked the comments from Lennox. We were all very confident but at the same time, we knew that we would have to be at or near our best to win the next three games.

All the Hartwick students went home for Thanksgiving break, so we decided to forgo going downtown. We were celebrating our victory in Joey's bedroom, listening to Bruce Springsteen, when a thought came to me.

The team and I were so focused on getting to the national championship game and winning it all, I forgot I had just played my last game in my Hartwick career on Elmore Field. The thought that I never would lead the team out to "Glad" blaring to an overflow crowd at Elmore made me feel quite sad for a few minutes.

Then I started thinking about all of the great memories I always would have from games we played on that field, and I felt a lot better. I just want to get to the sunshine in California and bring back that trophy.

Monday before training, Alden gave us all of the results from the weekend. Most importantly, we wanted to know who we were playing. Textile hammered Penn State 3-0 and would host us on Sunday afternoon. Clemson would play Brown, with the winner of that game matched up against our winner in the semifinals. The Midwest had SIU against Cleveland State, and out in the far West, two-time defending champion University of San Francisco was matched up against UCLA.

Normally the day after a game, the starters have a very light training session to help them physically recover. With the schedule for the national finals slated for back-to-back games on Saturday and Sunday, Lennox wanted to get us conditioned for that weekend's schedule.

Training was physically grueling and by the end of the session, we were exhausted. Jimmy and Alden were meticulous in our preparation. They left no stone unturned in preparing us for each match.

After training I weighed myself and to my surprise, I was 128 pounds. I thought over the last week and a half I would have put back on all of the weight I lost from the flu. I felt really good physically, so I guess a few pounds did not make a difference. It would give me an excuse to overeat on Thanksgiving, which was my favorite holiday of the year.

As the week progressed, there was a lot of talk among the players about Clemson. We knew that a semifinal match against Clemson would be a physical war and perhaps the most difficult game on our journey to win the championship.

Lennox called for a meeting Wednesday and addressed his concern that we should not be overconfident against Textile. Jimmy said there was a fine line between being confident and overconfident. He kept stressing how good Textile was and if we looked past them, the season could end on Sunday.

I think Jimmy's concern stemmed from the fact that we were pretty much in control for most of our regular-season matchup against them and neutralized Adrian Brooks.

Thursday morning, the first thing I did was call home. I had a lengthy conversation with my mother and father. I always felt better after I talked to my parents and this day was no different.

We would have a good training session, then have Thanksgiving dinner as a team.

We had really good training sessions the remainder of the week. There was not a lot of emotion displayed, with everybody so focused on Sunday's match. Saturday afternoon, we took Bluebird to Philadelphia to get settled in and hopefully have a good night's sleep.

Sunday, the temperature was in the mid-20s and very sunny. As we stepped onto the field at Temple Stadium, the playing surface felt hard. It seemed like it was frozen in many spots and although many of my teammates were hoping to wear studs, it seemed like for the time being, at least until it warms up more, our molded cleats would be more effective.

Adrian Brooks would be lining up on John Young's side of the field and Lennox decided to let John mark him man to man all over the field. I liked that decision for two reasons. First, John did a great job on him last game, and second, I would be allowed to hold in the central part of the field, which made it much easier for me to control the tempo of the game.

Like our last game against Textile, we wanted to keep possession of the ball for long periods of time and force Adrian Brooks and the other midfielders on Textile to expend lots of energy defending.

The game started out very tentative for both sides. We had lots of possession, but it was more passing the ball from one side of the field to another rather than attacking in the last third.

Textile was not committing many players into the attack and neither team created any quality opportunities in the first 15 minutes. At the 20-minute mark, Textile was awarded a free kick 25 yards from the goal. Johnny Nusum, Textile's huge powerful sweeper, came up to take the free kick. Nusum is a very intimidating figure and could strike the ball as hard as anyone in the country.

As per Aly's directions, we lined up the wall and prayed Nusum would shoot the ball over the top. Nusum approached the ball and struck it with such force, it was a blur as it sailed past the wall and went directly into Aly's well-positioned hands. We collectively let out a huge sigh of relief as we moved up the field.

The next quality chance of the game also came from Textile. Mike Mancke beat Gary Vogel out wide on the right, boring in on Aly, with his shot just sailing inches wide of the far post.

With four minutes left in the first half, I received a ball near the corner of the 18-yard box. As I made eye contact with Artie, he sprinted past his defender. He was first to my cross and volleyed a rocket that sailed just above the crossbar. That was our only good opportunity in the entire first half. We played entirely too cautious, waiting for a Textile mistake that never came.

At halftime, Lennox told us we were playing entirely too tentatively and then he added, "If we do not win this game, we are going to have to eat at McDonald's on the ride home."

In spite of the seriousness of the game, it was good to see Lennox joking with us and putting us at ease as we prepared to go out for the second half.

Right from the kickoff, you could sense that the game was about to open up. We both looked to push more numbers into the attack. In the 49th minute, Duncan overlapped to the end line and served a cross into the box. Artie received the cross and his shot had Textile keeper Dave Treschuk beaten—only to sail inches over the crossbar. The game started to go end to end, with both teams looking for that important first goal.

Fifteen minutes into the second half, Joey Ryan exhibited his impeccable dribbling skills, beating several Textile defenders out wide on the left, then unleashing a shot from 18 yards out. Treschuk went airborne and stretched as the ball went past him, striking the post.

The ball rebounded off of the post and Tommy Maresca followed up with a shot on goal that Treschuk, with catlike reflexes, bounced to his feet and punched over the crossbar for a corner kick.

On the subsequent corner kick, Treschuk came up with another outstanding save and we did not have anything to show for three quality chances.

Minutes later, Ryan put on another display of his dribbling abilities, beating two Textile defenders before he was pulled down to the ground just outside the 18-yard box, only yards from the end line.

As I stood over the ball, Textile lined up the same way it would defend a corner kick. Textile put a defender on the far post and the near post.

As the referee was pulling the wall back to get it 10 yards from the spot of the free kick, I noticed Tommy Maresca was standing unmarked on the six-yard line exactly parallel to the near post. The nearest Textile defender was their player standing on the near post and he was six yards from Tommy. All of the other Hartwick players that came up for the free kick were standing at the back post, waiting for the referee's whistle.

It was almost hard to believe what I was seeing: A player standing unmarked on the six-yard line. I wasn't sure if Textile didn't realize what it was doing, or thought I would not be able to get the ball around the wall to Tommy. Either way, I did not care. I was just thinking referee, please blow the whistle so I can take this free kick. Although the wait seemed like an eternity, it was only seconds.

The referee finally was satisfied with the location of the wall and blew his whistle. All of the Hartwick players at the back post just stood still as I approached the ball and curled the free kick around the wall directly to Tommy. Maresca jumped up and headed the ball past the outstretched hands of Textile keeper Treschuk to give us the very important first goal of the game.

After congratulating Tommy, I still could not comprehend how Textile would have left a player in Tommy's position unmarked like that.

We were in control of the game and we had Textile on its heels. Three minutes later, Aly collected a long through ball at the top of our 18-yard box and threw the ball towards me standing unmarked at the edge of the center circle. As the ball was in flight towards me, I made quick glances over my right shoulder and left shoulder.

I knew I had space and that Artie was unmarked. As the ball approached me, I arched my back and as I controlled the ball with my chest, I popped it over my head. I spun around and volleyed a 30-yard drive directly to Artie. He played the ball off to Joey as I sprinted forward.

Stevie made a run inside, creating a large space out wide on the right side. Out of the corner of my eye I could see Duncan flying up the sideline. Joey passed the ball to Stevie, who laid it back to me with Duncan continuing his run up the field. I played a diagonal pass into the penalty box directly into Duncan's path. John Nusum sprinted from his sweeper position, but Duncan beat him to the ball. As Duncan pushed the ball past the Textile sweeper he was tripped, and the referee blew his whistle and awarded us a penalty kick.

As in the Cornell game, John Young would take the penalty kick for us. John approached the ball, got Treschuk to lean to his right and calmly shot the ball into the left corner of the goal to give us a 2-0 lead.

The second goal took the wind out of Textile and the few attacks it mounted with time winding down were easily handled by Aly Anderson. Final score, 2-0. Three down, two to go.

The stands were filled with Hartwick alumni. There scouting the game were Al Miller and Timo for the Dallas Tornadoes; Terry Fisher, head coach for the Los Angeles Aztecs; and Francisco Marcos from the Tampa Bay Rowdies.

We had more good news that weekend. Alden had gone down to South Carolina yesterday to scout the Clemson-Brown quarterfinal game. Brown University scored a huge upset, winning 2-1.

Alden said Clemson did everything possible to intimidate the Brown players. He demonstrated how some of the Clemson players jumped into and tackled the Brown players by putting his foot up against the side of the knee of Ed Clough, our sports information director.

Brown lost several players through injuries in that game and Alden was not sure if they would be available the next weekend. Alden made a point that Brown deserved to win and we would have to be at our best if we wanted to get to the championship game.

My parents were attending a wedding that afternoon, so I had to wait until we got back to Oneonta to call them and give them the news that we won.

The team was not ecstatic on the bus ride back. Yes, we were happy but typically, we didn't show a lot of emotion. We were going to the Final Four, which would make most teams jubilant. But we were on a mission. For the seniors and juniors on this team, the only way we would be able to say we had a great season was if we won two games in Berkeley.

I thought about my contribution to the two goals we scored that day. The first was the result of my spending hundreds of hours in front of the wall at Nottingham Junior High, striking balls. Driving balls with my instep, bending balls with the outside of my foot, and curling balls with the inside of my foot.

The second goal started with my executing the Manfred chest trap. Ping Pong and I had spent so much time to master a skill that's rarely used in a game. This was the first time all season I had the chance to use the Manfred trap and it led to our second goal. I smiled, thinking about how sore and red my chest would be after a training session with Ping Pong when we were focusing on the different ways to chest trap a ball.

I thought Ping Pong had to get an assist for the second goal. His constant pushing me to master the ball paid huge dividends that day. Sometimes I thought I was the luckiest college soccer player in the country because I had Ping Pong to train with every day in the summer months for the previous five years.

After we stopped for dinner on the bus ride back to Oneonta, Lennox went over what the upcoming week would look like for us. He made it very clear that the next day, we would have a hard training session to get used to the back-to-back games next weekend.

We would have classes and training on Monday and Tuesday. After training on Tuesday, Hartwick College President Philip Wilder would lead a sendoff rally in Binder.

Wednesday, we would be taking a 7:20 a.m. flight out of Syracuse, arriving at the Oakland airport a little after noon. Wednesday afternoon, we would have a light training session on one of the University of California Berkeley practice fields. We would train Thursday again on the practice field, and were scheduled to have a short training session on Friday in Memorial Stadium, where the finals would be held.

Lennox said on Friday after training, we would be going into San Francisco for the afternoon, followed by a nice dinner somewhere near Fisherman's Wharf.

I thought it was hard to concentrate in class leading up to the Cornell game. But Monday in class, it was so much more difficult for me.

I decided that I would try to take notes of everything the professor lectured about so I hopefully could absorb the material later on at night. By the end of class, my hand was cramping up from writing so much.

Prior to the beginning of training, Alden went over his scouting report. Alden said Brown had two outstanding attacking players. Junior Peter VanBeek from Vauchesson, France was the leading goal scorer and sophomore Tom O'Brian led the team in assists. In the defense, Alden said they were led by a great sweeper in St. Louis-raised Ray Schnettgoecke.

Jimmy compared Brown to Cornell, saying they were very similar in playing style, meaning we should expect a very physical game. Training was grueling on Monday afternoon just as Lennox had promised.

Tuesday flew by and before we knew it, the alarm was going off at 4 a.m. Wednesday. We made the bus ride to the Syracuse Airport and had an uneventful flight to Oakland, with a one-hour layover in O'Hare Airport.

After we settled in at the hotel, we headed straight for the University of California at Berkeley to practice on one of its practice fields. Although we could feel the excitement, we were very tired from traveling. We made it through the warmup and went straight into some technical training. You could sense Lennox was not happy with our energy level.

Next, we went into some functional training, which had some combination play out wide, leading to a ball being served at the end line into the penalty box for two attacking players making runs. The only problem was that we had one poor cross after another. The crosses were of such poor quality that Aly was getting no work in the goal and Lennox was getting more upset by the minute. This went on for about five minutes.

The quality of our training session was absolutely terrible and finally, Jimmy could not take it anymore. He exploded and said, "Stop, stop. Greek, you go over there and serve the balls into the box. Everyone else form two lines, time your runs into the box and let's give Aly some work."

Lennox was furious. When Jimmy got like that you could almost see steam coming out of his ears. Jimmy was a perfectionist and despite the long travel day, he still expected perfection. The quality of the training exercise improved dramatically and we looked quite sharp the remainder of practice. That evening, we had a quiet dinner at the hotel and everyone went to bed early.

Thursday morning brought a surprise, as we were allowed to go train in Memorial Stadium. It was an exciting feeling walking into the 76,000-seat stadium we would be playing in on Saturday.

The first thing Lennox did while we were going through our warmup was to walk the dimensions to see how long and wide the soccer field actually was. To Lennox's disappointment, he found the field to be 2 1/3 yards narrower and eight yards shorter than Elmore Field.

That was not good news for us. We loved playing on Elmore Field, but it's one of the narrower fields we play on. We preferred big fields with a lot of width, which allowed us to spread out the opposing team and make it expend a lot of energy defending us.

The Memorial Stadium field would favor the very physical Brown team on Saturday. Despite the fact that the field is slightly narrower and a bit shorter in length than we expected, we still were elated to be playing on natural grass instead of AstroTurf.

Our training sessions on Thursday and Friday were very light, and it was difficult to go over our free kicks because scouts from Brown and the other finalists could be in the stands.

Friday afternoon, we headed to downtown San Francisco for some sightseeing and we ended the excursion by having a nice dinner on Fisherman's Wharf. The sourdough bread I had with my dinner was by far the best-tasting bread I had ever eaten. The rest of the evening was for us to relax and get mentally prepared for our 11 a.m. kickoff Saturday.

As I led the team onto the field Saturday morning, the weather conditions couldn't have been more perfect. It was sunny and 60 degrees. We had a good warmup and as a team, we were ready to punch our ticket into the championship game.

The game started with Brown high-pressuring us all over the field. Although we were the more experienced team and should have been more relaxed, we were not. Brown was all over us and we had a hard time putting two consecutive passes together.

In the third minute, Brown played a ball into our box that our defense didn't clear properly, and the ball dropped down to the feet of a Brown attacker, who first-timed the ball into the back of the net before Aly could even react. Brown was up 1-0 three minutes into the game.

Several Brown players turned toward us and started shouting, "You aren't so bleepin' good. You guys suck. You think you're so bleepin' great."

I'm not sure if I was more surprised that Brown scored against us so quickly or that several of its players verbally attacked us.

The game was only minutes old and we had no history with the Brown players. I could understand if we were well into the game and players were getting onto each other. But it was three minutes into the game and there was not a bunch of nasty fouls or any Hartwick players talking to them.

We didn't need more motivation than knowing we had to win to reach the championship game. But the goal and their verbal attacks just added more fuel to our desire.

The goal had the opposite effect on us from what you would think. Their score actually seemed to relax us. Immediately after the kickoff, we started to knock the ball around and get our rhythm. We started playing Hartwick soccer and Brown started spending a lot of time chasing the ball as we kept possession, probing their defense, looking for an opening.

What seemed like just minutes later, John Young hit a laser of a shot from 23 yards out, leaving Brown goalkeeper Ted VonGerichten helpless and tying the game 1-1. Brown's verbal taunts had been subsiding while its players chased the ball; the goal ended their oral attacks.

We controlled the game the remainder of the first half, but could not get the go-ahead goal. At halftime, we were very relaxed and confident.

Jimmy and Alden were very happy with our play, other than our momentary lapse in the third minute leading to the Brown goal. Going into the second half, we knew we needed to get the next goal. If Brown scored, it would pack it in defensively for the remainder of the game and make it difficult for us in the attacking third of the field.

But if we scored the next goal, eventually Brown would have to commit more players into the attack and we should be able to score more goals.

The second half started out just like the first half ended, with us stringing multiple passes together, keeping possession of the ball for long periods of time and Brown expending a lot of time and energy chasing the ball.

Early in the second half, a Brown defender made a long clearance of the ball from his 18-yard line and the Brown back line sprinted forward to play an offside trap.

I was standing in the center circle and when I saw the cleared ball land at the feet of Gary Vogel, I started sprinting forward. I timed my run so I was sprinting at top speed past the Brown defense just as Gary played the ball over the top.

I was so clear of the Brown defense that I allowed the ball Gary played to me to bounce twice as I watched the Brown goalkeeper initially hesitate before he finally sprinted off his line.

I allowed the ball to bounce one more time before I casually flicked it over the onrushing keeper, took two steps around Von Gerichten watching the ball roll towards the empty goal, and then before the ball even crossed over the goal line, I sprinted towards the corner flag, where all of the Hartwick fans were sitting. Seconds later, I was mobbed by my teammates. We scored the all-important second goal and we were not going to be denied a spot in the final.

Minutes later, Stevie Long did what he did best and beat several Brown defenders before getting to the end line and driving a low hard cross into the goal mouth. The ball deflected off of a Brown defender and found the back of the net for an own goal. The third goal took a lot of energy out of Brown.

Art finished the scoring off of an assist from John Young and put us up 4-1. What little hope Brown had of making a comeback was gone.

We played out the remaining minutes looking to expend as little energy as possible, just waiting for the referee to blow his whistle to end the game.

When the game finally ended, the Brown players were very congratulatory to us. I am not sure why they had that outburst after they scored the first goal of the game and do not think I would ever get the answer.

There was no celebrating in the locker room after the game. Jimmy and Alden addressed the team, with Lennox harping on the fact that we couldn't afford to make any mistakes, mental or physical, in the defense the next day. Our momentary lapse in the defense that day cost us a goal and he was unhappy about that.

Alden talked about preparing for the final the same way we have prepared individually for every game that year. He stressed not to change anything because it was for the national championship. Alden's exact words were, "Just do exactly what you always do the night before a game."

Lennox finished addressing the team in the locker room with, "We will all watch the game today and then have a team meeting after dinner to discuss our tactics."

Walking out of the locker room to grab lunch before the other semifinal game started, I thought it was a bit funny when Jimmy said we would discuss our tactics that night. One of the biggest differences between Jimmy and Timo is that Lennox had always felt we were the best team in the country and we just needed to execute exactly the way we played.

Timo was very different. We made lots of adjustments depending on who the opponent was. The teams my junior and senior year were much more talented than my first two years at Hartwick, so that also may have been a factor in Timo's constant changing of how we would play tactically.

31

I Have Been Waiting Four Years for This Game

The next day, I finally got to play in the game I had waited for since I entered Hartwick. I captained Junior High School Number 2 to the Trenton city championship in ninth grade. I captained St. Anthony's High School to the state championship in 12th grade, so it only made sense that the next day, I would captain Hartwick to the national championship in my senior year in college. It would be the perfect ending to my collegiate career.

Watching San Francisco and SIU Edwardsville warming up, I realized I wanted to play San Francisco in the final. They were the two-time defending national champion, had won something like 18 games in a row and was playing in what can be considered a home game, which should mean a bigger crowd to play in front of tomorrow if they won.

San Francisco had many very talented players, none more so than Andy Atuegbu and Tony Igwe. Nigerian-born Atuegbu was their playmaker and also a great goal scorer. Igwe was the heart and soul of the team.

Tony Igwe not only played in the 1968 Olympics for Nigeria as a 16-year-old but also started for the Nigerian men's national team for World Cup qualification games in 1969 and 1973. To say he had some experience in international soccer is quite an understatement.

SIU was led by All-American Greg Makowski, a defender who constantly looked to get forward and was very dangerous in the attack. SIU also had a very talented group of freshmen players, led by a goal-scoring machine in freshman Don Ebert.

We watched a very physical, aggressive, hard-fought game between two very good teams. The University of San Francisco edged out SIU Edwardsville 2-1 in overtime.

Back at the hotel, we had our team dinner followed by a team meeting. Lennox and Alden were meticulous in their scouting report for the University of San Francisco. They must have diagramed every free kick San Francisco had taken in the last four years.

We went over our defensive responsibilities. Duncan would be matching up with Andy Atuegbu. Atuegbu had his knee heavily bandaged in the semifinal, and the most dangerous attacking player for San Francisco looked like he was less than 100 percent fit.

Andy Atuegbu at less than 100 percent was still an extremely danger-ous player, from his powerful long-distance shooting to his vision, great passing ability and dribbling skills. Duncan has shut down the best wingers in the country for four years and I expected the same from him the next day.

Walking out of our team meeting and heading back to my hotel room, I could feel the excitement building inside me. I slept great the night before the two Robbie Cup Championship games and the night before the National Amateur Cup final, so I was confident I would get a good night's sleep that night, although the game the next day would be, by far, the biggest in my soccer career.

The moment my head hit the pillow, all I could think about was how we were going to win the national championship the next day. They were the last thoughts I had before waking up Sunday morning, Dec. 4.

During our pregame meal, everyone on the team seemed very relaxed, at least on the outside. I felt this excitement but at the same time a calmness, and the thought that we could actually lose today to a great University of San Francisco team never entered my mind.

Ping Pong flew out for the game and Tommy Maresca's parents flew in from Florida, along with a large group of fans from Oneonta. One of the downsides of owning a small business is that my parents couldn't make the trip to San Francisco.

The wait between our pregame meal and checking out of the hotel and heading to the stadium felt like forever. We finally boarded the bus and headed to the stadium.

In the locker room, everyone was business as usual, with Mitch checking out Aly's bruised left shoulder he received in the Brown game. Other than Aly's injury, the team came out of the Brown game in very good shape.

Lennox and Alden addressed the team just the way they had for the last two years. It was business as usual and Jimmy ended his talk with, "Greek, lead the team out."

As I exited the tunnel and stepped onto the playing field, I instantly felt chills and goose bumps throughout my body. It was a great feeling leading the Hartwick College soccer team out onto the field for the national championship game at Memorial Stadium.

We had a nice long warmup before the referee blew his whistle for the captains to come to the center circle for the coin flip. The referees introduced themselves, we had the customary coin flip for the ball and which goal we wanted to defend, and then I shook hands with the three tri-captains of the University of San Francisco.

Andy Atuegbo, Jimmy Boyle and Dag Olavson all wished me good luck as we shook hands. As captain of Hartwick, I had seen that after every coin flip, the opposing team captain or captains would shake hands with me and always wish me good luck.

I personally never understood this. Why would you wish the opposing team good luck when in reality, you hoped they had bad luck and you win the game?

In all of our games, I had never told an opposing captain good luck. As they wished me good luck, I would shake their hand and just nod my head. It didn't make sense to tell someone something that is so far from the truth.

I also was very superstitious and in 17 regular-season and NCAA Tournament games that year, I had yet to lose a game by not wishing the opposing captains good luck. I was not changing anything today with my center circle ritual. I hoped to end my career that day as the Hartwick captain that never lost a soccer game.

There were rumors that Bjorn Dahl, San Francisco's huge Norwegian center back, and leading scorer center forward Alex Nwosu would not play because of injuries they sustained in the semifinal match. But they lined up in their positions on the field as we prepared to start the game.

We were thoroughly prepared whether they played or not. We lined up for the opening kickoff and it was music to my ears when the referee finally blew his whistle to start the game.

The first few minutes of the game found both teams feeling each other out, and both teams' tactics were very obvious.

We were going to try and execute our short passing game, keep possession for long periods of time, and try to get the ball to our wingers in one-on-one situations against the Dons' outside backs.

The Dons' tactics are to high-pressure the ball, double team us when possible, win the ball back as quickly as possible and then look to counterattack with balls played to their front players.

Twenty minutes into the game, we'd had a good number of possessions and I was somewhat surprised that I was getting so many touches on the ball. The only problem was that our possessions weren't leading to any clear-cut opportunities on goal.

At the 23-minute mark, the Dons were awarded a corner kick. Our biggest concern entering the game was the massive height advantage the Dons had over us. We knew we had to try to minimize the number of corner kicks the University of San Francisco would get.

The ball was served to the far post, and as Aly stretched for the ball, it fell off of his fingertips. Zeren alertly cleared the loose ball out for another corner kick. The ensuing corner kick again was sent toward the far post. Aly clearly was obstructed and couldn't get to the ball. But once again, our defense was first to react and we cleared the ball out of danger.

Midway through the first half, I received a ball out wide on the left side around 35 yards from goal with some open space in front of me. As I dribbled towards our penalty box, the Dons' Roger Alphonso sprinted toward me and in one motion, I momentarily stopped the ball with the inside of my left foot and then immediately pushed it past the oncoming Alphonso with my right foot.

I continued dribbling forward. As I was approaching the corner of the 18-yard box, I could see Tony Igwe sprinting towards me. I thought because of his angle, I would be able to do the same stop-and-go move and get past him.

As the former Nigerian national team player came within several yards of me, I once again momentarily stopped the ball with my left foot and in the same motion pushed the ball past him with my right. Igwe couldn't have cared less about the ball and buried his knee into my thigh.

I crumpled to the ground, feeling the searing pain radiate from my thigh. After crushing me in the tackle, Tony threw himself down, rolling around and pretending he also was injured in the tackle.

The first thing I did when I got to my feet was to start stretching my quadricep to minimize the tightness I knew I was going to get in my thigh.

As our trainer Mitch ran over to me, I gave the referee an earful that Igwe deserved a red card or at least a yellow card. All this time, Igwe was still on the ground and the referee did not give me any indication whether he was going to card Igwe.

When Tony finally stood up, the referee went over to him and gave him a yellow card. From Igwe's perspective, it was a very good foul to take. I was going to get past him, heading directly into the 18-yard box and there was a lot of space to attack. It was one of those situations where you couldn't let the player and the ball both get past you. It was a mistake on my part. I made a bad decision thinking that I and the ball could get past him.

As I stood over the ball for the free kick, most of our attacking players were standing at the far post, leaving a lot of open space around the penalty spot. Tommy made a run into that space and as I crossed the ball, Tommy took one touch to control the pass and struck a shot on goal, which a defender blocked. Artie pounced on the rebound and a defender also blocked it before it could get to the goal.

They were our first real opportunities of the half. At around the 30-minute mark, San Francisco made two substitutions. Roger Alphonso, the Dons' central midfielder I was matched up with, was taken off and Anthony Gray came on. Also, Alex Nwosu, who Jeff Tipping shut down, was taken off and Dag Olafson came on.

At the 35-minute mark, San Francisco was awarded a free kick outside of our penalty box. The kick was directed towards the near post and Olafson beat Tipping to the ball, flicking it toward the back post.

John Brooks, the other huge center back for San Francisco, leaped above everyone and headed the ball directly toward the upper corner of the goal. Aly flung himself across the goal, tipping the ball over the cross-bar when it was just inches from going over the goal line. It was a brilliant save by Aly, which we had become quite accustomed to that season.

Late in the half, Tommy Maresca beat two defenders before he was fouled by Anthony Gray near the halfway line. Standing over the ball, I make a hand motion for Stevie Long to drag his defender inside, leaving a huge space out wide. John Young ran into the open space and the ball was delivered to him. He drove a very hard, low cross that froze University of San Francisco keeper Peter Arnautoff on his goal line as the ball rolled along the six-yard line, just inches out of the reach of our attacking players.

The remainder of the half did not result in any good opportunities for either team. San Francisco did a good job of limiting our chances in the attacking third and we did likewise with the Dons. Their best opportunities were off free kicks into the box, and that would be our biggest challenge in the second half.

Going into the locker room at halftime, I had two main concerns: Artie's knee and my quad. Artie had taken a real hard shot to his knee and was playing with a lot of pain. I was hoping he would be able to continue playing.

I knew that I had to do everything possible to keep my quadricep muscle from getting too tight or I wouldn't be able to run. I immediately went to the bathroom, grabbed a big glass of Gatorade and laid on the ground in a hurdler's stretch to keep my leg muscle loose. I kept my leg stretched until the minute before we had to go out for the second half.

As a team, we were very calm and as confident as ever that we would emerge as national champions. We knew that we had to do a better job defending against their corner kicks and free kicks around our 18-yard box. That was the real danger for us. In the attack, we were very confident they couldn't shut us down for another half.

As I lined up for the second-half kickoff, I could feel my quad throbbing and getting tighter. I kept stretching until the whistle blew to start the second half.

Just 2 1/2 minutes into the second half, we were awarded a free kick in our attacking half of the field. Duncan stood over the ball, getting ready to take the free kick.

As a team, we liked to leave space at the near post and then run into that area. Our belief was that more often than not, the first one to the ball would win the header, so our lack of height as a team didn't hinder us that much on our free kicks.

Duncan kicked the ball toward the near post. Artie sprinted toward the ball, with John Brooks within inches of him. Artie rose into the air and headed the ball one-half second before Brooks and Artie's heads collided. The Dons' U.S.A. Olympic keeper Peter Arnautoff had no chance and Artie's header found the back of the net. Three minutes into the second half and we were up 1-0.

Minutes later, Tony Igwe won a ball in his defending half and made a 50-yard run with the ball. As he approached the 18-yard box, he struck the ball with his left foot. The low hard shot got past the diving Aly Anderson, heading toward the far post with what looked like the equalizing goal. The ball hit the post, bouncing right back toward the center of the six-yard box. Aly sprung up like a cat and dove on the loose ball before Dag Olavson could react and knock the ball into the empty net.

The previous year in the semifinal against Indiana, we had some bad luck when one of its defenders punched the ball out of the goal with his hand and no penalty kick was called. This time it appears we had some good fortune.

As the half went on, San Francisco had a lot more urgency with its play and was starting to push more players into the attack.

San Francisco overplayed a long ball in our defensive third. Gary Vogel collected the errant pass and played it back to Aly. It was a rarity for Aly to punt the ball, as we tended to play short passes out of the back.

Aly rolled the ball back to Vogel, who played a short pass to Zeren out on the side of the 18-yard box. The Dons were chasing the ball and we were content keeping possession and looking for the right opportunity to go forward.

Zeren played the ball back to Aly, who rolled the ball to Jeff Tipping standing between the penalty spot and 18-yard line. Having stretched the Dons' front players chasing the ball, Tipping dribbled 25 yards up the field before Igwe confronted him.

Jeff played a low, hard pass toward Stevie Long, which skipped past Dons defender Jon Erik Skau. Stevie managed to collect the ball and avoided the sliding Bjorn Dahl, heading directly to goal with no other defenders in sight. Stevie slowed up as Arnautoff came off of his line. Stevie calmly beat Arnautoff to the near post, putting us up 2-0.

Sprinting to catch up to Stevie and celebrate, I think my mind went momentarily blank. I can't explain the euphoria I felt because I knew that leading 2-0, we were going to win the national championship. When the celebrations of the second goal were finished, I quickly refocused on the situation.

With the score, the time left in the game and the condition of my leg worsening by the minute, I knew I would be parking myself in front of our back four and would be defending the remainder of the game.

San Francisco started pushing everything it had into the attack, with center back John Brooks looking to get into our box and get his head to some crossed balls.

We absorbed everything the Dons had. Then they won a corner kick at the 87-minute mark. The corner kick was played to the near post, where it was headed onto the back post where inexplicably, Anthony Gray was standing totally unmarked and he headed the ball into the goal, giving San Francisco some newfound hope.

We didn't panic at all, playing out the last few minutes of the game just waiting for the referee to blow his whistle. Then we heard it: The referee's whistle ended the game.

At that moment I was standing near Joey Ryan. We both dropped to our knees and hugged in celebration. We did it. We did it. Going around and hugging all of my teammates and coaches was a surreal moment that I never will forget as long as I live.

As we gathered together for the trophy presentation, my mind raced back to Timo telling me I was not good enough to play at Hartwick, my tearful bus ride back to Oneonta after my first regular season game, and last year's devastating semifinal loss to Indiana. And right at this moment, the realization set in that in my last game ever wearing a Hartwick uniform, I had captained the Wick to the National Championship. I suddenly felt this great sense of accomplishment.

As the captain, I received the national championship trophy from the NCAA delegates. I kissed the trophy, raised it above my head, and as Aly and Duncan lifted me onto their shoulders, I felt like I was in heaven.

32

The Icing on the Cake

The years of training every day to improve myself as a player and to help make the team better did more than just help Hartwick College win a national championship (I cannot describe in words the sheer happiness and euphoria that brought me). It also led to my receiving numerous individual awards, truly the icing on the cake. My awards are listed below.

1977   Hermann Trophy winner

1977   *Soccer Monthly Magazine* College Player of the Year

1977   Division 1 First-Team All-American Team selected by
        the National Soccer Coaches Association of America

1977   *Soccer America Magazine* selection as one of the Nation's
        Top Ten Players.

Team Accomplishments

Below is a listing of team accomplishments, achieved only by having tremendously talented teammates, wonderful coaches and a little bit of luck.

1977   Hartwick College, Division One men's soccer national champions
1976   Hartwick College, Division One men's soccer third place
1976   Trenton Extension SC, Men's Amateur Cup finalist
1976   Trenton Extension SC, Men's New Jersey State Cup champions

1976   Hartwick College, Mr. Pibb Tournament, inaugural champions

1975   Hamilton Post 313, Junior Division New Jersey State Cup
        champions

1974   Hartwick College Division One men's soccer, third place

1974   Hamilton Post 313, Junior Division, Robbie International
        Soccer Tournament champions

1973   St. Anthony's High School New Jersey Parochial A
        state champions

1973   Hamilton Post 313 Junior Division, Robbie International
        Soccer Tournament champions

Hartwick College men's soccer team records during Gazonas' career:

1974-1975   10-4-3

1975-1976   9-3-1

1976-1977   16-1-1

1977-1978   16-0-2

Professional Playing Career

1978-1980   Tulsa Roughnecks   NASL

1981   Calgary Boomers   NASL

1981-1982   New York Arrows   MISL Champions

1982-1984   Kansas City Comets   MISL

After College

Shortly after Hartwick College won the NCAA national soccer championship, the Tulsa Roughnecks made me the third pick in the North American Soccer League draft. After three years with the Roughnecks, I was traded to the Calgary Boomers. After one year, the Boomers filed for bankruptcy and I became a free agent. I left the NASL and signed with the New York Arrows, defending champions in the Major Indoor Soccer League. We won the 1982-1983 MISL Championship. At the end of the season, I requested a trade and was sent to the Kansas City Comets.

In the middle of my sixth professional season, I suffered a season-ending knee injury. After a lengthy rehabilitation process, I returned the following season, but could not regain my pre-injury form. The following preseason the Comets released me and I decided to retire from professional soccer.

Several months later, the Kansas City Comets offered me the assistant coaching job position and I accepted it. I coached for two seasons before deciding to return to New Jersey and join my brother Andrew in Michele Lorie Cheesecakes, a frozen dessert manufacturer that he founded seven years earlier.

After 21 years of satisfying the sweet tooth of thousands of customers throughout New Jersey and eastern Pennsylvania, Andrew and I decided to retire. After one year of retirement I became a bit restless and I decided to write "The Billy Gazonas Story." I hope it inspires and motivates many to focus on their goals and reach for the stars.

I've been inducted into four Halls of Fame, I'm proud to say. They are the Hartwick College Athletic Hall of Fame; the Mercer County, N.J. Soccer Hall of Fame; the formerly St. Anthony's High School, now Trenton Catholic Academy Athletic Hall of Fame; and the American Hellenic Educational Progressive Association Athletic Hall of Fame.

Also, the Newark Star-Ledger named me one of the top 10 New Jersey high school soccer players of the 1970s.

Acknowledgments

In soccer, your teammates have a huge impact on team and individual success. When writing, I found the same need to be surrounded by talented individuals if I hoped to have any success.

So I feel very fortunate to have a wonderful supporting cast. Thank you to my publishing team: Bruce Goldberg, for his wonderful editing skills and guidance on many aspects of the book's development; Nick Zelinger with NZ Graphics for his ability to create front and back covers I can be proud of and his meticulous work on the layout; and Cara DeGette; for her superior trained eye in proofreading and editing anything that may have been missed. Thank you.

I have endless gratitude for Hartwick College Archivist Shelly Wallace for locating many special pictures that are in the book. A special thanks to the late Ed Clough, who shot many of the photos.

Words cannot thank enough the late sportswriter George O'Gorman, who also provided many of the book's photographs.

A special thanks to Glenn G. Pudelka for his timely guidance and advice.

My gratitude also goes to the many individuals that read and often re-read the manuscript, providing me with constructive criticism and suggestions. You know who you are and are well aware how thankful I am for your advice. Thank you so much.

I feel so fortunate to have been blessed with many talented teammates. At the top of the list is the late Glenn "Mooch" Myernick. All of you helped make me the player I developed into. Without you, there would not be a book. Thank you.

I also was fortunate to have special coaches in my life. They all contributed greatly: Ernie and Paul Tessein with Hamilton Post 313; Timo Liekoski, Jim Lennox and Alden Shattuck with Hartwick College; and Charles "Ping Pong" Farrauto, Trenton Extension S.C., who also was a mentor.

Finally, special thanks to the most important individuals in my life. The unwavering support from my daughters Stephanie, Stacie, Sydnie, and Colette helped me throughout this project. Thanks to my brother Andrew, who always has been there for me. And I have major gratitude for my wife Wanda, who always was willing to share her thoughts, whether I would like them or not, and often sent me back to rewrite a paragraph again and again.

About the Author

I did not attend an Ivy League university and major in English Literature. As a matter of fact, English was one of my worst subjects. Although I am an avid reader, I find writing difficult and intimidating, especially when one considers the works of so many brilliant authors who are so magical with their words.

I did not create this story; I lived it. "The Billy Gazonas Story" took many years to complete. If not for that will to win that God blessed me with, I do not think I ever would have finished this book.

The most important aspect for me to convey to you is what I went through, my roller coaster of emotions. The fears, embarrassments, elations, devastating defeats, jubilation in victory, and the drive and passion that I felt every day throughout my four years at Hartwick College.

If you are able to feel what I was going through, then I will consider this book a success.

Billy Gazonas

Made in United States
North Haven, CT
06 May 2022

18969052R00192